Blake's Margins

Blake's Margins

An Interpretive Study of the Annotations

Hazard Adams

McFarland & Company, Inc., Publishers
Jefferson, North Carolina, and London

ALSO BY HAZARD ADAMS—*Poetry:* The Farm at Richwood and Other Poems. *Fiction:* The Truth About Dragons; The Horses of Instruction; Many Pretty Toys; Home. *Nonfiction:* The Academic Tribes; Academic Child: A Memoir. *Literary criticism:* Blake and Yeats: The Contrary Vision; William Blake: A Reading of the Shorter Poems; The Contexts of Poetry; The Interests of Criticism; Lady Gregory; Philosophy of the Literary Symbolic; Joyce Cary's Trilogies: Pursuit of the Particular Real; The Book of Yeats's Poems; Antithetical Essays in Literary Criticism and Liberal Education; The Book of Yeats's Vision: Romantic Modernism and Antithetical Tradition; Four Lectures on the History of Criticism and Theory in the West; The Offense of Poetry. *Edited volumes*: Poems by Robert Simeon Adams; Poetry: An Introductory Anthology; Fiction as Process (with Carl Hartman); William Blake: Jerusalem, Selected Poetry and Prose; Critical Theory Since Plato (third edition with Leroy Searle); Critical Theory Since 1965 (with Leroy Searle); Critical Essays on William Blake.

LIBRARY OF CONGRESS CATALOGUING-IN-PUBLICATION DATA

Adams, Hazard, 1926–
 Blake's margins : an interpretive study of the annotations / by Hazard Adams.
     p.   cm.
 Includes bibliographical references and index.

 ISBN 978-0-7864-4536-3
 softcover : 50# alkaline paper

 1. Blake, William, 1757–1827 — Criticism and interpretation.
 2. Blake, William, 1757–1827 — Knowledge — Literature.
 I. Title.
 PR4147.A62   2009
 821'.7 — dc22   2009034519

British Library cataloguing data are available

©2009 Hazard Adams. All rights reserved

No part of this book may be reproduced or transmitted in any form or by any means, electronic or mechanical, including photocopying or recording, or by any information storage and retrieval system, without permission in writing from the publisher.

Cover art: Thomas Phillips, *William Blake,* oil on canvas, 36 ¼" × 28 ⅜", 1807 (National Portrait Gallery, London)

Manufactured in the United States of America

McFarland & Company, Inc., Publishers
  Box 611, Jefferson, North Carolina 28640
  www.mcfarlandpub.com

To
my students
over the years

Table of Contents

Preface   1
Introduction   3

1. Annotations to Johann Caspar Lavater's *Aphorisms on Man*   7
2. Annotations to Emanuel Swedenborg's *Heaven and Hell*, *Divine Love and Divine Wisdom*, and *Divine Providence*   28
3. Annotations to Bishop Richard Watson's *An Apology for the Bible*   61
4. Annotations to Sir Francis Bacon's *Essays Moral, Economical, and Political*   81
5. Annotations to Henry Boyd's *A Translation of the* Inferno *of Dante Alighieri*   97
6. Annotations to Sir Joshua Reynolds's *Discourses on Art*   109
7. Annotations to J. C. Spurzheim's *Observations on the Deranged Manifestations of the Mind, or Insanity*   139
8. Annotations to Bishop George Berkeley's *Siris*   150
9. Annotations to William Wordsworth's *Poems* and Preface to *The Excursion*   160
10. Annotations to Robert John Thornton's *The Lord's Prayer, Newly Translated*   177
11. Addendum   193
12. A Note on Blake's Reading   195

Index   199

Preface

This book is really my extension of a graduate seminar I offered at the University of Washington in 2005. In it, the students and I were engaged mainly with William Blake's annotations. There is no doubt that ideas explored by those students have crept into my text. I thank them for their interest, their serious attention, and their contributions. They were: Michael Deblois, Travis Landry, Katy Magusa, Andrew Meyer, Paige Morgan, Jeff Resta, Elizabeth Rubasky, Arendt Speser, and Kelly Walsh. The aim of this book is to provide a critical and interpretive commentary on all of the known extant annotations that William Blake made to books. His annotations to three books by Swedenborg and two by Wordsworth have survived, and I have devoted single chapters to the books by those authors. In a chapter entitled "Addendum" I have noted one alleged annotation by Blake from a lost book and one so-called annotation from one of his own watercolors. Otherwise I have devoted a chapter to each book with the intention that each chapter should stand alone as a separate essay. In some places I have directed the reader to pages in other chapters, and as a result I have occasionally repeated points. References in parentheses and brackets are either to page numbers or section numbers of the editions of the books Blake annotated, as indicated in the footnotes. References with page numbers preceded by E are also made to David V. Erdman's *The Complete Poetry and Prose of William Blake*, revised edition, New York: Anchor Books, 1988. In quotations from Blake I have preserved Blake's occasionally eccentric spelling and punctuation. Underlinings in quotations from others are Blake's except where noted.

I should like to acknowledge with thanks the help of Jeanne Moskal, Raimonda Modiano, and Leroy Searle, who read certain chapters and made helpful suggestions. The last brief chapter "A Note on Blake's Reading" would not be possible without previous work by the late Geoffrey Keynes and by Gerald E. Bentley, Jr., from which I have collected most of the information. The only part of this book that has previously appeared, since considerably revised and expanded, is the chapter on the annotations to Sir Joshua Reynolds's *Discourses on Art*, which in an earlier version was published in *Blake and His Time*, edited by Robert N. Essick and Donald Pearce (Bloomington: Indiana University Press, 1978), and reprinted in my *Antithetical Essays in Literary Criticism and Liberal Education* (Tallahassee: Florida State University Press, 1990).

I am indebted to the Huntington Library for the reproductions of pages of Watson's *Apology for the Bible* on pages 64 and 74.

Introduction

I have written this commentary on Blake's annotations less for scholars well acquainted with Blake's writings and art than for people who want to learn more about Blake's thought and for students in the early stages of study of his work. We have no idea how many books Blake may have annotated. Eleven have survived to find places in libraries in England and the United States. One other, Spurzheim's *Observations on the Deranged Manifestations of the Mind*, is lost; but Edwin J. Ellis and William Butler Yeats transcribed Blake's annotations for their edition of Blake's writings published in 1893. Blake's annotations to Wordsworth's poem *The Excursion* were not made in a book, but instead on four separate sheets still in existence. Thus we have thirteen surviving sets of annotations made by Blake. It is likely that he annotated other books, whether his or those of acquaintances. Indeed, he wrote in the annotations we have that he had read and annotated Edmund Burke on the sublime and the beautiful, John Locke on human understanding, and Francis Bacon's *Advancement of Learning*. It was not unusual in Blake's time for people to annotate books lent to them or presented to them for that purpose. Blake's annotations to Wordsworth's poems were of the latter sort. Often it seems that Blake thought he was writing them not merely for acquaintances but for a larger audience. It turns out that he was right about this.

Almost everyone who has written on Blake has quoted from his annotations, and some have depended heavily on them for their own arguments. Much of what we think we know of Blake's thought has its source in them. The earliest surviving annotations were made in a book published in 1788 and read by Blake in that year. Blake was then 31 years old. He made his last surviving annotations in 1827 not long before his death in the same year. The annotations thus cover thirty-nine years of his working life, over which time he developed and expressed his views on many things. The books he annotated took up a variety of subjects — religious, philosophical, economic, psychological, artistic, poetic, and historical. The annotations provide us with a sense not only of what he was thinking at various times in his life, but also of the breadth of his curiosity and interests as well as ways he reacted to the writings of others. They give us considerable insight into his character and personality over time. Blake read with enthusiasm. He interpreted. He complained, often brilliantly. He praised, and he criticized, often harshly. He could praise and then criticize. He marked without comment passages to remember or those he especially admired. He underlined. He edited, sometimes crossing out and emending, sometimes to express views opposite to those of the writer. He sometimes provided a "preface" of his own.

Blake was fundamentally self-educated. We know that he attended Henry Parrs's Drawing School, was apprenticed to the engraver James Basire, and studied at the Royal Academy of Art; but he had no formal education in the usual sense. We know from his writings, his visual art, and the reports of others that he read widely. His own library, as much as we know of it, was eclectic. In my last chapter, I attempt briefly to give some idea of the range of his reading.

I have taken up the annotations in the order in which they appear in David V. Erdman's *The Complete Poetry and Prose of William Blake*. The books are presented there in the order in which Erdman thought Blake annotated them, and I have no reason to disagree with his decisions, even though some of them are speculative.

Recent scholars have often depended on Erdman's edition, in which annotations are usually preceded by brief passages to which Blake seems to be responding. Often, however, it is the whole text to which an annotation responds, or it is the drift of an argument over a considerable space. I have sought to provide a better sense of the context of Blake's remarks than is possible in an edition such as Erdman's, or, for that matter, any edition likely to be produced.

There has not been much written that directly and exclusively deals with the annotations. Morton D. Paley has written two informative articles on the annotations to Watson's *Apology for the Bible* and Thornton's *The Lord's Prayer*, and, as the reader will see, I am in their debt. His essay on Blake and Swedenborg, though with more general intent than mine, also deals with the annotations. Thomas McFarland has written "Synecdochic Structure in Blake's Marginalia." There are facsimile editions of Lavater's *Aphorisms on Man* and Watson's *Apology*, both with Blake's annotations. They have helpful introductions by R. J. Shroyer and G. Ingli James, respectively.

More recently, H. J. Jackson has written an interesting book on reading

and publishing in the romantic period, and she has emphasized marginalia.*
Her brief discussion of Blake is excellent on his usually methodical use of annotation as "step-by-step refutation" (158). She declares, "In the context of reading practices of the period, Blake is hardly eccentric at all. He talked back to his books and, like certain other readers, he took steps to disseminate his opinion in a form of manuscript publication" (170). If this was not a way of reaching more than a very few readers in his day, it certainly became successful in the latter part of the twentieth century. Jackson offers fine brief discussions of Blake's annotations to Bacon (159–61), Watson (161, 164–6), and Reynolds (166–9), and she quite correctly remarks, "The effect of Blake's system of annotation was to make manuscript marginalia an integral part of the book and thus *publish* his quarrel with the author as the book circulated" (169).

The one book addressed to the annotations, though a little over half of the book passes before the annotations are discussed, has aims quite different from mine. This is *The Torn Book: UnReading William Blake's Marginalia* by Jason Allen Snart.† It is a textual study, narrowly conceived to emphasize the materiality of texts and virtually to ignore what Snart calls the "content" and I call the thought of Blake's annotations. He writes, "I am less interested in *what* Blake writes in the margins than by the fact that he writes them there at all" (111). His aim is to establish a material basis for reading: "It is the question surrounding how annotations exist on the page that matters for the present study, and what implications these have for our reading of the annotations and for our reading of other moments in Blake" (130). It is clear that the material context for Blake's engraved writings is important for a reading of his poems, but Snart's book, to my mind, does not demonstrate how the materiality of the annotations functions to affect the thought we draw from them, though it does lead us to take note of the rhetoric. Jackson has rightly pointed to the "layout and visual effect of his notes" (169). Blake's aim here was to be rhetorically persuasive. Snart's book, it seems to me, is an example of how notions of textuality and indeterminateness of meaning, emphasized in deconstruction and postmodernism generally, have found their way into academic textual studies, with the usual time lag and occasional oversimplification that have always occurred when philosophical notions have

---

*H. J. Jackson, *Romantic Readers: The Evidence of Marginalia*, New Haven and London: Yale University Press, 2005. This was preceded by her *Marginalia: Readers Writing in Books*, New Haven and London: Yale University Press, 2001. One can very profitably consult William St. Clair, *The Reading Nation in the Romantic Period*, Cambridge: Cambridge University Press, 2004 for a thorough study of reading habits, literary production, manufacturing, and selling in the period.
†Jason Allen Snart, *The Torn Book: UnReading Blake's Marginalia*, Selinsgrove, PA: Susquehanna University Press, 2006.

finally influenced literary criticism and theory. Still, at the level on which he is deliberately writing, Snart makes a number of interesting observations.

What I have done will perhaps not satisfy those for whom only their own inspection of the books would be adequate. Recourse may be had to the two facsimile editions, but they offer at best only moderately successful reproductions of the annotations. In some other cases, the original is in a deteriorated condition, and in certain places the annotations are difficult or impossible any longer to read. Erdman recovered some of these, and some that were available to him are now virtually unreadable. We depend today on his transcriptions. That they have lost their materiality is no reason to ignore them.

In the chapters that follow, I have tried to give attention to the larger intellectual contexts of the books and Blake's remarks. I hope that without prolixity I have selected what will most profit the reader.

1

Annotations to Johann Caspar Lavater's *Aphorisms on Man*

Henry Fuseli's translation of Lavater's *Aphorisms* was published in 1788.*
Blake's annotations to an unbound copy are probably his earliest that have
been discovered. He had engraved the frontispiece for the book from a sketch
by Fuseli. Lavater and Fuseli (then Füssli) had been friends since their atten-
dance at the Collegium Humanitatis and the Caroline College in Zurich.†
Indeed, together they found themselves in serious difficulty for having published a tract that accused a magistrate in Zurich of corruption. They fled to
Germany, Fuseli not returning even though the magistrate was proved to be
guilty and had to make restitution of stolen funds.

Both Fuseli and Lavater had been ordained ministers in the Zwinglian
Reformed Church.§ On his return to Zurich, Lavater pursued his vocation
and continued to do so all of his life. Fuseli did not, abandoned Christianity, emigrated to England, and embarked there on a literary and artistic career
that brought him fame. Though they found themselves in disagreement over
many things, Fuseli and Lavater remained friends, and Lavater warmly dedicated *Aphorisms* to Fuseli:

**Aphorisms on Man, Translated from the Original Manuscript of the Rev. John Caspar Lavater,
Citizen of Zurich. London: Printed for J. Johnson, St. Paul's Churchyard, 1788. The copy that
Blake annotated is in the Huntington Library. A facsimile edition of this copy, with a valuable
introduction by R. J. Shroyer, was published by Scholars' Facsimiles and Reprints, Delmar, NY,
1980.

†For a good short account of their relationship, see Marcia Allentuck, "Fuseli and Lavater:
Physiognomical Theory and the Enlightenment," *Studies in Voltaire and the Eighteenth Century*
55, 1967, 89–112.

§Huldreich (or Ulrich) Zwingli (1484–1531) was a critic of Luther and debated him over
church doctrine. Among other things, Zwingli held that the Lord's Supper was a commemo-
ration rather than a ritual sacrament. He also opposed celibacy of the clergy and was himself
married.

Take, dear observer of men, from the hand of your unbiassed friend, this testimony of esteem for your genius.

All the world knows that this is no flattery; for, in an hundred things, I am not of your opinion; but, in what concerns the knowledge of mankind, we are nearer to one another than any two in ten thousand [p. iii].*

On the title page of his copy, Blake drew a heart that contained the printed name of Lavater, enclosing in it his own signature, indicating his high regard for the book.

Lavater (1741–1801) had a very active career as a writer and was well acquainted with many of the luminaries of his time. He edited a moralistic journal in the 1760s, wrote poetry, made several translations, and composed pietistic religious works. His fame, however, came as a result of his writings on physiognomy, especially *Physiognomische Fragmente zur Beförderung der Menschenkenntnis und Menschenliebe* (1775–1778), translated into English as *Essays on Physiognomy* from a revised French edition.† This edition included some engravings by Blake after Fuseli, who probably arranged for Blake to do them. There were several translations into other languages.

Physiognomy can be traced back into ancient times, but it came into prominence in the eighteenth century as what today we would call a pseudo-science and persisted, though always controversial, into the nineteenth before being discredited.§ In short, it claimed that character is revealed by the study of bodily and especially facial features. It may be contrasted to phrenology, which involved principally the shape of the skull and divided the skull's surface into several areas that were supposed to express various characteristics of personality.**

Physiognomy seems to have only a modest presence in *Aphorisms* except

---

*Unprefixed numbers refer to the numbers of the aphorisms. Numbers prefixed by E indicate pages of *The Complete Poetry and Prose of William Blake*, newly revised, ed. David V. Erdman, New York: Anchor Books, 1988 (used throughout this book). Underlinings in the quotations are Blake's and usually express his agreement. The publisher seems to have misnumbered, there being no aphorisms 190 to 199.

†*Essays on Physiognomy, Designed to Promote the Knowledge and Love of Mankind*, ed. T[homas] Holloway, tr. H[enry] Hunter. 3 vols. London: J. Murray, 1789–98. There was another translation into English in 1798 by Thomas Holcroft. For an account of G. C. Lichtenberg's strong criticism of Lavater's physiognomy in his time, see J. P. Stern, *Lichtenberg: A Doctrine of Scattered Occasions*, Bloomington, IN: Indiana University Press, 1959, 89–93. On Lavater's book and Blake's engravings for it, see Mary Lynn Johnson, "Blake's Engravings for Lavater's *Physiognomy*: Overdue Credit for Chadoweicki, Schellenberg, and Lips," *Blake: An Illustrated Quarterly*, 38, 2 (Fall 2004), 52–74.

§For contemporary discussions of physiognomy, see *Physiognomy in Profile: Lavater's Impact on European Culture*, eds. Melissa Percival and Graeme Tytler, Newark, DE: University of Delaware Press, 2005.

**Blake annotated a work on madness by the prominent phrenologist, J. C. Spurzheim. See below, pp. 139–49.

for Lavater's view, appearing frequently, that the inner self is expressed by external appearance. Physiognomy and phrenology would certainly have been of interest to writers and artists, even if they did not believe in these pseudo-sciences, for, of course, in the arts, from cartoons to the naming of fictive characters, outward appearance often expresses character.

The Aphorisms

There is not a lot of difference between an aphorism and a maxim. Indeed the Oxford English Dictionary treats the two as synonyms. Other dictionaries tell us that an aphorism is a brief statement expressing a general truth or principle of conduct.* It is perhaps surprising that Lavater's aphorism 591 says, "Maxims are as necessary for the weak, as rules for the beginner: the master wants neither rule nor principle; he possesses both without thinking of them." It appears that either Lavater (or perhaps Fuseli) sees a difference between maxim and aphorism or he regards his reader as occupying a space between weakness and mastery. In his dedication to Fuseli, he writes that his book will be useful for "every class of men, from the throne to the cottage" (p. iii).

The aphorisms are not organized by topic, but on occasion two or more of them with the same theme are grouped together. Also, the first few serve as a sort of introduction. These are about human nature in general, and they attracted Blake's interest, offering the notion of both sameness and difference among men:

1. Know, in the first place, that mankind agree in essence, as they do in their limbs and senses.
2. Mankind differ as much in essence as they do in form, limbs, and senses — and only so, and not more [1–2].

Blake calls these aphorisms "true Christian philosophy far above all abstraction" (E584). They clearly influenced Blake's early tract *All Religions Are One*, as Shroyer points out (p. xxi).

Elsewhere, Lavater declares that there are only three classes of men, "the retrograde, the stationary, the progressive" (371). Later, however, he offers other sets of distinctions. For example, aphorism 418 declares that he knows only "three classes of men — those who see the whole, those who see but a part, and those who see both together." A more extensive set appears even

---

*J. P. Stern, *op. cit.*, writing on Lichtenberg, discusses the nature of literary aphorisms at length, 186–226.

later: the singular, the original, the extraordinary, the great, and the sublime, set in a hierarchy:

> ... the *sublime* alone unites the singular, original, extraordinary, and great, with his own uniformity and simplicity: the *great*, with many powers, and uniformity of ends, is destitute of that superior calmness and inward harmony which soars above the atmosphere of praise: the *extraordinary* is distinguished by copiousness, and a wide range of energy: the *original* need not be very rich, only that which he produces is unique, and has the exclusive stamp of individuality: the *singular*, as such, is placed between originality and whim, and often makes a trifle the medium of fame [600].

Of these types, Lavater writes most often of the great. His principal interests are in human character and how it is properly or improperly expressed in the relation of self to others. "Character" appears frequently in *Aphorisms*. In aphorisms 105 and 106, Lavater writes of three types of character: there are positive and negative characters and "an immense class of mere passives." In 112, he adds the categories of firm, quick, and slow, all of which can be detected in the way a person answers with "yes" or "no." He believes that character is illuminated in the "rapid moments of joy and of grief" (160). He very much values consistency of character, which extends to a person's speaking and writing: "Who writes as he speaks, speaks as he writes, looks as he speaks and writes — is honest" (114). He admires the capacity for self-subsistence and, especially, one's regard for both self and others.

Consistency is connected to Lavater's view that virtue lies between vicious extremes, a mean in the Aristotelian sense. Thus he values "economy of words without scarcity, and liberality without profusion" (392). He values serene seriousness, neither anxious nor careless (394). He praises calmness of speech, prudent silence, self-composure, patience, and the ability to be a good listener, to subdue one's anger and that of others (217), and to make neither too much nor too little of oneself (188). Other things he praises are justness, sincerity, generosity, humility, neatness, modesty, forgiveness, sympathy, and energy. He likes laughter and gladness: "The glad gladdens — who gladdens not is not glad" (28). He much admires disinterested goodness.

On the other hand, there are many things of which he speaks ill: hypocrisy, lying, especially calumniation, arrogance, affectation, indolence, cruelty, vanity, forwardness, egotism, insolence, impertinence, obstinacy, jealousy, pretension, impetuosity, evasiveness, shallowness, slovenliness, crawling, oppressiveness, and pedantry.

From his mentions of God, it appears that for Lavater man's relation to the deity is radically personal. He declares that an impersonal God does not exist (552), and he seems to hold that God is made in man's image as much as man is made in God's: "As the interest of <u>man, so his God — as his God, so he</u>" (13). Thus we may see God in man (138, 408), and if one has no self-confidence, one has none in God (216). He praises "hearty participation in the joys and griefs of others" as proper expressions of one's humanity and religion (431). He praises what he calls "<u>the most refined Epicurism</u>" as the "<u>purest religion</u>" and goes on to write, "<u>He, who in the smallest given time can enjoy most of what he never shall repent, and what furnishes</u> enjoyments, still more unexhausted, still less changeable — is the most religious and the most voluptuous of men" (366). Lavater consistently sees one's relation to God as the same as one's proper relations with others: "As you receive the stranger, so you receive your God" (340).*

The aphorisms frequently speak of the importance of the relation of self to others, especially friendship, which Lavater seems to have placed before anything else in human relations. He emphasizes the serene seriousness of those alone "formed for friendship" (394). The whole study of man is "the doctrine of unisons and discords between ourselves and others" (18). The mean is present here, Lavater asserting that a warm, neither cold nor fervid, character is the best for friendship (212). He values the unobserved act of goodness, a princely, modest act of giving, and the capacity to enjoy the greatness of others (203); but he praises the ability to conceal joys, suspicious of any impulse to show off (208). He believes that a person can be known by observing his friends and enemies (150), that no one loves who is not loved (219). He believes also that feeling free in the presence of another makes that other person free (86). Generally, Lavater emphasizes empathetic identification with others, even the importance, for one's own improvement, of understanding an enemy (325). Knowledge of what one loves or hates in another provides knowledge of oneself. Lavater extends his notion of empathy to nature itself when he says that discovery of the good in inanimate things is "sagacious," in animate things "liberal" (291).

Lavater offers a number of aphorisms on the importance of what to take note of in others, the purpose being self-betterment. This requires understanding the strict difference between wishes and will:

> Who has many wishes has generally but little will. Who has energy of will has few diverging wishes. Whose will is bent with energy on *one*, *must* renounce the wishes for *many* things. Who cannot do this is not stamped with the majesty of human nature. <u>The energy of choice, the unison of various powers for one is only *will*, born under the agonies of self-denial and renounced desires</u> [20].

---

*F. Ernest Stoeffer in *German Pietism During the Eighteenth Century* (Leiden: E. J. Brill, 1973) provides a concise account of Lavater's religious views, 253–56.

Blake underlines the last sentence and writes "regeneration" (E584). "Admirable!" is written alongside, but it appears to be in another hand. Energy and vigor impress Lavater, especially under command of will; it must have durability, supported by strength. Leopold Damrosch sees in Blake's later writings a definite suspicion of human will.* He notes also Blake's decisive declaration, "Will is always Evil" (E602) in the annotations to Swedenborg, not much later, if at all, than those to Lavater. However, Blake's underlining above seems to indicate approbation. In his annotations to Swedenborg's *Divine Love and Divine Wisdom*, however, Blake, as does Swedenborg, later, sees possible good in the will (below p. 37–8).

There is, for Lavater, such a thing as genius, which among other attributes, is the ability to "produce what none else can" (23), to make "quick use of the moment" (91), to intuit truth "not preceded by perceptible meditation" (93), to possess the gift of prophecy (413), and to see the "whole in the parts, and the parts in the whole" (418). There is also saintliness. Geniuses and merchants who never lie are saintly (332). Saints do good nearly unconsciously (343).

Lavater praises discrete silence and unobtrusive behavior, but he likes harmless merriment (55). Aphorism 328 says, "Keep him at least three paces distant who hates bread, music, and the laugh of a child." After underlining, Blake writes, "the best in the book" (E590).

The Annotations

In the concluding aphorism, Lavater makes a suggestion to his readers: "If you mean to know yourself, interline such of these aphorisms as affected you agreeably in reading, and set a mark to such as left a sense of uneasiness with you; and then shew your copy to whom you please" (643). Blake takes up at least the first part of this invitation, though his writing is for the most part marginal and not interlinear. In addition to making comments, he underlines what he seems to like and marks with an X what he does not like. Often he appends the word "uneasy" (sometimes coupled with "very" or "rather") and, on a few occasions, "false." Sometimes he uses what Erdman calls a square dagger to indicate strong approval.† On the last page he writes,

---

*Leopold Damrosch, Jr., *Symbol and Truth in Blake's Myth*, Princeton, NJ: Princeton University Press, 1980, esp. 133–38.
†H. J. Jackson suggests that Blake's method of annotation was probably influenced by Lavater's suggestion. See her *Romantic Readers: The Evidence of Marginalia*, New Haven and London: Yale University Press, 2005, 158.

1. *Lavater's* Aphorisms on Man 13

> I hope no one will call what I have written cavilling because he may think my remarks of small consequence For I write from the warmth of my heart. & cannot resist the impulse I feel to rectify what I think false in a book I love so much. & approve so generally [p. 224, E600].

After this, Blake writes a long criticism of Lavater's "principles," which I shall discuss shortly.

It is fair to say at the outset that although Blake praises Lavater, in personality and with respect to what they valued in personality, if not character, they were quite different from each other. This is often reflected in the aphorisms that Blake marks "uneasy."

It is clear that Blake did not simply read once from beginning to end, for in his annotation to aphorism 3 he directs *his* reader to his remarks on aphorisms 533 and 630, where in turn he refers the reader to 549 and 554. These aphorisms and comments constitute a group of considerable interest, and I shall eventually take them up.

The two most interesting and important annotations from a philosophical point of view are 532 and Blake's summary comments on Lavater on blank pages 225 and 226 at the end of the book. Lavater says:

> Take from Luther his roughness and fiery courage; from Calvin his hectic obstinacy; from Erasmus his timid prudence; hypocrisy and fanaticism from Cromwell; from Henry IV. his sanguine character; mysticism from Fenelon; from Hume his all-unhinging wit; love of paradox and brooding suspicion from Rousseau; naiveté and elegance of knavery from Voltaire; from Milton the extravagance of his all-personifying fancy; from Raffaelle his dryness and nearly hard precision; and from Rubens his supernatural luxury of colours:— deduct this oppressive exuberance from each; rectify them according to your own taste—what will be the result? Your own correct, pretty, flat, useful—for me, to be sure, quite convenient vulgarity. And why this amongst maxims of humanity? that you may learn to know this exuberance, this leven, of each great character, and its effects on contemporaries and posterity—that you may know where d, e, f, is, there must be a, b, c: he alone has knowledge of man, who knows the ferment that raises each character, and makes it that which it shall be, and something more or less than it shall be [532].

Blake's comments follow:

> Deduct from a rose its redness. from a lilly its whiteness from a diamond its hardness from a spunge its softness from an oak its heighth from a daisy its lowness & rectify every thing in Nature as the Philosophers do. & then we shall return to Chaos & God will be compelld to be Excentric if he Creates O happy Philosopher
>
> Variety does not necessarily suppose deformity, for a rose & a lilly. are various. & both beautiful
>
> Beauty is exuberant but not of ugliness but of beauty & if ugliness is adjoined

to beauty it is not the exuberance of beauty. so if Rafael is hard & dry it is not his genius but an accident acquired for how can Substance & Accident be predicated of the same Essence! I cannot conceive

But the substance gives tincture to the accident & makes it physiognomic

Aphorism 47. speaks of the heterogeneous, which all extravagance is. but exuberance not [E596-6].

Blake's comment is well-known to scholars as a statement critical of John Locke's distinction between what he called the primary and secondary qualities of experience. The former are the measurable qualities of an object; the latter are those that Locke believes belong only to our perceptions, that is, "different ideas of several colours, sounds, smells, taste, etc."* These latter, Locke says, are "sensible" and are produced by the power of the "insensible *primary qualities*" (76). But how this can occur Locke does not venture to say. Blake, like George Berkeley preceding him, raises the question of how we can know that an object composed only of the primary qualities really exists, since we experience only the secondary. For Blake, this raises the question of whether God's creation as we experience it is, under Locke's system, possible at all; for all that is left is a chaos of jostling particles. The charge Blake makes that under these conditions, "God will be compelld to be Excentric if he Creates," requires us to understand Blake's view of God as imagination in the sense of visionary creation, that is, creation literally by sight. This is identical in act to the human imagination, which proceeds from each of us. Thus Blake identifies each human imagination with God's and thinks of imagination as the human being. God is the image of man and man the image of God. Human beings correctly image God as human, beyond which imagination cannot go. Without that limit there would be chaos. Imagination thus proceeds from a center of perception to encompass and humanize all existence.

The process of center expanding to that circumference is God acting in man. Every act of perception is centric. Without this, God would be thrust out and away from the act of imagination and become "excentric," and there would be no center to imagine *from*, leaving only a qualitative blankness like what Berkeley called an "abstract general idea."† This is the world that, although devoid of the secondary qualities, Blake yet tries to imagine in *The Book of Urizen* and in his description of the travels of Urizen in *The Four Zoas*. There is no place to stand in that world. God's creation of such a world would have to be not an imaginative projection but entirely alien, unknowable.

---

*John Locke, *An Essay Concerning Human Understanding* (1690), II, 8, London: Everyman, 1977, 76.

†George Berkeley, "The Principles of Human Knowledge," *Berkeley's Philosophical Writings*, ed. David M. Armstrong, New York: Collier Books, 1965, 51.

Blake's next point has to do with sameness and difference. He refuses to privilege one over the other. He asserts that "variety does not necessarily suppose deformity," and goes on to imply that every object has its own form, that beauty has many shapes. One of the foremost qualities of beauty for Blake is exuberance. In *The Marriage of Heaven and Hell*, he declares, "Exuberance is Beauty" (E38), and here he insists that exuberance is not an accidental part of a beautiful object but instead belongs to its essence. (A good many critics of Blake have either not seen or simply disregarded the comic exuberance in Blake's work.)

Here we come upon a verbal thicket that requires a little clearing up, at least an effort to do so. For a long time, even back to Aristotle, there has been some overlapping of or changing places of "essence" and "substance," both of which appear here. Aristotle called essence sometimes form, sometimes matter, sometimes concrete being or individual thing. He sometimes divided substance into primary (the individual) and secondary (the species), and sometimes he thought of it as the ultimate substratum. The matter is complicated by his using the Greek *ousia* for both essence and substance, as well as being. Later usage never recovered from this multiplicity of meanings. In modern times, the two words seem to mean the same thing: the quality of something that needs nothing else for its existence. Thus we find phrases such as "essential being" used by philosophers. This introduces the Aristotelian notion of accident, which is something belonging to a thing that a thing does not need to have in order to be what it is. Accident is also an attribute that cannot exist on its own except, I suppose, insofar as we are thinking of it as a word "accident" denoting an attribute. Some attributes of a thing are not accidental but essential. The problem in all of this is that it is not clear whether we should be talking about things or words.

Blake's essence seems to be the individual imaginatively created thing itself, different from both Locke's and Kant's thing, both of which are the unknown and unknowable substratum of an appearance, and different as well from the indeterminate substratum of the Scholastics, which unites with form to make a thing. Blake's point in the discussion of Lavater in this passage is that those qualities Lavater attributes to the people he mentions are, for Blake, not accidents but substantial, undetachable parts of the essence of each, just as the redness of a rose is part of the rose's essence. Essence, then, is fundamental identity, and substance here seems to be very nearly a synonym for it. Blake's use of these terms may seem more Scholastic than Aristotelian, but still not quite. To think of Blake's usage of either in connection with a rigorously Aristotelian or Scholastic definition would be to force them where they don't want to go.

Blake employs "substance" in his essay on the Canterbury pilgrims: "...Accident ever varies, Substance can never suffer change nor decay.... Chaucer's characters ... are the physiognomies or lineaments of universal life" (E532–3). When Blake speaks here of substance, the passage in Aristotle's terms would seem to refer to what Aristotle calls "secondary substance." J. L. Ackrill may be helpful here:

> A *substance*— that which is called a substance most strictly, primarily, and most of all — is that which is neither said of a subject nor in a subject, e. g. the individual man or the individual horse. The species in which the things primarily called substances are, are called *secondary substances*, as also are the genera of these species. For example, the individual man belongs in a species, man, and animal is a genus of the species; so these — both man and animal — are called secondary substances.*

However, for Blake, all substances maintain themselves as *images* having their source in imagination. Here Blake rejects any notion that any life or thing can be expressed or known through or in abstract universals. For him, there can be no distinction between things and their qualities. Qualities, here "physiognomies and lineaments," are not to the imagination at any one time simply accidental properties of a substance; they are, in the case of the pilgrims Blake imagines, imaginative universals, as Giambattista Vico called them.†

In Blake's comment on Lavater, substance seems to be an essence when it is thought of as an actual imaginative projection. Accident is not predicated of either. Still, Blake argues, substance can affect ("tincture") the accidental. The accidental would be blended, so to speak, with substance in any particular appearance (the physiognomic; Lavater emphasizes facial appearance). However, it is difficult to understand how there can be any accident if imagination is the creator. Blake seems to regard Raphael's hardness and dryness as substantive. His deep respect for Raphael, expressed elsewhere, suggests this, as well as the implication generally in Blake's writings that elements of character or genius are not accidental. On the other hand, Blake may be treating Raphael's hardness and dryness as accidental but tinctured, that is, influenced by substance; but I think that, with respect to Raphael, Blake is criticizing Lavater for separating a substantive characteristic from essence.

Blake then distinguishes between exuberance, which is substantive of beauty, and extravagance, which is characterized by heterogeneity. In apho-

---

*J. L. Ackrill, *A New Aristotle Reader*, Princeton: Princeton, NJ: Princeton University Press, 1987, 7.
†On Vico's distinction between abstract and imaginative universals relative to Blake's views, see my *The Offense of Poetry*, Seattle, WA: University of Washington Press, 2007, esp. 144–7, 161–71.

rism 47, cited here by Blake, Lavater identifies heterogeneity with what is "impertinent ... in character, actions, works of art and literature." Heterogeneity here refers to a certain formlessness bordering on the chaos that Blake mentioned earlier in his comment. Neither Blake nor Lavater likes disorder.

Blake's remarks at the end of the book (blank pages 226–7) carry on his discussion of accident. Here he summarizes what he objects to in Lavater:

> There is a strong objection to Lavater's principles (as I understand them) & that is He makes every thing originate in its accident he makes the vicious propensity not only a leading feature of the man but the Stamina on which all his virtues grow. But as I understand Vice it is a Negative — It does not signify what the laws of Kings and Priests have calld Vice we who are philosophers ought not to call the Staminal Virtues of Humanity by the same name that we call the omissions of intellect springing from poverty
>
> Every mans leading propensity ought to be calld his leading Virtue & his good Angel But the Philosophy of Causes & Consequences misled Lavater as it has all his cotemporaries. Each thing is its own cause & its own effect Accident is the omission of act in self & the hindering of act in another, This is Vice but all Act is Virtue. To hinder another is not an act it is the contrary it is a restraint on action both in ourselves & in the person hinderd. for he who hinders another omits his own duty. at the time
>
> Murder is Hindering Another
>
> Theft is Hindering Another
>
> Backbiting. Undermining C[i]rcumventing & whatever is Negative is Vice
>
> But the or[i]gin of this mistake in Lavater & his cotemporaries, is, They suppose that Womans Love is Sin. in consequence all the Loves & Graces with them are Sin [E600-1]

Blake thinks that Lavater reverses accident and essence, making accident the original essence or substance of an individual. He believes this because he has concluded that Lavater thinks man's essence is sin, rather than in every case an accident or omission of a positive act. It is, as he calls it a "negative." Lavater nowhere in *Aphorisms* says that man's essence is sin, but Blake knows he is a Protestant clergyman and assumes that he accepts the doctrine of original sin as expressed by the biblical story of Eve and the apple. There is no suggestion in *Aphorisms* that woman is originally responsible for sin. Indeed, there is little about women in the book (see only 450 and 539, both being on the whole complimentary). However, Lavater frequently refers to villains, knaves, and hypocrites *as if* these indicate "staminal" essences, definers of character in some men. On the other hand, as we shall see, he is not consistent about this.

For Blake, sin or vice (which I doubt he distinguishes from each other) is the lack or absence of something in the intellect. Frequently it is "error." Thus he can say, as he does when Lavater tells of certain villainies, "to hell till he [the villain] behaves better" (309, E590).* Always it is a failure of action because of some lack or simply a failure to act, and it can be a hindrance to others. It creates a situation in which a positive ethical relation to another is violated.

Perhaps a clarification of Lavater's views can be made by consulting aphorism 489 and Blake's response. Lavater says:

> An entirely honest man, in the severe sense of the word, exists no more than an entirely dishonest knave: the best and worst are only approximations of those qualities. Who are those that never contradict themselves? yet honesty never contradicts itself: who are those that always contradict themselves? yet knavery is mere self-contradiction. Thus the knowledge of man determines not the things themselves, but their proportions, the quantum of congruities and incongruities [489].

Blake responds:

> Man is a twofold being. one part capable of evil & the other capable of good that which is capable of good is not also capable of evil. but that which is capable of evil is also capable of good. this aphorism seems to consider man as simple & yet capable of evil. now both evil & good cannot exist in a simple being. for thus 2 contraries would. spring from one essence which is impossible. but if man is considerd as only evil. & god only good. how then is regeneration effected which turns the evil to good. by casting out the evil. by the good. See Matthew XII. Ch. 26. 27. 28. 29 vs [E594]

Lavater thinks here of honesty and dishonesty as only approximate descriptions of human character and acts. No one is either wholly evil or wholly good. Knowledge of character must end up, then, as the result of a judgment of the proportion of good to evil in a person's behavior. Blake believes that Lavater has a conception of man as simple, that is, possessing a single essence, but he thinks that Lavater contradicts himself when he sees good and evil mixed together in man, because Lavater makes these two substances, which are incompatible, spring from the same essence. Blake's view is that man's essence is goodness and that evil is a lack or absence, a "negative" or an accident that can be cast away without destroying the being and integrity of what is left, the fundamentally good being, but also a being capable of evil. Something lapses in a man's behavior that we call in its negativity evil.

Blake cannot see how there can be "regeneration," the casting away of

---

*It is of interest to know that one of those Lavater criticizes here is "he who blasphemes a book, a work of art." Blake adds, "mark that I do not believe there is such a thing [hell] literally. But hell is the being shut up in the possession of corporeal desires which shortly weary the man for <u>all life is holy</u>."

the negative evil, if that evil is a substantive part of man's essence. What remained would be only part of a man. In the passage Blake cites from St. Matthew, Jesus declares that evil cannot cast out evil. For Blake, this means that a negative does not have the power to act.

I now return to Blake's concluding criticism of Lavater. Consistent with what he has to say about good and evil, Blake remarks that every man's leading propensity is his leading virtue, evil being a negative. Blake follows this by implying a criticism of the views of causality that he says are held by Lavater and "all his cotemporaries." It is not clear to whom Blake refers here. Aristotle's fourfold theory of causes seems to have been generally accepted in the time, especially among churchmen. In Blake's mind, Lavater's "cotemporaries" must have included David Hume (1711–1776), whose account of causation Blake read. Hume rejected as unsatisfactory all empirical explanations of the relation of cause to effect. Blake's critique of modern notions of cause is grounded not on Hume's skepticism, however, or, for that matter, Locke's earlier, rather messy empirical effort. These, like all empirical approaches to this matter, are irrelevant to his views, which are logically independent of them. Blake's radical position is that everything arises from and exists in an original and endless act of imagination in which we all participate. Strictly speaking, nothing ever precedes the creative act as its cause, and its effect is what imagination produces and contains in its act. Further, by synecdoche, a trope central to Blake and which he takes literally, man's individual acts of imagination are God's. Imagination *as act* is what is. Thus, "Each thing is its own cause & its own effect" (E601). Also, every act is virtuous, and all hindrance is negative, as he next indicates. Here the imaginative act is an ethical imperative and absence of act an ethical failure, a void.

Finally, Blake, in his critique of Lavater's substantive idea of woman's original sin, says that sin, the idea of which he opposes, would have to include all the "Loves and Graces" of women.

These criticisms, which drive to fundamental issues and thus indicate Blake's severe reservations, also reflect Blake's disagreement with Lavater over severity of judgment, itself. Lavater writes, "Who begins with severity, in judging of another, ends commonly with falsehood" (36) and "The smiles that encourage severity of judgment, hide malice and insincerity" (37). Blake replies, "false" to both of these aphorisms and remarks of the first of them, "Severity of judgment is a great virtue" (E585). To the second he asserts, "Aphorisms should be universally true," recognizing that 37 might be true in some cases. Here Blake clearly means that one should speak out forthrightly, and elsewhere he expresses that view. When Lavater says, "He who, when called upon to speak a disagreeable truth, tells it boldly and has done, is both bolder and milder than he who nibbles in a low voice, and never ceases nibbling." Blake remarks, "damn such" (302, E590).

All of these criticisms are preceded, however, by Blake's very favorable general comment about *Aphorisms*, part of which I have quoted earlier. The rest follows:

> Man is bad or good. as he unites himself with bad or good spirits. tell me with whom you go & Ill tell you what you do
>
> As we cannot experience pleasure but by means of others. who experience either pleasure or pain thro us. And as all of us on earth are united in thought, for it is impossible to think without images of somewhat on earth — So it is impossible to know God or heavenly things without conjunction with those who know God & heavenly things. therefore, all who converse in the spirit, converse with spirits.
>
> For these reasons I say that this Book is written by consultation with Good Spirits because it is Good. & that the name Lavater. is the amulet of those who purify the heart of man [p. 225, E600].

The chain of comments that I earlier mentioned as indicating that Blake didn't merely read from beginning to end sends us from aphorism 3 to both 533 and 630. Aphorism 533 sends us to 554, and 630 sends us also to 554 and to 459. These are important because they express some of Lavater's and Blake's notions of the relation of man to the world and to God. Aphorism 3, underlined by Blake, reads as follows: "As in looking upward each beholder thinks himself the centre of the sky; so Nature formed her individuals, that each must see himself the center of being." We are referred to 533 where Lavater writes:

> I have often, too often, been tempted, at the daily relation of new knaveries, to despise human nature in every individual, till, on minute anatomy of each trick, I found that the knave was only an *enthusiast* or *momentary fool*. This discovery of momentary folly, symptoms of which assail the wisest and the best, has thrown a great consolatory light on my inquiries into man's moral nature; by this the theorist is enabled to assign to each class and each individual its own peculiar fit of vice or folly; and, by the same, he has it in his power to contrast the ludicrous or dismal catalogue with the more pleasing one of sentiment and virtue, more properly their own.

Blake responds:

> man is the ark of God the mercy seat is above upon the ark cherubims guard it on either side & in the midst is the holy law. man is either the ark of God or a phantom of the earth & of the water if thou seekest by human policy to guide this ark. remember Uzzah II Sam VI Ch:
> > knaveries are not human nature knaveries are knaveries. See N 554
> > this aphorism seems to me to want discrimination [E596]

Here, as he has before, Lavater sees people as possessing a type of vice or folly and a type of sentiment and virtue. Though elsewhere he seems to speak of knaves as being *essentially* knaves, here he presents us with the idea of momentary knavish behavior. This seems to be closer to Blake's view that all evil is an absence or negative, but Lavater proceeds to assign tendencies toward particular follies to individuals as if they are part of each person's essence. Lavater is consoled by this. For one, thing, it does not conflict with his physiognomic views and at the same time allows him to maintain optimism about humanity.

Blake's response seems, at first, quite oblique. He accurately describes the Ark of the Covenant. In William Smith's description, "it contain[ed] inviolate the Divine autograph of the two tables, that 'covenant' from which it derived its title."* 1 Kings 8 tells us, as does Blake, that cherubim guarded it. It signified the most holy place in the sanctuary of the temple and prevented any idol from being placed there. Uzzah (2 Samuel 6, 6) made the fatal mistake of placing his hand on the ark and taking "hold of it." God smote him, and he died on the spot. Blake offers his own reading of this event. He identifies the ark with man and Uzzah's act as an attempt to dominate and control human imagination by imposition of some "human policy." He does not think that a knavery should be explained away as a momentary appearance of a usually hidden part of human nature. Knaveries are what they are, falling under Blake's notion of negatives. The connection to aphorism 33 lies in Blake's identification of human imagination with the ark and thus with God. That relation becomes the subject, for Blake, of his comment on 630. Lavater writes:

> A *god*, an *animal*, a *plant*, are not companions of man; nor is the *faultless*— then judge with lenity of all; the coolest, wisest, best, all without exception, have their points, their moments of enthusiasm, fanaticism, absence of mind, faint-heartedness, stupidity — if you allow not for these, your criticisms on man will be a mass of accusations or caricatures.

Blake comments:

> It is the God in <u>all</u> that is our companion & friend, for our God himself says, you are my brother my sister & my mother; & St John. Whoso dwelleth in love dwelleth in God & God in him. & such an one cannot judge of any but in love. & his feelings will be attractions or repulses
> See Aphorisms 549 & 554
> God is in the lowest effects as well as in the highest causes for he is become a worm that he may nourish the weak
> For let it be rememberd that creation is. God descending according to the weakness of man for our Lord is the word of God & every thing on earth is the word of God & in its essence is God [E599]

---

*William Smith LL.D., *Smith's Bible Dictionary*, New York: Pyramid Books, 1967, 49.

Lavater refers here to some pagan deity (*a* god, not God) as distanced from man along with animals and plants. He proceeds to imply, as he has in 533, that no one is faultless. The whole passage expresses Lavater's desire to be charitable and to abjure severity of judgment. Blake rejects the distance that Lavater accepts between man and anything else and expresses, as he often does elsewhere, the empathetic friendship, indeed brotherhood and even identity of God with all things. I am not certain whether Blake is quarreling with Lavater and assuming Lavater really refers to God, not a god, or is merely extending a statement Lavater has made. The reference to St. John seems to be to no specific passage but rather to John's emphasis on the notion that we are all God's children and therefore, it follows, one family.

Blake's comments on 549 and 554 express this view, but in different ways. In his response to 549, Blake calls Lavater's remark "true worship": "He who hates the wisest and best of men hates the Father of men; for, where is the Father of men to be seen but in the most perfect of his children," but Blake erases the two "hates" and replaces them with "loves." In response to 554, Blake reasserts a fundamental belief; Lavater has written, "The enemy of art is the enemy of nature; art is nothing but the highest sagacity and exertion of human nature; and what nature will he honour who honours not the human?" Blake responds, "human nature is the image of God" (E597). He has not yet decided that "nature" is a word carrying the connotation of alienation from imagination and thus reality, as he does in his annotation to Wordsworth (below p. 166, E665).

It is also interesting that here Blake says nothing about art. Indeed, most of his surviving remarks about art come later in his career. We have, however, seen that he responds positively to Lavater's objection to those who "blaspheme" books and works of art and to Lavater's aphorism 506: "the poet, who composes not before the moment of inspiration, and as that leaves him ceases — composes, and he alone, for all men, all classes, all ages." Blake comments, "Most Excellent" (E595).

The aphorisms and responses reveal the difference of temperament between Lavater and Blake despite their many agreements. Lavater emphasizes calmness of will and in general calmness in all things. Blake is often made "uneasy" by this, as when Lavater remarks, "There is no mortal truly wise and restless at once — wisdom is the repose of minds" (226), or when Lavater connects energy to patience (276) or praises silence. Both hate indolence (487, E594) and distinguish between will and the powers of concentration of energy on the one hand and wishes, which, as Lavater says, can "run over into loquacious impotence" (25). But Blake is willing to go further: When Lavater says, "He alone is good, who, though possessed of energy, prefers virtue, with the appearance of weakness, to the invitation of acting brilliantly ill" (409), Blake responds, "Noble But Mark Active Evil is better than Passive Good" (E592), expression of an attitude straight out of *The Marriage of Heaven and Hell*.

Lavater is never impulsive and dislikes impulsiveness. Blake tends to identify energy with passion. When Lavater does let himself go and say, "Fear the boisterous savage of passion less than the sedate grin of villainy" (63), Blake responds with, I think, relief, "bravo" (E586), as if at last Lavater has shown some passion, himself. But Lavater is hardly praising passion here, which he usually identifies with excess and often distrusts: "Between passion and lie there is not a finger's breadth" (333). Blake replies, "Lie, is the contrary to Passion" (E590), recognizing it as a calculated deception.

Blake frequently supports excess against Lavater's advice for prudence and restraint. He is "uneasy" when Lavater says, "He who goes one step beyond his real faith, or presentiment, is in danger of deceiving himself and others" (414, E592). Certainly this could be called dangerous, but Blake worries that caution of this kind can bottle up genius. Even with respect to "immature, impetuous wishes," Blake is "uneasy" with Lavater's criticism that such a wisher will be dragged "by stern repentance ... bound and reluctant, back to the place from which he sallied" (607, E598).

Blake's remark, "weak is the joy that is never wearied" (E584), expresses his general suspicion of Lavater's praise of evenhandedness, patience, and fear of excess of any kind. Related to this is a distrust of Lavater's identifying genius and energy only with the creation of durable, indelible things (E587). One may suspect that Blake has in mind here fear for his own work and the possibility that it might suffer destruction. Furthermore, Blake is "uneasy" when Lavater says, "He is much greater and more authentic, who produces one thing entire and perfect, than he who does many by halves" (440, E593), knowing that some works of genius are unfinished, as *The Four Zoas* would come to be.

At the same time, Blake values Lavater's apparent approval of laughter ("I love laughing," Blake remarks) when Lavater says that many vigorous minds are unable to abstain from laughing and that he is suspicious of "scarce smiles" and "sneerers" (54, E585, and 59, E585). But characteristically, Lavater mentions his dislike of immoderate laughter as well as the "horse-laugh," a sign of "brutality of character" (58). Blake underlines Lavater's praise of the power of gladness (13, 28, E585), which is related to Lavater's emphasis on the importance of fellowship, empathy, and, above all, friendship. The last two of these Blake also values. The following is marked "excellent" and part of it is underlined: "Let the unhappiness you feel at another's errors, and the happiness you enjo<u>y in their perfections, be the measure of your progress in wisdom and virtue</u> (278, E589).

An important disagreement Blake has with Lavater is over the matter of forgiveness. It has been well and thoroughly discussed by Jeanne Moskal, and I report on her findings here. The forgiveness at issue is forgiveness of another human being, not God's forgiveness. Moskal points out that Blake differs with Lavater on two matters: "The first one is that Lavater's description of the process of forgiveness omits the initial stage of the victim's resentment against the offender.... Blake's second count against Lavater — a more profound objection, I believe — is that Lavater omits any possibility of the offender's change of heart, or, as Blake puts it, of his regeneration."* This seems to me correct. I think, however, that although the second objection is more profound in a religious and ethical sense, the first is as profound about human behavior in a psychological sense. With respect to the first sense, Blake thinks Lavater is psychologically distant from the victim. Blake, no doubt looking into his own responses, sees that Lavater's attitude reveals a failure of empathy and a refusal to recognize an important aspect of human nature. According to Blake, one's immediate response to an offense is inevitably resentment. Blake's comment on aphorism 608 reveals how far he will go to acknowledge passion against Lavater's dislike:

> LAVATER: He submits to be seen through a microscope, who suffers himself to be caught in a fit of passion [608].
> BLAKE: & such a one I dare love [E598].

Blake endorses forgiveness, but only after the victim calms his resentment and the offender changes his ways:

> LAVATER: The frigid smiler, crawling, indiscreet, obtrusive, brazen-faced, is a scorpion-whip of destiny — avoid him! [477]
> BLAKE: & never forgive him till he mends [E594]

On the matter of change of heart, Moskal refers to Blake's use of the word "regeneration," which is connected in her view to his friendliness to Methodism. Moskal rightly notes Lavater's "distrust of fanaticism, emotion, and mystery" (80). At the same time, it is clear, as I have indicated, that Lavater is inconsistent about whether knavery is but a momentary failure or an essential quality of a knave.

In short, Blake puts a high value on exuberance ("Beauty is exuberant"

---

*Jeanne Moskal, "The Problem of Forgiveness in Blake's Annotations to Lavater," *Studies in Philology*, 86, 1 (Winter 1989), 71. See also her *Blake, Ethics, and Forgiveness*, Tuscaloosa & London: University of Alabama Press, 1994, esp. 49–56.

[E595]), laughter, passion, and energy. He identifies these qualities with forthrightness and sincerity. Included here is enthusiasm, which Lavater identifies, as did many others at the time, with an excess of religious passion. Oddly enough, Lavater was on occasion suspected of being an enthusiast, but he is hardly exuberant and thinks exuberance is likely to be oppressive. He mistrusts passion and emphasizes the strength and energy of patience.

Blake outrightly declares only four of the aphorisms "false." Two of them (36 and 37) have to do with severity in the judgment of acts of others. Lavater seems to equate severity with a lack of kindness. He also implies that severity may be impulsive and the judgment might have to be changed: "Who begins with severity, in judging of another, ends commonly with falsehood" (36). Lavater seems to be thinking about an *a priori* notion, a prejudiced one. Blake values severity ("a great virtue" [E585]) as forthrightness and equates it with decisiveness and clarity. He certainly practiced it later in his judgments of other artists.

Blake marks aphorism 39 "uneasy" and later "false." It reads: "Who, without pressing temptation, tells a lie, will, without pressing temptation, act ignobly and meanly." It is possible here that Blake has in the back of his mind traditional attacks on poets as liars and the value of a good story. In any case, he remarks, "a man may lie for his own pleasure. but if any one is hurt by his lying will confess his lie" (17, 39, E585). He then advises his reader to look at aphorism 124, which he thinks contradicts 39: "Who has a daring eye, tells downright truths and downright lies." To this he says, "most True" (E587).

Religious Views

Of Lavater's "refined Epicurism" Blake remarks, "True Christian philosophy" (366, E591), though in later years he turned against Epicurus. He endorses Lavater's remarks about God, such as the following: "Let none turn over books, or roam the stars in quest of God, who sees him not in man" (408, E592). He enthusiastically endorses Lavater's rejection of an impersonal God (552, E596).

Lavater and Blake seem to agree about religious sectarianism. Blake approves of aphorism 339 by underlining the following part of it: "who adheres to a sect has something of its cant" (E590). However, Blake quarrels with Lavater about superstition when Lavater writes: "Superstition always inspires littleness, religion grandeur of mind: the superstitious raises beings inferior to himself to deities" (342). Blake rewrites this, substituting "hipocrisy" for "superstition" and "hypocrite" for superstitious." His comment follows:

no man was ever truly superstitious who was not truly religious as far as he knew
True superstition is ignorant honesty & this is beloved of god & man
I do not allow that there is such a thing as Superstition taken in the strict sense of the word
A man must first deceive himself before he is thus Superstitious & so he is a hypocrite
Hipocrisy. is as distant from superstition. as the wolf from the lamb [E 591].

Later, Blake comes back to this matter, insisting that superstition as such is innocent and is a bugbear to reason only when it is attached to hypocrisy. He does not comment when Lavater esteems "the reasonable part of incredulity and the respectable of superstition" (443). Blake's motive in his remarks appears to be maintenance of respect for the religious innocence of children and the uneducated.

Blake on Blake

In a few cases, when Blake marks an aphorism with "uneasy," he is expressing uneasiness about either his own past or present self. These are of interest because one finds few statements in Blake's writings that are other than those forthrightly expressing opinions. When Lavater says that one can know that a man is good if his friends are good and his enemies bad, Blake is "uneasy" because he fears he has "not many enemies," implying that perhaps to be good he should have more of them (151, E 587). He is also uneasy when Lavater remarks, "To know yourself perfectly you have only to set down a true statement of those that ever loved or hated you." Blake declares that he cannot do this (619, E599). He admits he has been guilty of the fault of jealousy in human friendships and hopes to "mend" (588, E 597), but he hopes he does not flatter himself when he says that he enjoys the greatness of others and "forgets his greatest qualities in their greater ones" (203, E588).

Blake hated hypocrisy as much as anything, yet he is uneasy about his ability to follow the advice of aphorism 638: "Let the cold, who offers a nauseous mimickry of warm affection, meet with what he deserves — a repulse; but from that moment depend on his unreconcilable enmity." Blake responds that he does not know how to do this but "will try to do it the first opportunity" (E 600). There is no record of his managing to do it, and reminiscences treat him as affable and of good nature.

Of his past actions Blake regrets that he has done what Lavater warns against: "Distrust your heart and the durability of your fame, if from the stream of occasion you snatch a handful of foam; deny the stream, and give its name to the frothy bursting bubble" (486). Blake is "uneasy," but not because he disagrees, and writes, "this I lament that I have done" (E594). He is uneasy as well about one or more of his past acts. Another aphorism evokes a comment that he has changed his view:

> LAVATER: The fool separates his object from all surrounding ones; all abstraction is temporary folly [624].
>
> BLAKE: uneasy because I once thought otherwise but now know it is Truth [E 599]

He did not change his mind again on this matter.

2

Annotations to Emanuel Swedenborg's *Heaven and Hell, Divine Love and Divine Wisdom,* and *Divine Providence*

Emanuel Swedenborg (1688–1772), Swedish son of a Lutheran clergyman, began his career as an engineer, served as a governmental overseer of mines, was appointed to the Swedish House of Nobles and the Swedish Royal Academy, and produced several scientific studies including a voluminous work on mineralogy and books on anatomy and physiology. In 1745, he experienced a vision that transformed his life, and thereafter he devoted himself to theological writings that brought him fame and in some cases made him the object of controversy.

His books were written in Latin, and Blake is known to have read in translation all or part of at least five. His annotations to three of them, published in 1784, 1788, and 1790, have survived. It appears that by 1789 he had read and annotated *Heaven and Hell* and read *Earths in Our Solar System,* which he calls in an annotation *Worlds in Universe.* The year 1790 seems to have been a critical one for Blake's attitude toward Swedenborg, for in that year he began to write his satirical work, largely directed at Swedenborg, *The Marriage of Heaven and Hell.* Furthermore, if we read through all the annotations we find that they begin with notes that mark what he regarded as important ideas; however, they later tend to be intermixed with occasional unfavorable responses until in *Divine Providence* they are mainly negative. It must be added that later in life Blake's attitude seems to have softened to ambivalence or guarded respect. Henry Crabb Robinson reports in his *Reminiscences,*

> Blake said, "[Swedenborg] was a Divine teacher. He has done much good, and will do much. He has corrected many errors of Popery, and also of Luther and

Calvin. Yet Swedenborg was wrong in endeavouring to explain to the rational faculty what the reason cannot comprehend. He should have left that."*

In *The Marriage of Heaven and Hell*, begun in 1790, Blake deals harshly with Swedenborg. He plays with Swedenborg's prophecy that the Last Judgment would occur in 1757, the year also of Blake's birth. This was to be the year that the spirit of Jesus in the form of the New Church would appear on earth. The old church passes away and "all things are become New." These are the words in the "Propositions" offered at the first general conference in 1798 of the New Jerusalem Church, founded on the writings of Swedenborg.† But Blake, who with his wife attended the conference, observes, "It is now thirty-three years [Jesus's age when he was crucified] since its advent," and all that is left of Swedenborg's writings are "the linen clothes folded up" (E34), the body of them gone from the tomb. "Swedenborg has not written one new truth ... he has written all the old falshoods"§ (E43). Blake's disillusionment seems to have begun not long after he and his wife attended the conference. There were 42 propositions offered and accepted, and 32 resolutions based on them were passed unanimously. Blake may have accepted all of them at the time, if indeed he voted. Among the propositions that he would have accepted were the following:

> IV. That to believe Redemption to have consisted in the passion of the cross, is a fundamental error of the Old Church; and that this error, together with that relating to the existence of Three Divine Persons from eternity, hath perverted the whole Christian Church, so that nothing is left remaining in it.
>
> V. That all prayers directed to a Trinity of distinct persons, and not to a Trinity conjoined in One Person, are henceforth not attended to, but are in heaven like ill-scented odours.
>
> VII. That the doctrines universally taught in the Old Church, particularly respecting Three Divine Persons, the Atonement, Justification by Faith alone, the Resurrection of the material Body, &c., &c., are highly dangerous to the rising generation, inasmuch as they tend to ingraft in their infant kinds principles diametrically opposite to those of the New Church, and consequently hurtful to their salvation [Hindmarsh, 122].

---

*Henry Crabb Robinson, *Diary, Reminiscences, and Correspondence*, selected and edited by Thomas Sadler, London: Macmillan and Co., 1869, II, 304.
†Robert Hindmarsh, "An Account of the First General Conference of the Members of the New Jerusalem Church, London, April13–17, 1789," reprinted in *Blake and Swedenborg: Opposition Is True Friendship*, eds. Harvey F. Bellin and Darrell Ruhl, West Chester, PA: Swedenborg Foundation, 1985, 124.
§On *The Marriage of Heaven and* Hell and Blake's changing views of Swedenborg see Martin K. Nurmi, *Blake's "Marriage of Heaven and Hell": A Critical Study*, Kent OH: Kent State University Bulletin, Research Series III; Morton D. Paley, *Energy and the Imagination: A Study of the Development of Blake's Thought*, Oxford at the Clarendon Press, 1970, and Paley's "'A New Heaven is Begun': Blake and Swedenborgianism," in *Blake and Swedenborg*, details cited in footnote 2 above, pp. 15–34.

However, Blake seems soon to have concluded that the New Church was the Old come again as Antichrist and with the trappings of what he later came to call "outward Ceremony" (E274). Proposition 34, for example, states that "external Forms of Worship, agreeable to the doctrines of the New Church are necessary" (124).

Airy Nothing

I treat separately here Blake's first annotation in *Heaven and Hell*.* It responds on the half-title page to a quotation there from *A Midsummer Night's Dream*, written and somewhat misquoted by someone else, perhaps a previous owner: "And as Imagination bodies forth y forms of things unseen — turns them to shape & gives to airy Nothing a local habitation & a Name" Sh.† Blake objects here to the attribution of the words to Shakespeare and not to Theseus, the character who speaks them. He writes, "Thus fools quote Shakespeare The Above is Theseus's opinion Not Shakespeares You might as well quote Satans blasphemies from Milton & give them as Miltons opinions" (E601). This is interesting because early commentators made the same mistake about the speakers of Blake's *Songs*, and some later critics carelessly identified speeches by characters in the long poems as expressing Blake's views. Blake's annotation can be taken as a reminder to readers of how not to read his own works and indeed any piece of imaginative writing.§

There is another aspect of the passage from Shakespeare that, as Morton D. Paley has pointed out, clashes with Blake's view. Paley quotes Alexander Gilchrist's comment that Blake objected to the phrase "airy nothing" on the ground that "things imagination saw were as much realities as were gross and tangible facts."** Paley also points out that in the follow-

---

*A Treatise concerning Heaven and Hell, and of the Wonderful Things therein, as Heard and Seen, by the Honourable and Learned Emanuel Swedenborg, of the Senatorial Order of Nobles in the Kingdom of Sweden. Translated from the Original Latin [by William Cookworthy and Thomas Hartley]. Second edition. London: Printed by R. Hindmarsh, No. 32, Clerkenwell-Close; London, 1784. The copy that Blake annotated is in the Houghton Library of Harvard University. Except where otherwise noted, all quotations from this work and others by Swedenborg will be cited by section number rather than page, as is the custom with Swedenborg's works.

†The correct quotation according to *The Riverside Shakespeare* is:
    And as imagination bodies forth
    The forms of things unknown, the poet's pen
    Turns them to shapes, and gives to airy nothing
    A local habitation and a name.

§On this matter of dramatic form in imaginative works see my *The Offense of Poetry*, Seattle: University of Washington Press, 2007, 113–127.

**Morton D. Paley, *Energy and the Imagination*, 212. Alexander Gilchrist, *Life of William Blake*, London: J. N. Dent & Sons Ltd.; New York: E. P. Dutton & Co Inc., 318.

ing passage Blake uses one of the lines from *A Midsummer Night's Dream* in *Milton*:

> Some Sons of Los surround the Passions with porches of iron & silver
> Creating form & beauty around the dark regions of sorrow,
> Giving to airy nothing a name and a habitation
> Delightful! With bounds to the Infinite putting off the indefinite
> Into most holy forms of Thought [E125]

These lines seem to refer to the creation of a frame for those "dark regions," thereby transforming an abstraction, "sorrow," into apprehensible shape by art.

It seems, then, that Blake's response to Theseus's statement reflects three important attitudes: that poems are always dramatic in form and that the imagination does not fabricate illusions, being instead the power to experience and express beyond that which could be apprehended by the so-called passive reception of sense data. Finally, it expresses Blake's suspicion of vagueness and his (and Swedenborg's) dislike of abstractions.

Heaven and Hell: Theological Vision

The brief account that follows of Swedenborg's most popular and best-known work emphasizes elements that either influenced Blake or have similarities to or differences from his views. Blake's annotations to *Heaven and Hell* are but two in number. However, they have interest in that they seem to show Blake adopting Swedenborg's position. I shall discuss them after an account of key ideas expressed in the work.

Bernhard Lang declares, "The best way to summarize the contents of *Heaven and Hell* is to reconstruct its teaching in the form of a maplike representation of the universe."* Lang's map presents the world of earth at the center, the world of spirits surrounding it, Swedenborg's "hells" and "heavens" (of which there are three each) below and above respectively, and God, or the Lord, surrounding the whole, providing a circumference. Lang points out that Swedenborg uses both vertical and centric metaphors to describe this universe, with God both above, surrounding, and within. However, as we imagine this map we must remind ourselves that Swedenborg's universe is a spiritual one, and is actually spaceless and timeless, totally interior to the

---

*Bernhard Lang, "Introduction," *Heaven and Its Wonders and Hell, Drawn from Things Heard & Seen* by Emanuel Swedenborg, translated from the Latin by George F. Dole, West Chester, PA: Swedenborg Foundation, 2000, 12. This is the most recent translation of that work.

mind, though not an airy nothing. Indeed, it is offered to us in excruciating detail and with much repetition.

The whole of *Heaven and Hell* is a report on what Swedenborg has learned of the structure of the universe and the character of angels from his conversations with angels themselves. In his preface, he writes:

> The secrets revealed in the following work are concerning heaven and hell, and the life of man after death, subjects which the church now o'days hardly knows any thing of, though described in the written word; nay, many who were born and live within the pale of it deny them, saying in their hearts, Who ever came from thence to shew us of these things: left therefore the like incredulity, which chiefly reigns among the learned and worldly wise, should infect the simple in heart, and the simple in faith; it has been granted to me to associate with angels, and to converse with them, as man does with man; and also to see the things that are in the heavens and in the hells, and this now for thirteen years together; and also to describe the things so seen and heard, in order that hereby the minds of the ignorant may be enlightened, and an end put to incredulity [p. 3].

I now discuss five points fundamental to Swedenborg's theological vision and important to compare to Blake's views:

Angels: There have not been, or are there now any angels or devils who were not once human beings. They are all people who have died, but they do not know that they are dead. Indeed, they have reached real life. There are two classes of angels, heavenly and spiritual, those representing love for God and those of a lesser heaven representing love of neighbors. They have human forms that resemble them as they were in the prime of life.* Their faces accurately reflect their feelings at all times. Their writing and their thoughts are one, for their writing accurately represents their thoughts. They possess identity with God, God being in them and they in God. As such, they are all individuals, but they compose a single angelic community that is one human form. They rightly believe that all the good they do comes from God and nothing good comes from the self. They serve as teachers to newcomers to heaven, who must learn what the earliest people knew, the ancient knowledge of symbols and images that on earth has been erased. Occasionally, we are told, fraudulents sneak into heaven:

> It sometimes happens, that hypocrites from beneath insinuate themselves into some angelical societies, who have learned to conceal their interior state to the form of good peculiar to such Societies respectively, that they may pass for

---

*Blake departs from Swedenborg here, if we are to trust his remark to Henry Crabb Robinson about his vision of and conversation with Milton. Robinson writes, "As he spoke of Milton's appearing to him, I asked whether he resembled the prints of him. He answered, 'All.'—'What age did he appear to be?'—'Various ages—sometimes a very old man.'" *Diary, Reminiscences, and Correspondence*, II, 309.

angels of light; but such can make no long tarrying there, for they presently begin to feel an inward anguish and pain, to change countenance, and to be struck in a manner lifeless, through the Influx of the life-powers of the angels so contrary to their own; on which they cast themselves headlong into hell among their fellows, without daring to ascend again;... [48].

Blake may have taken part of his idea for the false kind of angel who appears in *The Marriage of Heaven and Hell* partly from Swedenborg's hypocrites. Blake's angel is a parodic inversion. In one "Memorable Fancy," a phrase parodying Swedenborg's "Memorable Relations," an angel attempts to instruct the narrator about the afterlife. The angel is certain that he is destined for hell: "O pitiable foolish young man! O horrible! O dreadful state! consider the hot burning dungeon thou art preparing for thyself to all eternity, to which thou art going in such career" (E41). But the narrator responds to the angel with an opposite vision, in which Swedenborg's heavy works provide ballast that brings them both down to earth. In another "Memorable Fancy," a devil, who represents active energy against the fixity of mind of the angels, irritates one of them so that the angel's face changes color: "The Angel, hearing this, became almost blue, but mastering himself he grew yellow, & at last white pink & smiling," at which point he unleashes violent curses at the devil (E43). As in Swedenborg, the angel's face reveals his feelings, but Blake's angel is capable of a hypocritical smile.

Time and Space: In heaven there is no measurable time or space, only changes of what Swedenborg calls states (of spirit or mind). What is temporal for us on earth is for angels a state. Eternity is an infinite state, not an infinite stretch of time; and spatial relations are determined by people's inner or spiritual natures. Closeness to God or to others or distances from them are states of mind. Motion is a change of one's state. The terms devil and Satan refer to states of mind. Though people are described as in states, it is more accurate to say that states are in people. God does not condemn people to hell. Hell is a state of mind that arises from self-love and/or love of the world of earth rather than love of God, neighbor, and heaven. Imagined as a single entity, hell is a single devil, heaven a single angel. Blake's "states," a word that comes up in the longer poems, are also interior to the mind, and one of them is called Satan.*

Correspondences: There is nothing natural or earthly to which something spiritual does not correspond, even though it may be by opposition. Everything in heaven corresponds to something in us. The human being is a heaven

---

*On states in Blake's work, see *Milton* II, plate 32, ll. 23–35 (E132); on Satan as a state, see *The Four Zoas* VIII, 109 (E378).

in miniature, a microcosm. This notion in Swedenborg repeats the traditional occult idea, attributed to Hermes Trismegistus, that what is above has a correspondence below; but the idea is also a "horizontal" one: What is inside has an outer correspondence. The Swedenborgian correspondence between heaven and hell is an inversion, directions are reversed, and hell is upside-down. Blake offers a similar view in his imagery of the natural or fallen man, upside-down with his parts in grotesque, disturbing relation to each other.*

Equilibrium: The world, including hell, is a product of action and reaction controlled by God, who provides the necessary balance between good and evil. Without that balance there would be a collapse into chaos. The world of human spirits exists halfway between heaven and hell, and in this equilibrium we are free to accept God's good or our evil. We are born into evil by heredity, and its sum has increased with every generation, requiring a greater and greater effort to dispel it. One's self-love, with which everyone is born, is evil. Blake calls this the "selfhood," and Milton, in *Milton*, declares that it "must be put off & annihilated" (II, 40, l. 36 [E420]). For Swedenborg, equilibrium can exist only if God has some other — us — to love. Otherwise his love would have to be directed toward himself. Blake's notion of contraries as it is expressed in *The Marriage of Heaven and Hell* tends to oppose Swedenborg's equilibrium in that it suggests energy and strife rather than balance and stasis.

Will and Understanding: These words are related to volition and rationality respectively. We have will from birth; and, though it is initially evil from heredity, it makes possible our being open to the influx of God's goodness and our being formed by it. Rationality, or understanding, opens us to truths and is formed by them. Our birth into hereditary evil has been brought down to us from the creation, when will and understanding were separated from each other (as seems to be the case in Blake's *Book of Urizen* and his later works). The evil in our will can be gradually dispelled. On the flyleaf of *Divine Love and Divine Wisdom*, Blake seems to be expressing a similar view, which is drawn from *Heaven and Hell*, sections 424 and 425, but it actually differs from that of Swedenborg's, as I shall show in the next section. Blake does not write annotations to 424 and 425.

In his few annotations to this volume, Blake is interested in the angels who instruct those who have just arrived in heaven. He (or someone else) marked in the margin the following from sections 333 and 334. The passages illustrate Swedenborg's tendency toward pedantic detail, hardly what Blake would have dignified as "minute particulars":

---

*On the upside-down man see my *William Blake: A Reading of the Shorter Poems*, Seattle, WA, University of Washington Press, 1963, 35–44.

[333] Little children are of different dispositions, some like the Spiritual, some like the Celestial Angels: such as are of the former class, appear in Heaven stationed to the left hand; those of the latter class, to the right hand: and all Little Children in the Grand Man or Heaven, are in the province of the eyes; such as resemble the Spiritual Angels, in the province of the left eye; and such as resemble the Celestials, in the province of the right eye; and that because the Lord appears to the Angels of his Spiritual Kingdom, fronting the left eye; and to the Angels of the Celestial Kingdom, fronting the right eye; see above, n. 118. Little Children being thus in the province of the eyes, denotes them to be under the immediate guardianship and protection of the Lord.

[334] How Infants [who have died] are educated in Heaven shall here briefly be told. They are first taught to speak by those that have the care of them: their first utterance is only a kind of affectionate sound, which, by degrees, grows more distinct, as their minds become furnished with ideas; for the ideas of the mind springing from the affectionate part, immediately give birth and form to the speech of Angels, as mentioned above, n. 234 to 235.

But he (or someone else) partially erased the mark.

Blake marked and commented on section 513, which reads,

> The angels appointed for instructors are from several societies, but chiefly from such as are in the north and the south, as their understanding and wisdom more particularly consist in the distinct knowledges of good and truth. The places set apart for instructing are towards the north, and are various, well-ordered, and divided, according to the particular classes of the disciples to be instructed in heavenly things....

These symbolic directions may have been taken up by Blake in his long poems, the area of the north being that of Los, identified with the imagination, and that of the south Urizen, identified with rationality or understanding. Blake, in his note refers us as follows: "See N 73 Worlds in Universe. for account of Instructing Spirits" (E602). The passage is in Swedenborg's book, popularly titled *Earths in the Universe*, an English translation of which was published in 1758. It reads as follows:

> The Spirits who instruct, apply themselves also to the left Side of the Persons instructed, but more to the Front; they reprove likewise, but mildly, and presently teach them how they ought to live: They appear also of a darkish Hue, yet not like Clouds as the former, but as if they were clad in Sackcloth: These are called Instructors, but the former Chastisers. When the instructing Spirits are present, angelic Spirits are present also, sitting close to the Head, and filling it in a peculiar Manner; their Presence likewise is perceived there like a mild and gentle Aspiration, for they are afraid of Man's perceiving the least Pain or Anxiety from their Approach and Influx; They govern the chastising and instructing Spirits, preventing the former from putting Man to more Pain than is permitted by the Lord, and prompting the latter to teach what is true. During the Time that a chastising Spirit was with me, there were present also angelic

Spirits, who kept my Countenance in a constant Smile and Chearfulness, and the Region about the Lips prominent, and my Mouth a little open; this the Angels easily effect by Influx, when it is permitted of the Lord: They said, that with the Inhabitants of their Earth, they induce such a Countenance when they are present.*

The final annotation refers to the imaginative location of hells. In Swedenborg hell is both one and many, as is heaven. It is a community of devils (as many as those who have died and condemned themselves). It also is seen as one devil:

> ...there is a society of infernals answering to every society of angels, according to the nature of opposites.... According to these manifold distinctions in evil, and their nearer or more remote distances from one another, are the several Hells divided and regulated with the utmost exactness and congruity. There are also Hells under Hells, communicating with one another, some by passages, and some by exhalations, according to the agreement or affinity betwixt evil and evil. That the Hells are so many and various, appears from it's being given to me to know, that under every mountain, hill, rock, plain, and valley, there were particular Hells of different extent in length, breadth, and depth. In a word, both Heaven and the World of Spirits may be considered as convexities, under which are arrangements of those infernal mansions [588].

In his annotation, Blake is interpreting Swedenborg: "under every Good is a hell. i. e. hell is the outward or external of heaven. & is of the body of the lord. for nothing is destroyd" (E602). However, he is also emphasizing a relation of the inner world to the outer that is similar to his own imagery.

Visionary Theology: Divine Love and Divine Wisdom

Much of what is written in *Divine Love and Divine Wisdom* is an elaboration on topics in *Heaven and Hell*.† However, Swedenborg is less interested in mapping the spiritual universe and emphasizing the role of angels in his instruction by them than he is in offering the fundamentals of a theol-

---

*Concerning the Earths in our Solar System which are called Planets; and concerning the Earths in the Starry Heavens; together with an Account of their Inhabitants, and also of the Spirits and Angels there From what has been Seen and Heard. Now first translated from the Latin of the Hon. Emanuel Swedenborg. Published at London by the Author, in the Year 1758. London: Printed and Sold by R. Hindmarsh, No. 32 Clerkenwell-Close.

†*The Wisdom of Angels, concerning Divine Love and Divine Wisdom, translated from the original Latin of the* Hon. *Emanuel Swedenborg,* London : Printed and Sold by W. Chalkin, Grocers Court, Poultry, 1788. The translation is by Nathaniel Tucker. The copy that Blake annotated is in the British Library.

ogy. Blake's first annotations are on the flyleaf, and the first of these cites section 425 of *Heaven and Hell*, in which Swedenborg discusses the will and evil. However, the relevant discussion really begins in section 424, which I quote in full:

> It is provided that men should be able to think from the intellectual part separately from the will, to the end that he may be reformed and changed; for he is reformed by means of truths, and these appertain to the intellect, as was said before. Man is born into the world with natural propensities to evil, whence it is that he is so swallowed up in the love of self, as to grudge and covet the good things of others, and to take pleasure in their loss if it may turn to his gain, being only intent on the honours, riches, and pleasures of this world: now that this malignity of his nature may be reformed, he is endowed with the power of apprehending truths in his understanding, that he may thereby counteract and subdue the evil affections in his will: hence it is that he can speculate truths in his intellect, and bring forth into speech, and act according to them; yet they are not properly his own till they be dictated from his heart and will, and flow spontaneously into his life and actions; and where this is the case, the thoughts of a man's mind, or understanding, constitute his faith; and the thoughts of his heart or will, constitute his love; and so his faith and love, like his understanding and will, are united and agree in one [424].

This is followed, in 425, by,

> As for therefore as truths in the understanding are conjoined with good (*bonis*) in the will, and consequently, as far as any one is freely actuated thereby in the practical manifestation of them, so far he has Heaven in himself, or is in a heavenly state; for, as was said before, the conjunction of good and truth is Heaven in the soul; but as far as falses (*falsa*) in the understanding are conjoined with evil in the will, so far a man has Hell in himself, or is in a hellish state; for the conjunction of false and evil constitutes Hell; but as far as truth in the understanding is not united with good in the will, so far man is in a middle state between both; ... [425].

This is not the whole of section 425, but it is the part Blake seems to be commenting on. From these passages, it appears that Swedenborg is not quite consistent about whether the will is entirely evil or has some good in it. Blake tries to overcome this inconsistency. (Parts of the annotation are very hard to read. I accept Erdman's conjectures about certain words [in brackets], being able to do no better):

> There can be no Good-Will. Will is always Evil It is pernicious to others or selfish If God is any thing he is Understanding He is the Influx from that into the Will Thus Good to others is benevolent Understanding can [?&does] Work [?harm] ignorantly but never can? the Truth [be ?evil] because Man is only Evil [when he wills an untruth]
>
> H[eaven] & Hell Chapter 425 [E602]

This follows from 424. However, in 425 above, Swedenborg declares that there is "good in the will as well as evil." The problem is the separation of the will from understanding, will being identified with volition and desire. However, Blake seems to be putting Swedenborg into his own words when he says that God is influx of understanding into the will, which would then make the will, though evil from birth by heredity, partly good from birth, and having the potential to become one with the understanding. (The two were separated in the creation.) Here Blake must be identifying God's understanding with sympathetic identification, though it is referred to as "thought" in the second annotation, which is below:

> Understanding or Thought is not natural to Man it is acquired by means of Suffering & distress i.e. Experience. Will, Desire, Love, Rage, Envy, & all other Affections are natural, but Understanding is Acquired But Observe. without these is to be less than Man. Man could ?never [have received] ?light from heaven ?without [aid of the] affections one would be ?limited to the ?five [?heavens &] ? hells [& live] in different periods of time
>
> Wisdom of Angels 10 [E602]

If Erdman is right about "five," Blake is wrong, there being only three heavens in Swedenborg's system; and it is by no means clear why man would be limited to the heavens under the conditions stated or what that could possibly mean. Understanding is not natural to man ("natural" does not have the pejorative meaning here that it has later in Blake), as it also is not in Swedenborg (if we identify it with what Swedenborg called "wisdom"). It is provided, like all things good, by God. "Wisdom of Angels 10" may refer either to *Divine Love and Divine Wisdom* or to *Divine Providence*. The passage from the latter seems to me the more likely:

> *That the Good of Love is not Good, except so far as it is united to the True of Wisdom, and that the True of Wisdom is not True, except so far as it is united to the Good of Love.* Good and Truth derive from their Origin, Good in it's Origin is in the Lord, in like Manner is Truth, because the Lord is Good itself and Truth itself, and these two in Him are one; hence it is that Good in the Angels of Heaven and in Men of the Earth is not Good in itself, except so far as it is united to Truth, and that Truth is not Truth in itself, except so far as it is united to Good [10].

Blake writes a separate annotation to passage 10 from *Divine Love and Divine Wisdom*. I will discuss it later.

Divine Love and Divine Wisdom is divided into five parts, and I will discuss the content of and Blake's annotations to each:

Part One: Much of this part is concerned with God's relation to his creation, and much repeats what we have already learned from *Heaven and Hell*:

In the world of spirits there is neither space nor time as we think we know them. Rather, there are "states," which are internal to the spirit, distance in the spiritual world being the difference between two states of mind. Eternity is not of an infinite length; it is a state that an angel is in, or it is something within an angel. God is present everywhere, but not in physical space or time, which are unreal. God's divinity and love infuse everything.

Nothing can be created out of nothing. God created (or rather continually creates) by sending forth everywhere not his divine self but his divine nature and presence: love and wisdom. His love, the only true kind of love, is love of another, not of the self. The created universe is the object of God's love and is a necessity. Otherwise, his love could be only of himself, a false love, which would be impossible for him.

Likewise, his wisdom is also the essence of divinity. What Swedenborg says about this in section 49 is confusing because it seems to conflict with the notion of the influx of divine love. Swedenborg is trying to maintain a distinction here between the divine (or God) and divinity (an influx into man in the forms of love and wisdom):

> With respect to God, it is not possible that he can love and be reciprocally loved by others, in whom there is any Thing infinite, or any Thing of the Essence and Life of Love in itself, that is, any Thing Divine; for if there was any Thing infinite, or of the Essence and Life of Love in itself; that is, any Thing Divine in them, then it would not be beloved by others, but it would love itself; for Infinite or the Divine is one, if this existed in others, it would be itself, and it would be essential Self Love, whereof not the least is possible in God; for this is totally opposite to the Divine Essence; wherefore it must exist in others, in whom there is nothing of the self-existent Divine; ... [49].

Blake supposes a possible semantic disagreement: "False Take it so or the contrary it comes to the same for if a thing loves it is infinite Perhaps we only differ in the meaning of the words Infinite & Eternal" (E604). Swedenborg wants to identify God and man but not commit the heresy of calling Man God (though God is a man, or has a human form). Also, he wants to avoid the charge of pantheism. Thus we have the distinction between divinity and the divine. It is a difficult balancing act, and Blake resists it. The whole matter is connected to Swedenborg's notion of the opposition of action (God's) and reaction (man's), but Swedenborg converts reaction into action in the following:

> There is from God in every created Thing a Reaction, Life alone hath Action, and Reaction is excited by the Action of Life: This Reaction appears as if it appertained to the created Being, because it exists when the Being is acted upon; thus in Man it appears as if it was his own, because he does not perceive any otherwise than that Life is his own, when nevertheless Man is only a Recip-

ient of Life. From the Cause it is, that Man, from his own hereditary Evil, reacts against God; but so far as he believes that all his Life is from God, and every Good of Life from the Action of God, and every Evil of Life from the Reaction of Man, Reaction thus becomes correspondent with Action, and Man acts with God as from himself [68].

Blake, employing language from *The Marriage of Heaven and Hell*, declares, "Good and Evil are here both Good & the two contraries Married" (E604). But it is not that simple in *The Marriage of Heaven and Hell*, as the evil there is not connected with the original evil that Swedenborg sees in the creation but with energy. The usual notions of good and evil are annihilated and replaced by passivity and activity respectively. Devils symbolize activity, and Blake sides with them against the passive angels.

For Swedenborg, in the physical or natural world our thought is entangled in concepts of abstract space and time. Angels think in a different way; they have no notion of what is meant if one says divinity fills space, but they do understand if one says infinity fills everything. God's divinity — his love and wisdom — is everywhere present as influx from his essence. He is not in himself everything. In an annotation to section 70, where this is discussed, Blake says, "Excellent" (E604). If one thinks spatially, infinity becomes only the largest extension of space, the ultimate size of nature. Physical images, of course, seem to involve space, but in the spiritual world angels see things only *as if* they are in space, space being only the appearance *we* see. In the spiritual world, thought has nothing to do with length, breadth, and height:

> The merely natural man thinks by Ideas which he has acquired from the Objects of Sight, in all which there is Figure derived from Length, Breadth and Heighth, and from Form terminated by them, which is either angular or circular; these are, manifestly in the Ideas of his Thought concerning the visible Things on Earth, and they are also in the Ideas of his Thought concerning invisible Things, as Things civil and moral; he does not indeed see them, but still they are there as continuous. Not so the Spiritual Man, especially the Angel of Heaven; his Thought has nothing in common with Figure and Form deriving any Thing from the Length, Breadth, and Heighth of Space, but from the State of a Thing as grounded in it's State of Life: Hence instead of Length of Space, he thinks of the Good of a Thing, grounded in the Good of Life, instead of Breadth of Space the Truth of a Thing, grounded in the Truth of Life, and instead of Heighth the Degrees of these; thus he thinks from the Correspondence which is between Things spiritual and natural [71].

Because divinity is everywhere and abstract space is unreal, small things and large things are the same as well as different. Swedenborg's principal trope, like Blake's, is synecdoche, taken literally, that is, not merely as a rhetorical figure.

> That the Divine is the same in Things the greatest and most minute, may be illustrated by Heaven and the Angels there: the Divine in the whole Heaven and the Divine in an Angel is the same, wherefore also the whole Heaven may appear as one Angel. It is the same with the Church and the Man of the Church. The greatest Body in which the Divine is, is the whole Heaven, and also the whole Church, the least is an Angel of Heaven and a Man of the Church. Sometimes a whole celestial Society hath appeared to me as one angelic Man; and it was told to me that it could appear as a great Man or a Giant, and as a little Man or an Infant; and this because the Divine is the same in Things the greatest and most minute [79].

By the same token, divinity is equally in what we think of as both the largest and smallest things.

Swedenborg begins Part 1 by asserting that the essence of God, or the Lord, is love and wisdom. Love and wisdom are two things that are also one thing, though love is prior in importance to Swedenborg, as it is in this part. Love is identified with will and volition. It can be perverted, as it is in hell, when it is self-love or love of earthly things. Love is also identified with justice, wisdom with judgment and understanding. But to speak about love only in the abstract is to fail to grasp it as an influx from God that inheres always in specific acts.

> Doth it not happen that in Proportion as the Affection which is of Love groweth cold, the Thought, Speech and Action grow cold also? And that in Proportion as it is heated, they also are heated? But this a wise Man perceiveth, not from Knowledge that Love is the Life of Man, but from Experience of this Fact [1].

Blake adds, "They also percieve this from Knowledge but not with the natural part" (E602). Knowledge is obtained from specific experiences and not from apprehension of generalizations about life, which would be passive acceptance like the passive reception of sense data. This interpretation seems endorsed by Swedenborg's next statement:

> No one knoweth what is the Life of Man, unless he knoweth that it is Love; if this be not known, one Person may believe that the Life of Man is only to feel and to act, another that it is to think, when nevertheless Thought is the first Effect of Life, and Sensation and Action the second Effect of Life [2].

Blake's remark is: "This was known to me & thousands" (E602), important because Blake does not limit visionary experience only to a favored few. Love precedes everything else. All else are effects of it for better or worse, and this means that wisdom is an effect of love.

Swedenborg proceeds to discuss one of his paradoxes: That we experience images, but they are not really temporal or spatial:

> That the Divine or God is not in Space, although he is omnipresent, and present with every Man in the World, and every Angel in Heaven, and every Spirit

> under Heaven, cannot be comprehended by any merely natural Idea, but it may be by a spiritual Idea: The Reason why it cannot be comprehended by a natural Idea, is, because in that Idea there is Space [7].

Here Blake is interested in the distinction between a spiritual and a physical, or natural, idea: "What a natural Idea is —," he writes (E603). However, the distinction is not clear at this point, since all images ("ideas" in Locke's and Berkeley's language) seem to have a spatial character. Swedenborg tries to clarify by invoking the nature of the inner "state":

> Nevertheless, Man may comprehend this by natural Thought, if he will only admit into such Thought somewhat of a spiritual Light; wherefore first of all, something shall be said concerning spiritual Ideas and the Thought thus derived: A spiritual Idea doth not derive any Thing from Space, but it derives every Thing appertaining to it from State: State is predicated of Love, of Life, of Wisdom, of the Affections, of the Joys thence derived, in general of Good and of Truth [7].

Blake marks some of this and identifies a spiritual idea with what he here calls a "Poetic idea" (E603). Interpreting Swedenborg's view of how angels experience the deity, Blake comments, "He who Loves feels love descend into him & if he has wisdom may percieve it is from the Poetic Genius which is the Lord" (E603). A little later, Blake mentions again the poetic genius, which is central to his early tract *All Religions Are One* (E1) and can be identified in his later works with imagination. It is, for him, the power of spiritual insight, and he identifies poetic expression with it. Swedenborg has written, "The Negation of God constitutes Hell, and in the Christian World the Negation of the Lord's Divinity" (13). Blake responds, "the Negation of the Poetic Genius" (E603).

Blake proceeds to observe that Swedenborg has made a distinction between "the natural and spiritual as seen by Man," which Blake converts into two kinds of people: "Man [spiritual man] may comprehend. but not the natural or external man" (E603).

Swedenborg's solution to his paradox is that angels and spiritual men can see an "appearance" of spatiality and yet realize it is an appearance only. No abstract notion of space should be drawn from it.

The next matter has to do with the identity of man and God. Swedenborg states that in the three heavens the only idea that angels have of God is that of a man (11). This calls forth from Blake a statement that at first seems to indicate that it is a human limitation that human beings imagine God as a man, but then Blake adds a further comment. The whole annotation is as follows:

2. *Swedenborg's* Heaven and Hell...   43

> Man can have no idea of any thing greater than Man as a cup cannot contain more than its capaciousness But God is a man not because he is so percieved by man but because he is a creator of man [E603].

It turns out that, man is right to have imagined (within that limitation) God to be a man, for everything spiritual to Blake, and to Swedenborg, has an identity by synecdoche with the divine. Man is made by God in God's image. Swedenborg writes,

> What has been said may be illustrated by the following Extract from a small Treatise, published some Time ago. "The Gentiles, particularly the Africans, who acknowledge and worship one God the Creator of the Universe, entertain an idea of God as of a Man, and say that no one can have any other Idea of God; When they hear that many form an Idea of God as existing in the Midst of a Cloud, they ask where such are" [11].

The passage evokes in Blake one of his best-known annotations:

> Think of a white cloud. as being holy you cannot love it but think of a holy man within the cloud love springs up in your thought. for to think of holiness distinct from man is impossible to the affections. Thought alone can make monsters, but the affections cannot [E603]

The passage expresses Blake's, and Swedenborg's, distrust of abstractions, and it edges up to a disagreement Blake seems to have with Swedenborg (a very important one): Swedenborg thinks God is a man, but he does not think that man is God or *a* god. However, if Crabb Robinson has reported accurately, in his later years Blake seems to have come to think that both are true, though in the first part of the quotation below he seems to be Swedenborgian:

> "[Blake said] We are all co-existent with God, members of the Divine body. We are all partakers of the Divine nature." In this, by-the-by, Blake has but adopted an ancient Greek idea. As connected with this idea, I will mention here, though it formed part of our talk as we were walking homeward, that on my asking in what light he viewed the great question concerning the deity of Jesus Christ, he said, "He is the only God. But then," he added, "and so am I, and so are you" [II, 302–3]

The matter turns somewhat on the difference between essence and identity that is the subject of Swedenborg's remark later and Blake's long response. First Swedenborg:

> What Person of sound Reason doth not perceive, that the Divine is not divisible; also that a Plurality of Infinites, Uncreates, Omnipotents, and Gods is not possible? If another, who hath no Reason, should say that it is possible there may be several Infinites, Uncreates, Omnipotents and Gods, provided they have the same Essence, and that thereby there is one Infinite, Uncreate, Omnipotent and God — is not one and the same Essence but one and the same Iden-

tity? and one and the same Identity is not communicable to many; if it should be said that one is from the other, then he who is from the other is not God in himself, and nevertheless God in himself is the God from whom all Things are [27].

Blake:

> Answer Essence is not Identity but from Essence proceeds Identity & from one Essence may proceed many Identities as from one Affection may proceed. many thoughts Surely this is an oversight
>   That there is but one Omnipotent Uncreate & God I agree but that there is but one Infinite I do not. for if all but God is not Infinite they shall come to an End which God forbid
>   If the Essence was the same <u>as the</u> [Blake's underlining] Identity there could be but one Identity. which is false
>   Heaven would upon this plan be but a Clock but one & the same Essence is therefore Essence & not Identity [E604]

Blake's response reveals his rigorous commitment to a principle of synecdoche as a fundamental idea about the real. It turns out to be more rigorous than Swedenborg's. Blake assumes that it is an oversight that Swedenborg identifies essence with identity. Blake does not (though they may not mean the same thing by "identity"). He believes that to make the two terms the same would limit infinitude to God alone and would mean that different identities could not exist except apart from the divine, destroying the synecdochic relation of God to man (and to angels) that Swedenborg has heretofore expressed. If there were but one essence and one identity there would be no emanation of love and wisdom. All individuality and difference would disappear, and the universe would be but a machine, leaving God alone to love only himself.

Near the end of Part One, an annotation responds to Swedenborg's return to the need for man to "elevate his mind above the Ideas of Thought which are derived from Space and Time" (69). If this is accomplished, one "shakes off the Darkness of natural Light and removes <u>its Fallacies</u> from the Center to the Circumference" (E604). Center and circumference are familiar to Blake's readers from his later poems. Here Swedenborg means that things are thrust outside the spirit, gotten rid of, negated. Blake may have found this statement useful, but his treatment of the terms is different. In *The Marriage of Heaven and Hell*, reason is the circumferential boundary holding energy in check and preventing anarchy. In the later poems, a center is "selfish," a contraction to the point that everything is outside the self as a potential enemy. A circumference is something that needs to be expanded in order for the imagination to take in as much reality as it can. If, on the other hand, Swedenborg means only the difference between what is interior and spiritual and what is external and earthly, then Blake offers a similar view.

Part Two: Here Swedenborg presents an odd notion that dominates his discussion throughout. It is that there are two suns, one that shines above in the spiritual world and one in the physical. They are related only by correspondence. The sun of the spiritual world is alive; God's love and wisdom, spiritual warmth and light respectively, emanate from it. Another way of discussing this is to say that the divine sun is internal to man and the earthly sun external. The earthly sun is dead, being merely fire, and gets its light and warmth from an infusion of spiritual light and warmth. The spiritual sun is not in time or space. Blake, who claims that in the body one can have visionary experiences, uses a compatible imagery in his *A Vision of the Last Judgment*:

> What it will be Questioned When the Sun rises do you not see a round disk of fire somewhat like a Guinea O no no I see an innumerable company of the Heavenly host crying Holy Holy Holy is the Lord God Almighty I question not my Corporeal or Vegetative Eye any more than I would Question a window concerning a Sight I look thro it & not with it ... [E565–6].

It takes the inner spirit to see spiritual truth, not the bodily self.

Angels are as they are by virtue of what comes from God; what we are born with, and is ours alone, is evil. Swedenborg returns to the question faced in Part One, whether we are one with God's essence or are objects infused with God's love and wisdom:

> Let every one beware of falling into that execrable Heresy, that God hath infused himself into Men, and that he is in them, and no longer in himself; when nevertheless God is every where, as well within Man as without him, inasmuch as he is in all Space without Space, as was shown above, n. 7 to 10, and 69 to 72; for if he was in Man, he would not only be divisible, but also included in Space, yea Man also might then think himself to be God: This Heresy is so abominable, that in the spiritual World it stinks like a dead Carcase [130].

Later in Part Two Swedenborg discusses the three components of everything: ends, causes, and effects. The end (or purpose) of everything is in the spiritual sun, from which emanates God's love and wisdom. The causes are in the physical world, and the effects are in the physical world. In the larger sense, the result is the return of all things to that union with God, lost in the creation and fall.

Blake's four annotations to Part Two all deal with Swedenborg's suns. Swedenborg heads sections 163–66 with the following:

> That without two Suns, the one living and the other dead, there can be no Creation. The Universe in general is distinguished into two Worlds, the spiritual and the natural; in the spiritual World Angels and Spirits dwell, in the natural World Men dwell: These two Worlds are entirely alike as to the external

Face of them, so much alike that they cannot be distinguished; but as to the internal Face of them, they are entirely unlike [163].

Why does Blake call this "False philosophy according to the letter. but true according to the spirit" (E605)? Because, for Blake, the dead sun does not really exist and should for Swedenborg be only symbolic. In another annotation Blake says, the dead Sun is only a phantasy of evil Men" (E605). In the strictest sense, the dead sun is not even a creation except as a false idea. Swedenborg writes,

> Now forasmuch as these two Worlds are so distinct, there is a Necessity that there should be two Suns, the one from which all spiritual Things are and the other from which all natural Things are; and forasmuch as all Things spiritual in their Origins are living, and all Things natural from their Origin are dead, and the Suns are their Origin, it follows that the one Sun is living and that the other Sun is dead, also that the dead Sun itself was created by the living Sun from the Lord [164].

Blake responds, "how could Life create death" (E605). It appears that Blake is claiming everything created is alive in the sense that it is the product of an imagination, thus part of a living being. Swedenborg's argument is as follows:

> The Reason why a dead Sun was created is to the End that in the Ultimates all Things may be fixed, stated, and constant, and that thence Things may exist which are to be permanent and to endure: On this and no other Ground Creation is founded: The terraqueous Globe, in which, upon which, and about which, such Things exist, is as it were the Basis and Firmament, for it is the ultimate Work, in which all Things close, and upon which they rest [165].

This sounds rather like Blake's idea in the later poems that is later called by critics the consolidation of error, that is, the idea that with the giving of form to and then clarification of error the error ceases to delude. With the eventual consolidation of all error the Last Judgment will occur, revealing that everything is a mental, not physical creation. Blake responds, "[all things] exist literally about the sun & not about the earth" (E605), but spiritually, or imaginatively, the earth, from which imagination sends forth its visions is really the expanding human center. Thus Blake thinks Swedenborg contradicts what should be his view.

Part Three: The subject here is what Swedenborg calls "degrees" ("levels" in the most recent translation). There are degrees of love and wisdom, degrees of light and warmth, and consequent degrees of atmosphere. There are vertical and horizontal degrees. These are distinct from each other from lower to upper or outer to inner, and they are related in their distinctness to the relation of ends to causes to effects (purpose, means, and result in the most recent translation), with ends the sum and substance of all three. Gradual degrees are like the movement from light to shade, warmth to coldness, hard to soft. The three heavens of the spiritual world are three degrees:

> These Differences may in some Measure be comprehended by these considerations, that the Thought of Angels of the supreme or third Heaven are Thoughts of Ends, and the Thought of the Angels of the middle or second Heaven are Thoughts of Causes, and the Thoughts of the Angels of the lowest or first Heaven are Thoughts of Effects. It is to be observed, that it is one Thing to think from Ends, and another to think of Ends; also that it is one Thing to think from Causes, and another to think of Causes; as also that it is one Thing to think from Effects, and another to think of Effects; the Angels of the inferior Heavens think of Causes and of Ends, but the Angels of the superior Heavens from Causes and from Ends, and to think from these is of superior Wisdom, but to think of these is of inferior Wisdom. To think from Ends is of Wisdom, to think from Causes is of Intelligence, and to think from Effects is of Science [202].

By inverse correspondence, there are also degrees of hell:

> THAT THE THREE DEGREES OF THE NATURAL MIND, WHICH IS FORM AND IMAGE OF HELL, ARE OPPOSITE TO THE THREE DEGREES OF THE SPIRITUAL MIND, WHICH IS A FORM AND IMAGE OF HEAVEN. That there are three degrees of the Mind, which are called the natural, spiritual and celestial, and that the human Mind consisting of these Degrees looks towards Heaven and turns itself spirally thitherward, was shown above; hence it may be seen, that the natural Mind, when it looks downwards, and circumflects itself towards Hell, in like Manner consists of three Degrees, and that each Degree thereof is opposite to a Degree of Mind, which is Heaven [275].

When Swedenborg speaks of ends, causes, and effects, he wants to make sure that our thought is not lost in such abstractions. This is connected to his view, like Blake's, that no phenomenon is abstract; and it leads to his emphasis on good works:

> ...because every Thing civil, moral and spiritual, is not any Thing abstracted from Substance, but they are Substances, for as Love and Wisdom are not abstract Things but are a Substance, as was shown above, n. 40 to 43, so in like Manner all Things, which are called civil, moral and spiritual; these indeed may be thought of abstractly from Substance, but still in themselves they are not abstracted [209].

This leads to the declarations "the whole of Charity and Faith is in Works" and "Charity and Faith without Works are like Rainbows about the Sun which vanish and are dissipated by a Cloud" (220). Blake agrees and adds a complaint against ritual, "The Whole of the New Church is in the Active Life & not in Ceremonies at all" (E605). He aligns himself as Protestant more radically than do the Swedenborgians. Swedenborg believes rationality, as does Blake, can go astray into abstractions enabling people to validate whatever they want to (267).

Blake's main concern in this section (as it will also be in Part Four) is the distinction between natural, or earthly, man and spiritual man. He is aware of Swedenborg's difficulty in maintaining the clarity of the distinction, since Swedenborg sometimes refers simply to "man" and the reader must decide by the context which he is talking about. Blake is particularly interested in this matter because of his belief in the possibility of spiritual vision in *this* world. It is clear from the cross referencing in his annotations that he has studied sections 181 to 267 carefully.

The first annotation points to the problem of expression. Swedenborg has said,

> Angels feel that Heat, and see that Light, whereas Men do not, by Reason that Men are in natural Heat and Light, and so long as this is the Case, they do not feel spiritual Heat, except by certain Delight of Love, nor do they see spiritual Light except by the Perception of Truth [181].

Blake responds by trying to clarify: "He speaks of Men as meer earthly Men not receptacles of spirit, or else he contradicts N257" (E605). Further along, Swedenborg writes, "...if he becomes an Angel [after death] ... then he speaks Things ineffable and incomprehensible to the natural Man" (239). Blake's comment emphasizes "natural": "Not to a Man but to the natural Man" (E606). Later, in Part Four, he tries to straighten out what might be and probably is an inconsistency. Swedenborg writes,

> That there is such a Difference between the Thoughts of Angels and Men, was made known to me by this Experience: They were told to think something spiritually and afterwards to tell me what they thought of; when this was done and they would have told me, they could not, saying that they could not express themselves: It was the same with their spiritual Speech, and the same with their spiritual Writing, there was not any Word of spiritual Speech, which was like a Word of natural Speech; nor any Thing of spiritual Writing like natural Writing, except the Letters, each of which contained a distinct Sense [295].

How then could Swedenborg have understood what the angels said? Blake responds, "they could not tell him in natural ideas how absurd must men be to understand him as if he said the angels could not express themselves at all to him" (E607). This doesn't quite erase Swedenborg's problem here, but it does suggest that angels' speech to men can somehow transcend the difference between spiritual and natural speech. It is either this, or Swedenborg is claiming for himself extraordinary powers. Swedenborg goes on to invoke correspondence:

> But what is wonderful, they said, that they seemed to themselves to think, speak, and write in their spiritual State, in the same manner as man does in his natural State, when nevertheless there is nothing similar: From which Circum-

2. *Swedenborg's* Heaven and Hell... 49

stance it was evident, that Natural and Spiritual differ according to Degrees of Altitude, and that they have no Communication with each other but by Correspondences [295].

Section 257 follows on Swedenborg's statement that the natural or earthly man "cannot be elevated into Wisdom itself" (256), but 257 declares that even before he dies he may come into wisdom "by laying asleep the Sensations of the Body, and by the Influx from above at the same Time into the Spirituals of his Mind" (257). Blake remarks, "this is while in the Body" and adds "This is to be understood as unusual in our time but common in ancient" (E606). Further, Swedenborg has written in 257,

> ...the natural Mind is capable of being elevated to the Light of Heaven, in which the Angels are, and of perceiving naturally what the Angels do spiritually, consequently not so fully; but still the natural Mind of Man cannot be elevated into Angelic light itself.... Man, by Means of his natural Mind elevated to the Light of Heaven, can think with Angels, yes speak with them, but then the Thought and Speech of the Angels flow into the natural Thought and Speech of the Man, and not *vice versa*, wherefore the Angels speak with man in natural Language, which is the Man's Mother Tongue.

Blake offers, as a second reason for a reader's possible misunderstanding, the following comment, attributing misunderstanding to a materialist attitude: "Many perversely understand him. as if man while in the body was only conversant with natural Substances. because themselves are mercenary & worldly & have no idea of any but worldly gain" (E606). In all of this, Blake seems to be a friendly interpreter.

Blake's longest annotation in Part Three follows a discussion of degrees. Swedenborg has written,

> These three Degrees of Altitude are named Natural, Spiritual and Celestial, as was said above, n. 232: Man, at his Birth, first comes into the natural Degree, and this increases in him by Continuity according to the Sciences, and according to the Understanding acquired by them, to the Summit of Understanding, which is called Rational: Nevertheless the other Degree which is called Spiritual, is not hereby opened; this Degree is opened by the Love of Uses derived from Things intellectual, supposing this Love of Uses to be spiritual, which Love is Love towards our Neighbour [237].

Blake's statement is complicated:

> Study Sciences till you are blind
> Study intellectuals till you are cold
> Yet Science cannot teach intellect
> Much less can intellect teach Affection [This follows along with Swedenborg's view that love is always prior to wisdom]
> How foolish then is it to assert that Man is born in only one degree when

> that one degree is reception of the 3 degrees. two of which he must destroy or close up or they will descend, if he closes up the two superior then he is not truly in the 3d but descends out of it into meer Nature or Hell
>   See N 239
>   Is it not also evident that one degree will not open the other & that science will not open intellect but that they are discrete & not continuous so as to explain each other except by correspondence which has nothing to do with demonstration for you cannot demonstrate one degree by the other for how can science by brought to demonstrate intellect, without making them continuous & not discrete [E605–6].

Section 239, to which Blake directs us, says that everyone has "a natural, spiritual and celestial Will and Understanding, in Power from his Birth, and in Act whilst they are opening." The translation is odd. I think the meaning is that they are in action from the beginning. Blake is insisting, as has Swedenborg previously, on the discreteness of vertical degrees and that one cannot lead gradually to the next. Correspondence of science to love and intellect, or wisdom is like that of natural language to the language of angels. Though they mirror each other, they cannot be understood on the same principle. Most fundamental of the degrees is that of love and affection, which is also the end to which things should tend. It is expressed by the will, which is not led by the understanding (241, 244). Blake marks this assertion.

Finally, it is important to consider Blake's last annotation to Part Three, which follows on this nearly summary statement:

> ...the natural Man can elevate his Understanding to superior Light as far as he desires it, but he who is principled in Evils and thence in Things false, does not elevate it higher than to the superior Region of his natural Mind, and rarely to the Region of his spiritual Mind; the Reason is, because he is in the Delights of the Love of his natural Mind, and if he elevates it above that the Delight of his Love perishes; it is elevated higher, and he sees Truths opposite to the Delights of his Life, or to the Principles of his own self-derived Intelligence [267].

Blake responds by declaring for an elevation to a spiritual degree that some wrongly think is selfish, irrational, and even perhaps crazed. Intelligence, for Swedenborg and Blake, is never that of or via the selfhood. Demonstration is a word that Blake always identifies with an operation of the mind that objectifies and distances everything from the individual, annihilating God's gift of love and wisdom: "Who shall dare to say after this that all elevation is of self & is Enthusiasm & Madness & is it not plain that self derived intelligence is worldly demonstration" (E606).

Part Four: Swedenborg begins this part by repeating assertions made in *Heaven and Hell*: The creation was not from nothing but from a substance, essential being, God himself. However, nothing in creation is God; God, and the whole heaven, is a person. Love and wisdom are not mere abstractions, but are occurrences that have specific forms. The true sun is not God but instead an emanation of divine love and wisdom. The natural sun is dead; it is fire only.

In his annotations, Blake's interest lies in the difference between spiritual and natural ideas and presages his contemptuous treatment of what he calls "nature" in the later poems. He begins by commenting on Swedenborg's statement about what constitutes the sun, which follows:

> Forasmuch as the Things, which constitute the Sun of the spiritual World, are from the Lord, and not the Lord, therefore they are not Life in itself, but are void of Life in itself; in like Manner as the Things which exhale from an Angel, or a Man, and constitute the Spheres about them, are not the Angel or the Man, but are from them, void of their Life; which no otherwise make one with the Angel or Man, than in that they accord with them, being derived from the Forms of their Body, which were the Forms of their Life in them [294].

Blake observes, "The assertion that the spiritual Sun is not Life explains how the natural Sun is dead" (E606).* The distinction between God, who is life itself, and the spiritual sun, with life derived from God and not intrinsic to it, leads us to look further downward toward the sun of nature and the dead physical universe.

Spiritual ideas and natural ideas are the subject of the next section, in which Swedenborg repeats yet another idea:

> This is an Arcanum, which the Angels by their spiritual Ideas can see in Thought, and also express in Speech, but not Men by their natural Ideas; because a thousand spiritual Ideas make one natural Idea, and one natural Idea, and one natural Idea cannot be resolved by Man into any spiritual Idea, much less into so many: The Reason is, because they differ according to the Degrees of Altitude, which were treated in Part the Third [294].

It is important to Blake to remind us (as he had in Part Three), that man can still have spiritual thoughts while in the natural body. Otherwise Swedenborg would be contradicting section 257. Blake always insists on the possibility of imagination and vision: "How absurd then would it be to say that no man on earth has a spiritual idea after reading N 257" (E607). That section is, for Blake, a major moment in Swedenborg's argument. Blake annotated it and refers to it twice.

After this, Blake's interest turns to Swedenborg's discussion of process

---

*Henry Crabb Robinson reports that Blake said to him, "I have conversed with the spiritual Sun. I saw him on Primrose Hill. He said, 'Do you take me for the Greek Apollo?'—'No,' I said; 'that' (pointing to the sky) 'is the Greek Apollo. He is Satan'" (II, 306).

in the natural world, which images the spiritual. In the spiritual world process is, of course, entirely internal: "from first Principles to Ultimates, and from Ultimates to first Principles" (316). In the natural world there is a resemblance to this in the life cycles of plants and animals. Blake comments, "A going forth & returning" (E607), presaging a corresponding movement at the very end of *Jerusalem*:

> All Human Forms identified even Tree Metal Earth & Stone. all
> Human Forms identified, living going forth & returning wearied
> Into the Planetary lives of Years Months Days & Hours reposing
> And then Awakening into his Bosom in the Life of Immortality
> [E258]

Swedenborg's description of all this is complicated (296–304), culminating in the following:

> Forasmuch as there is such a Progression of the Fibres and Vessels in a Man from first Principles to Ultimates, therefore there is a similar Progression of their States; their States are the Sensations, Thoughts and Affections; these also from their first Principles <u>where they are in the Light</u>, pervade to their Ultimates, where they are in Obscurity; or from their first Principles, where they are in Heat, to their Ultimates where they are not <u>in Heat</u> [304].

Blake is probably right in attributing the cause of this to a diminishment of light and heat as one approaches the ultimate in nature, that is, death. Natural heat and light, as Swedenborg says (315), "only open Seeds," but the power to do this comes from influx from the spiritual world. Blake marks this observation and makes an important comment on the following:

> It is to be observed, that the Heat, Light and Atmospheres of the natural World conduce nothing to this Image of Creation, but only the Heat, Light and Atmospheres of the Sun of the spiritual World; these latter carry along with them that Image, and cloathe it in the Form of Uses of the vegetable Kingdom [315].

Blake responds, "Therefore Natural earth & Atmosphere is a Phantasy" (E607). Blake's conclusion is more radical than Swedenborg's. For Swedenborg, there *is* a natural world. Blake won't grant it even the status of existence.

Part Five: Blake's interest here is in Swedenborg's treatment of the relation of love to wisdom or understanding, a subject that has been central to all three of his books. Divine love is prior in power in that it determines the wisdom anyone can possess, but it can't accomplish anything in human form without "marriage" to wisdom. Love is expressed by the will. First comes the will's desire for knowledge, which in turn produces a desire for truth and gives rise to thought.

The first annotation is to a passage that mentions memory. Blake says of the following "Note this" (E607), and he both brackets and underlines a lot of it:

> Thought indeed exists first, because it is of the natural Mind, but Thought from the Perception of Truth, which is from the Affection of Truth, exists last; this Thought is the Thought of Wisdom, but the other is Thought from the Memory by the Sight of the natural Mind. All the Operations of Love or of the Will out of the Understanding have not Relation to the Affections of Truth, but to the Affections of Good [404].

Blake marks this probably because Swedenborg says that the memory is an inferior form of thinking. As readers of Blake know, for him memory is indeed inferior because in his time it is identified with the theory of association of ideas, a mechanical combining of so-called experiences. In his marking certain passages Blake expresses his interest in the force of love and will. Swedenborg says, of course, that everything of value is influx from the Lord. Love is the active force; it acts on the understanding:

> From these Things it may be seen, that Love or the Will joins itself to Wisdom or the Understanding, and not that Wisdom or the Understanding joins itself to Love or the Will [410].

Blake also marks the statement "Understanding does nothing from itself" (412). Swedenborg goes on to remark, "it does not perceive nor think from itself, but all from the addactions which are of the Love" (412). This power of love enables "Wisdom or the Understanding" to "receive the Things which are of the Light from Heaven, and perceive them" (413), that is, truths. Blake marks this and several statements related to it. Clearly, mention of the capacity to perceive appealed to him, also the reiteration that love is the fundamental power enabling the understanding to function in concert with it, and also that the understanding can defile love.

Section 421 begins, "THAT LOVE OR THE WILL IS DEFILED IN THE UNDERSTANDING, AND BY IT, IF THEY ARE NOT ELEVATED TOGETHER." Blake brackets this and writes, "Mark this they are elevated together." Swedenborg calls this relationship a "marriage":

> Love however, or the Will, cannot be elevated by any Thing of Honour, Glory or Gain as it's End, but through the Love of Use not so much for its own Sake, as for the Sake of it's Neighbour; and forasmuch as the Love is not given but from Heaven by the Lord; and it is given by the Lord when Man shuns Evil as Sins, therefore by these Means Love or the Will also can be elevated, and without these Means it cannot: Love however, or the Will, is elevated into the Heat of Heaven, but the Understanding into the Light of Heaven, and if they are both elevated, a Marriage of them is effected there, which is called the celestial Marriage [414].

Blake, revealing that he has attended Swedenborgian meetings, comments, "Is it not false then, that love recieves influx thro the understanding as was asserted in the society" (E608). Further, he notes that heredity has caused the impurity of love: "Therefore it was not created impure & is not naturally so" (E608); and he wants to emphasize that love gets nothing from the understanding but actively joins it in "marriage."

Finally, Blake's interpretation of section 432 to indicate that Swedenborg imagines a twin birth of heaven and hell points to Swedenborg's opposition of reaction to action and his view that to maintain equilibrium in the universe the opposition is required as it is in every individual: "...it was shown in the Light of Heaven, which shone upon it, that the interior Compages of this little Brain was, as to its Situation and Fluxion, in the Order and Form of Heaven; and that its exterior Compages was in Opposition to that Order and Form" (432).* "Heaven & Hell are born together," Blake adds (E609). In this section, Swedenborg returns to a distinction he made elsewhere between the inner or spiritual world of heaven and the external, outer, material world of hell. With a similar imagery, Blake later contrasts a spiritual imagination with a materialistic, fallen reason.

Divine Providence: The Question of Predestination

Swedenborg's *Divine Providence* repeats many of the arguments made in *Divine Love and Divine Wisdom*.† There is no change from views expressed there and in *Heaven and Hell*: The Divine is the one fundamental substance, and the image of the divine is in everything. Human beings have will or volition, which is their freedom, and understanding or reason. However, both of these powers come from God, who is the source of all life and goodness. We only *think* we live on our own, but our positive thoughts and acts are the result of an influx from the divine.

Swedenborg's new emphasis is on God's providence. The word comes from the Greek *pronoia*, or forethought, and the Latin *providere*, to foresee. In the New Testament, the word signifies God's provision for the future. Swe-

---

*According to the Oxford English Dictionary "compages" is "a whole formed by the compaction or juncture of parts, a framework or system of joined parts, a complex structure."

†*The Wisdom of Angels concerning the Divine Providence. Translated from the Latin of the Hon. Emanuel Swedenborg.* London: printed and Sold by R. Hindmarsh, Printer to His Royal Highness the Prince of Wales. No 32 Clerkinwell-Close, 1790. The copy that Blake annotated is in the British Library.

denborg frequently mentions it. Providence is the way in which God, with love and wisdom, governs us (1). It is said to control everything (197). Its aim is our salvation, ultimately the continual creation of a heaven, which is the community of angels, all formerly human beings (323, 331–2). God provides not only for the spiritual or internal world, but also for the external world of animals, vegetables, and minerals (332). Providence strives for the ultimate marriage of all goodness with truth, which is expressible by our will and understanding, reuniting those things that were separated in the creation (9, 21). Like Blake, Swedenborg identifies creation and fall with a primordial division. Providence moves toward the recreation of a whole, a communal angelic person in God's image (47), thus united with him (102), though containing individualities that are microcosms or literal synecdoches of that whole. Providence would unite us with God, but there must be evil for us to be able to discern the good from it and freely choose the good and true. In other words, we must have freedom and rationality (234). Thus we live between heaven and hell, though these are really in us. What we do with our own freedom and reason (24) cannot be forced on us from the outside. We are free to choose good or evil. God charges no one with evil. It is we who make the choice of it (322). His providence gives us the power to understand what is good and true.

We are infused by God's love and wisdom and are thus predestined, but only to the extent that a place in heaven is prepared for us, though we may not accept it. What we think is our decision for the good and true is really a gift to accept from God or to reject. Our decision for evil and a place in hell is ours and not predestined. That decision expresses a false, perverted love. Swedenborg identifies it with love of self, inherited from our parents. We have the power eventually to put it off along with love for the external world.

The idea of predestination has always been a problem for theologians, and probably the best that can be said is that there is a paradox in it.* Packer and Jeffrey write as follows:

> The biblical theme of predestination has ... two focal centers. From one standpoint it belongs to the doctrine of God, affirming that whatever happens under God's sovereign providence was foreordained. In this respect it broaches problems such as the existence of evil and the suffering of the innocent. Varying conceptions of God's personhood, rationality, wisdom, goodness, freedom, foreknowledge, and power in relation to his world produce different understand-

---

*The paradox is comically treated by Anatole France in *Penguin Island* (1908), where the Lord declares, "In order not to impair human liberty, I will be ignorant of what I know, I will thicken upon my eyes the veils I have pierced, and in my blind clear-sightedness I will let myself be surprised by what I have foreseen." New York: Random House, 1933, 32.

ings of foreordination, and issues of theodicy (is God arbitrary? Is he the author of sin? Are his ways justifiable?) press down on the whole discussion.... From another standpoint, however, biblical predestination belongs to the doctrine of grace, affirming that God saves some (not all) of a guilty, helpless, corrupt humanity, according to his own free and sovereign choice.*

They refer to St. Augustine, who, according to them, offers the following view: "God in sovereign freedom, foreseeing all, chooses out of the corrupt mass of sinful humanity those whose hearts and wills he would change" (637).

Swedenborg could argue that his own view is closer to the scriptures than Augustine's or later Calvin's. W. R. F. Browning writes,

> The scriptures do not so much affirm predestination as a rational deduction within a philosophy of theism as give expression to a glorious sense of God's graciousness. God has a plan to deliver human beings from the power of sin — this is predestined: People may freely accept or reject this offer [Phil. 2:12].†

Swedenborg's view is close to this. Some human beings condemn themselves to hell as a result of their free choice of evil and their perverted love for it. Evil, for Swedenborg, is an abuse of freedom and rationality (15). It is entirely negative (19). God's gift of freedom means that he cannot rid us of evil without our own action (156). However, that action is really an acceptance of the influx of his divine love and wisdom, always part of us, though tainted from heredity with the evil of self-love. Our regeneration is a process rather than a sudden event. There is no instant salvation. That must come through our actions.

Blake makes thirteen annotations to *Divine Providence* and the preface by its translator Nathaniel Tucker. Nine of them involve the issue of predestination. They are all critical of Swedenborg and are of two sorts. First, Blake interprets Swedenborg's notion of God's foreknowledge and his enrollment of human beings in heaven or hell as predestination. Second, Blake objects strenuously to Swedenborg's claim that after death those who in life loved evil are incapable in the afterlife of changing for the better. They are condemned for eternity to the hell of their own making. Swedenborg's notion here that there can be no change after death has nothing to do with predestination in the traditional sense, and Blake is wrong to accuse him of predestination on this basis.

---

*A Dictionary of Biblical Tradition in English Literature, ed. David Lyle Jeffrey. Grand Rapids MI, 1992, 636–7. Written by Jeffrey with James I. Packer.

†W. R. F Browning, *A Dictionary of the Bible*, Oxford and New York: Oxford University Press, 1997, 301. The passage from Philippians 2:12 reads: "Wherefore, my beloved, as ye have always obeyed, not as in my presence only, but now much more in my absence, work out your own salvation with fear and trembling."

With respect to the first issue Blake misreads Swedenborg, perhaps deliberately, though Swedenborg does occasionally say something that might strike one as implying predestination. Blake simply misinterprets what Swedenborg means by enrollment. In an annotation to the translator's preface, Blake identifies the whole notion of providence as Tucker sees it with predestination. Tucker writes, "...if we allow a *general* Providence, and yet deny a *particular* one, or if we allow a *particular* one, and yet deny a *singular* one, that is, one extending to Things and Circumstances most *singular* and minute, what is this but denying a *general* Providence?" (v). Blake responds, "Is not this Predestination?" (E609). But Blake is confusing or perhaps conflating predestination with either determinism or providence, the latter of which is seen as expressing God's purpose for good in the universe. As Browning describes it, "God is responsible not only for making but also for preserving the created order, and history is a process moving ever onwards towards an end, which God foresees" (306). Predestination is not about what individuals do on earth, determined or not, but instead about their fate after death. It appears that Blake is objecting particularly to Tucker's notion of a "singular" providence, which seems to apply to individual lives on earth. Blake apparently chooses to think that predestination implies that each life on earth is determined in every detail.

This aside, there is an annotated statement by Swedenborg that Blake reads as if it implies predestination in the traditional sense. Where Swedenborg speaks of a place in heaven or hell prepared or provided, Blake assumes that he means by these words predestination. In section 69, Swedenborg writes,

> But the Man who doth not suffer himself to be led to, and enrolled in Heaven, is prepared for his Place in Hell; for Man from himself continually tends to the lowest Hell, but is continually with-held by the Lord; and he, who cannot be with-held, is prepared for a certain Place there, in which he is also enrolled immediately after his Departure out of the World; and this Place there is opposite to a certain Place in Heaven, for Hell is in Opposition to Heaven; wherefore as a Man Angel, according to the Affection of Good and Truth, hath his place assigned him in Heaven, so a Man Devil, according to the Affection of Evil and the False, hath his Place assigned him in Hell; for two Opposites, disposed in a similar Situation against each other, are contained in Connection [69].

Blake responds, "What is Enrolling but Predestination" (E609). In addition, in his annotation to section 185 Blake refers the reader to section 203, "Where he says a Place for Each Man is Foreseen & at the same time Provided" (E610). Blake apparently thinks, as have many, that the claim of God's foreknowledge inevitably means a belief that people are predestined to hell or heaven.

Swedenborg, though he does believe in such foreknowledge, does not think that this denies human free will. As for the matter of God's providing a place in heaven or hell, Blake interprets "enrollment," when it is coupled with foreknowledge, to mean predestination; but Swedenborg means only that a place is reserved in heaven for everyone, though some will choose the place also provided in hell. Blake finds Swedenborg's language is section 69 confusing and wonders whether some people will occupy both places (simultaneously?). This reflects either his own confusion or points out Swedenborg's inconsistency.

It is perhaps easy, but inaccurate, to read section 185, which follows, as Blake does, to indicate predestination:

> That this is the Case, cannot better be known than from the Case of Men after Death in the spiritual World, where the greatest Part of those, who in the natural World became great and rich, and in Honours respected themselves alone, and also in Riches at first speak of God, and of the Divine Providence, as if they acknowledged them in their Hearts: But whereas they then manifestly see the Divine Providence, and from it their final Portion, which is that they are to be in Hell, they connect themselves with Devils there, and then not only deny God, but also blaspheme; and then they come into such a Delirium, that they acknowledge the more powerful of the Devils for their Gods, and affect Nothing more ardently, than that they themselves also may be deified [185].

Blake writes, "What could Calvin Say more than is Said in this Number Final Portion is Predestination." He proceeds to return to the matter of provision: "See n 69 & 329 at the End & 277 & 203 Where he says a Place for each Man is Foreseen & at the same time Provided" (E610). But Swedenborg is referring to the eventual lot those will have if they persist in love for their evil ways. The choice is theirs.

Section 69 leads us to other sections where the second sort of criticism Blake makes is present. Swedenborg is adamant about eternal damnation for those who choose evil. Blake's objection to this, which he calls predestination against the traditional view of it, appears in two other annotations (277, 307), to which Blake has referred us. In the annotation to 277, Blake accuses Swedenborg of "Cursed Folly!" (E610) for writing,

> ...he who is in Evil in the World, the same is in Evil after he goes out of <u>the World; wherefore if Evil be not removed in the World, it cannot be removed afterwards</u>; where the Tree falls, there it lieth; so also it is with the Life of Man; as it was at his Death, such it remaineth; every one also is judged according to his Actions, not that they are enumerated, but because he returns to them, and does the like again; for Death is a Continuation of Life, with this difference, that then Man cannot be reformed [277].

He complains further, "Predestination after this Life is more Abominable than Calvins & Swedenborg is Such a Spiritual Predestinarian — witness this Number & many others. See 69 & 185 & 329 & 307" (E610). At 307 Blake writes, "Predestination" (E611), and at 329, in a sort of summary, he returns again to God's provision, "Read N 185 & There See how Swedenborg contradicts himself & N 69 See also 277 & 203 where [repeating his remark there] he says that a Place for Each Man is foreseen & at the same time provided" (E611). The accusation depends on our acceptance that in Swedenborg predestination either to heaven or to hell is inevitable. Swedenborg does say that all are predestined to heaven, but by this he means only that a place is provided there for those who choose it by their acts, but no one is predestined to hell in the traditional sense. The accusation also depends on an acceptance of Blake's notion that provision and enrollment must mean predestination. Swedenborg's language about provision is clear, but with respect to enrollment it is slippery, and there are several places where Blake could have noted this.

The annotations to *Divine Providence* clearly reflect Blake's growing distrust of Swedenborg's theology, and that distrust never left him, though his attitude softened in his later years. Blake's attitude toward priesthood did not. Two annotations to Tucker's preface show this. Tucker writes,

> Nothing doth *in general* so contradict Man's natural and favourite Opinions as *Truth* and that all the grandest and purest Truths of Heaven must needs seem obscure and perplexing to the natural Man at first View — until his intellectual Eye becomes accustomed to the Light, and can thereby behold it with Satisfaction [xviii–xix].

To the first part of this Blake replies, "Lies & Priestcraft Truth is Nature." The association he makes here between truth and nature is, of course, ironic. To the latter part he writes, "that is: till he agrees to the Priests interest" (E609). As the passage proceeds, however, Tucker gives a little more freedom to man's intellect than Blake allows with his comment:

> He will not therefore *hastily* reject which he does not *immediately* comprehend, or what at first Sight dazzles and thereby darkens his Sight, but waiting patiently for the Light to strengthen his intellectual Faculties and thereby to clear itself, and from the Beauty of what he *does* understand, being led to think favourably of what at present he *does not*, and to hope that he *may* understand it at a future Time, and upon a further Reading and Consideration, he will be cautious of passing rash Censure, and will rather judge not at all than judge unrighteous Judgment [xix].

Another anathema for Blake was kingship. He comments on this at 220, arguing that Swedenborg has contradicted himself. Swedenborg has written,

> Dignities with their Honours are natural and temporary, when a Man personally respects himself in them, and not the State and Uses, for then a Man cannot but think interiorly with himself, that the State was made for him, and not he for the State: he is like a King who thinks his Kingdom and all Men in it are for him, and not he for the Kingdom and the Men of which it consists [220].

Blake has remarked, "He says at N 201 No King hath such a Government as this for all Kings are Universal in their Government otherwise they are No Kings" (E610). Section 201 says,

> If it should be alledged, that the Divine Providence is an universal Government, and that not any Thing is governed, but only kept in its Connection, and the Things which relate to Government (*illaquae Regiminis sunt*) are disposed by others, can this be called an universal Government? No King hath such a Government as this; for if a King were to allow his Subjects to govern every Thing in his Kingdom, he would no longer be a King, but he would only be called a King, therefore would have only a nominal Dignity and no real Dignity: Such a King cannot be said to hold the Government, much less universal Government [201].

It is interesting that Blake does not take the opportunity to offer a dissent to this. Swedenborg's view would not be radical enough for Blake. This is another place where Blake, though influenced by Swedenborg in many ways, often went beyond him.

3

Annotations to Bishop Richard Watson's *An Apology for the Bible*

Blake annotated Watson's *Apology* (1796) in 1798.* The *Apology* was an answer to Part Two of Thomas Paine's *The Age of Reason*, published in 1795 after Part One in 1794. Paine attacked the Bible's historical accuracy and morality, offering a form of Deism. His book caused a considerable furor among the Anglican clergy in England and the Episcopalians in America and did harm to the reputation he had made as a political radical with *Common Sense* (1776). Blake, who was acquainted with Paine, agreed with his attack on kingship in that book, though certainly not entirely with his Deism.† In *Common Sense*, Paine wrote:

> In England a k — hath little more to do than to make war and give away places; which in plain term, is to impoverish the nation and set it together by the ears. A pretty business indeed for a man to be allowed eight hundred thousand sterling a year for, and worshipped into the bargain! Of more worth is one honest man to society, and in the sight of God, than all the crowned ruffians that ever lived.§

---

* *An Apology for the Bible, in a Series of Letters, addressed to Thomas Paine, Author of a Book entitled, the Age of Reason, Part the Second, being an Investigation of True and Fabulous Theology.* By R. Watson, D. D. F.R.S. Lord Bishop of Landaff, and Regius Professor of Divinity in the University of Cambridge. Eighth Edition. London: Printed for T. Evans, in Paternoster Row. 1797. The copy Blake annotated is in the Huntington Library.

† In an excellent essay, Morton D. Paley discusses Blake's relation to Paine, Joseph Johnson and others as well as Blake's annotations to Watson's *Apology*. He also offers information about Watson's career, including Watson's opposition to the American war and slavery. Watson, as Paley remarks, even "originally had high hopes for the French Revolution," and he supported Catholic emancipation. Paley's theme is the situation of 1798, when Blake made his annotations: "To Defend the Bible in This Year 1798 Would Cost a Man His Life," *Blake: An Illustrated Quarterly* 32, 2(fall 1998), 32–42. See also Florence Sandler, "'Defending the Bible': Blake, Paine and the Bishop on Atonement" in *Blake and His Bibles*, ed. David V. Erdman, West Cornwall CT: Locust Hill Literary Studies, 1990.

§Thomas Paine, *Common Sense, addressed to the Inhabitants of America* (1776), Isaac Kramnick, ed., London: Penguin Books, 1986. 81

Paine's attack is on hereditary right:

> England, since the conquest, hath known some few good monarchs, but groaned beneath a much larger number of bad ones, yet no man in his senses can say that their claim under William the Conqueror is a very honorable one. A French bastard landing with an armed banditti, and establishing himself king of England against the consent of the natives, is in plain terms a very paltry rascally original. — It certainly hath no divinity in it [77–8].

Though in 1804 Blake was acquitted in his trial for seditious utterances against the king, there is no doubt about a sentiment he held before that and, indeed, all his life: "Every Body hates a King" (E623). In Blake's poem *America*, Paine is grouped with Washington, Franklin, Warren, Gates, Hancock, and Lee. In that poem, Washington speaks, but his words come closer in sentiment to those of Paine:

> ...Friends of America look over the Atlantic sea;
> A bended bow is lifted in heaven, & a heavy iron chain
> Descends link by link from Albions cliff across the sea to bind
> Brothers & sons of America, till our faces pale and yellow;
> Heads deprest, voices weak, eyes downcast, hands work-bruised [E52].

A story persisted that in 1792 Blake warned Paine that his life was in danger and he should leave England. That is highly unlikely. G. E. Bentley, Jr., observes that others may have warned Paine.*

Certainly Blake had read with approval *Common Sense* and *Rights of Man* (1791). To the few readers of his *America* and *Europe*, there was no secret of his republicanism. Paine had influenced his work, and it is no surprise that Blake should have defended Paine against Watson, even though he objected to aspects of Paine's Deism.

The Age of Reason

Part One of *The Age of Reason* (1794), written in prison in France, is little more than half the length of the second part, which followed in 1795 after Paine was freed. Blake, being too protestant for any protestant church, is likely to have approved of Paine's early remark that he rejected the beliefs of all churches known to him and that "My own mind is my own church,"† though Blake would probably have substituted "imagination" for "mind."

---

*G. E. Bentley, Jr., *The Stranger from Paradise: A Biography of William Blake*, New Haven CT and London: Yale University Press, 2001, 113.
†Thomas Paine, *The Age of Reason, Being an Investigation of True and Fabulous Theology* (1794, 1795), Amherst, NY: Prometheus Books, 1984, 8.

Paine was most severe about what he regarded as hypocritical allegiance to beliefs not really held and to churches as national institutions. They were, in his view, "human inventions put up to terrify and enslave mankind, and monopolize power and profit" (4). At one time or another, Blake expressed similar views.

After a critique of all revelations reported at second hand, Paine finds the sources of the Christian church in heathen mythology. He proposes that Jesus preached a benevolent morality, opposed priestly corruption, and probably had in mind attainment of freedom from Roman rule. He argues that "prophet" originally meant "poet," that the Jewish poets deserved better than to be tied up with the supposed word of God, and that poets are not to be regarded as predictors of future events. In Paine's view, Jesus founded no new system, he did not intend to be crucified, and the church as system is contradictory to his character and teaching. Further, the doctrine of redemption foisted by the church on the people is a fraud founded by analogy with the notion of pecuniary debt.

Paine's form of Deism holds that the creation we behold, not the Bible, is the word of God. The creation is a universal language everywhere open to all. God is the first cause, a power superior to all things, and is incomprehensible. It follows that natural philosophy, or natural science, is the true theology and the rest human fabrication. In Paine's view, the principles of science are truth. The universe, of which there are probably many, displays those principles, and human beings attempt to apply them. Paine thinks the prevailing system of education in the dead languages of Greek and Latin at the expense of natural science is a disaster; all the useful books of the Ancients have been translated, and there is nothing more to learn from them. (However, Paine admits elsewhere that translation is always inaccurate.)

As for the Christian system of faith, it is based on preposterous myths of Satan, Adam, Eve, the apple, and uncorroborated revelations. It is a corruption of an ancient monotheistic belief. The three principal means of priestly imposition on people have been mystery, miracle, and prophecy. "The two first are incompatible with true religion, and the third ought always to be suspected" (61).

Paine's summary of Part One is as follows:

> *First*— That the idea or belief of a word of God existing in print, or in writing, or in speech, is inconsistent in itself.... These reasons, among many others, are the want of a universal language; the mutability of language; the errors to which translations are subject; the possibility of totally suppressing such a word; the probability of altering it, or of fabricating the whole, and imposing it upon the world.

Secondly— That the Creation we behold is the real and ever-existing word of God, in which we cannot be deceived. It proclaims his power, it demonstrates his wisdom, it manifests his goodness and beneficence.

Thirdly— That the moral duty of man consists in imitating the moral goodness and beneficence of God, manifested in the creation toward all his creatures. That seeing, as we daily do, the goodness of God to all men, it is an example calling upon all men to practise the same toward each other; and, consequently, that everything of persecution and revenge between man and man, and everything of cruelty to animals, is a violation of moral duty [69–70].

The second part of *The Age of Reason*, toward which Watson directs his response, is divided into two sections, one on the Old and one on the New Testament. Paine rejects the notion that the books ascribed to Moses, Joshua, and Samuel were really written by them. He notes Moses's villainous acts, points out internal contradictions, and mocks as preposterousness many Biblical accounts. He observes that the two books each of Kings and Chronicles are historical, and on this basis he regards the Jewish kings as, "in general ...

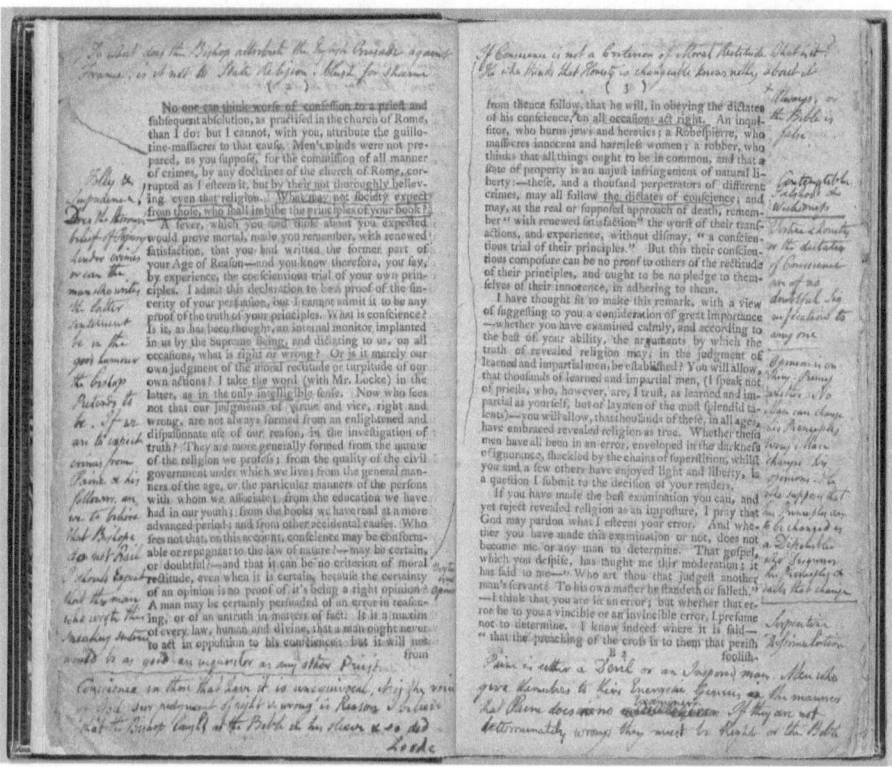

Margins to Watson's *Apology* barely contain Blake's scorn.

a parcel of rascals" (103) and their histories a "jumble of fable and of fact" (104). He holds that Job and Proverbs were not written by Jews, that the so-called prophets made false predictions, and that, in any case, they wrote in support of the views of the parties to which they belonged.

As for the New Testament, two different genealogies of Jesus's family are given, the four gospels offer different and sometimes conflicting accounts, and the books were probably not written by their alleged authors. Certainly none was an eyewitness. Paine regards the broadly accepted typological relation of the Old to the New Testament to be a fraudulent construction: "Between the Christian Jew and the Christian Gentile, the thing called a prophecy and the thing prophesied, the type and the thing typified, the sign and the thing signified, have been industriously rummaged up and fitted together, like old locks and pick-lock keys" (170). St. Paul's doctrine of bodily resurrection evokes Paine's sarcasm: "... as a matter of choice, as well as of hope, I had rather have a better body and a more convenient form than the present" (172–3).

In his conclusion, Paine admits the possibility of revelation, for God can do anything. However, he opposes anyone forcing his revelation on another without corroboration. In short, revealed religion as church doctrine is "a dangerous heresy and an impious fraud" (181). He repeats that God speaks only through his creation.

As to the "fragments of morality" (181) scattered through the Bible, Paine argues that they appear in most cultures. The New Testament exaggerates some of these, for example, the admonition to turn the other cheek and to love one's enemies, dogmas of "feigned morality" (182). They exaggerate the earlier notion that one should not seek revenge: "Those who preach this doctrine of loving their enemies are in general the greatest persecutors, and they act consistently by doing so; for the doctrine is hypocritical, and it is natural that hypocrisy should act the reverse of what it preaches" (183).

Paine concludes with a defense of Deism, which, he argues cannot be employed for purposes of despotism. The natural creation is the bible of the Deists and source of the principles of science, which are "eternal and of divine origin" (186).

Blake agreed with Paine about monarchy, the church, moral codes, prophets and poets, and the hypocrisy of loving one's enemy, but he often expressed his dislike of Deism, which he regarded as nature-worship. He would have disagreed with Paine about the role of imagination, because for him the natural world of the Deists is really a faulty projection of human imagination. Paine was explicit about his skepticism: "The natural bent of my mind was to science. I had some turn, and I believe some talent, for poetry;

but this I rather repressed than encouraged, as leading too much into the field of imagination" (49). For Paine, imagination led to fantasy and unreality. For Blake, imagination and visionary intensity constituted the real.

Watson and the Apology

Though by his own admission he knew nothing about chemistry, in 1760 Watson became professor of chemistry in Trinity College, Cambridge. He became Regius Professor of Divinity in 1771, a position obviously more appropriate to his talents, and Bishop of Landaff in 1782. The *Apology* first appeared in 1796 when he was 60. In his posthumous *Anecdotes*, he writes,

> In the beginning of the year 1796, I published "An Apology for the Bible," being a defence of that Holy Book against the scurrilous abuse of Thomas Paine. This little book, I have reason to believe, was of singular service in stopping that torrent of irreligion which had been excited by his writings. *David Dale of Paisley*, (I mention his name to his honour, his person I never saw), asked my permission, which was most readily granted, to print three thousand copies, to be distributed amongst his own workmen; many thousands were printed also at Dundee, and in other places of Scotland and England at a small price, without any profit or wish of profit to myself.*

The book was well received also by clergymen in America and Ireland. In America, the convention of the Episcopal Church of Connecticut sent a letter of thanks:

> The reputation which that writer [Paine] had obtained in this country by his political pieces during the American Revolution, and the great lukewarmness and indifferency towards the Christian Revelation visible among too many of our citizens, were very alarming circumstances, and led us to apprehend some ill effects from his writings; but happily for us, and we trust for the world at large, that so able a champion of Christianity has again taken the field, and so successfully combated its enemies. Happy we are to find that your excellent defence has (in this country), in a good degree, strengthened the faithful, confirmed the doubtful, roused the indifferent, and silenced the gainsayer. And we have reason to believe that it will, by the blessing of God, be a means of checking that spirit of infidelity among us, which has produced such horrid scenes of distress in a powerful nation of Europe [288–9].

From a meeting in Dublin of the Association for Discountenancing Vice, and Promoting the Knowledge and Practice of Religion and Virtue came a resolution praising the Bishop for standing forth as the "powerful defender

---

Anecdotes of the Life of Richard Watson. Bishop of Landaff, written by Himself, London: Cadell and Davies, 1817, 287–8.

of the Christian cause, in opposition to the attacks of infidel authors, and particularly those of Thomas Paine" (290). About a year later, Watson wrote a letter of praise to the poet William Cowper in which he deplored an age such as theirs, in which "religion is rejected, morality outraged, and the concerns of futurity lost in dissipation and sensual indulgence" (346). Watson praised Cowper for writing poems that "support the cause of piety and virtue" (346).

If Paine's book was often sarcastic, Watson's *Apology*, composed of ten letters addressed to Paine, was sometimes obliquely and often openly arrogant in its *ad hominem* attacks. At least once, it led Blake to complain mightily of viciousness. Watson writes:

> I begin with your preface. You therein state — that you had long had an intention of publishing your thoughts upon religion, but that you originally reserved it to a later period of life. — I hope there is no want of charity in saying, that it would have been fortunate for the christian world had your life been terminated before you had fulfilled your intention [1].

Blake responds in horror, " Presumptuous Murderer dost thou O Priest wish thy brothers death when God has preserved him" (E612), implying both Watson's arrogance and self-contradictory view of God's power.

Watson responds only to Part Two of Paine's work. It is clear from his tenth letter that he had not read Part One. From what he writes, it appears that he had not read *Common Sense*, for in his discussion of Paine's comments on Deuteronomy he seems not to know that Paine had attacked kings as well as priests. Not long into the first letter, he criticizes Paine for "much repetition and a defect of proper arrangement" (4), vowing to do the best he can to construe Paine's argument. He will, he writes, deliberately seek a popular audience and avoid "deep disquisitions concerning the authenticity of the Bible" (6). Thus he implies that there is for his defense a large body of support, too subtle, perhaps, for the mass of his readers.

Watson accuses Paine of a massive and serious disservice to the public:

> In accomplishing your purpose you will have unsettled the faith of thousands; rooted from the minds of the unhappy virtuous all their comfortable assurance of future recompense; have annihilated in the minds of the flagitious all their fears of future punishment; you will have given the reins to the domination of every passion, and have thereby contributed to the introduction of the public insecurity, and of the private unhappiness usually and almost necessarily accompanying a state of corrupted morals [1].

Much of Watson's early argument is devoted to a defense of the Pentateuch. Paine has questioned who wrote these books, and Watson seeks to straighten out confusion in Paine's idea of authenticity by distinguishing between a genuine book and an authentic one. The former is one written by the supposed author. The latter is one that is accurate, not merely fable or fantasy. A book can be authentic even if not genuine and inauthentic even if genuine. He admits that if Moses, Samuel, and others had lied about their authorship, there would be no reason to believe anything they say, but this is not, in his view, the case. Authenticity is not, for him, in doubt. That the books were written in the third person is no proof Moses did not write them, and anyway for centuries the Jews have affirmed the Pentateuch's authority, by which he apparently means, above all, authenticity.

As for the comparison of Jesus's miracles to those told about by ancient pagan writers, corroboration of the latter is weak, and the pagan writers merely describe "tricks of ancient imposters" (12). Watson proceeds to discuss the tradition of the Sabbath, defending it against Paine's attack.

He challenges Paine's claim that the Bible is not the word of God because it says that the Israelites were commanded by God to destroy the Canaanites even down to the women and children. Paine expresses shock at the viciousness of the act and cannot believe that God would have ordered it. Watson holds, in response, that God properly punished a wicked people and did what he did as a lesson to the Israelites to keep to the path of righteousness.

The letters take up and seek to refute Paine's arguments roughly in the order in which they are presented. In the third letter, which defends Moses's behavior, Watson criticizes Paine's historical evidence for its appearing to be presented by an "atheistical madman," not a Deist. In the fourth letter, Watson turns to Paine's critique of Joshua, Samuel, and Kings and defends the idea of the Jews as God's chosen people. The fifth and sixth letters proceed into the later books of the Old Testament and to a general defense of the biblical prophets, beginning with Isaiah:

> What shall be said of you, who, either designedly, or ignorantly, represent one of the most clear and important prophecies in the Bible, as an historical compliment, written above an hundred and fifty years after the death of the prophet? We contend, Sir, that this is a prophecy and not an history.... We will not, Sir, give up Daniel and St. Matthew to the impudent assertions of Porphyry and Voltaire, nor will we give up Isaiah to your assertion. Proof, proof is what we require, and not assertion: we will not relinquish our religion, in obedience to your abusive assertion respecting the prophets of God [50].

Watson accepts Isaiah 7:14 as a prophecy of Jesus's birth, but he does not attempt a defense of it as such. He defends Jeremiah's authenticity and honesty and accuses Paine of misunderstanding the prophets: "... you wholly mistake their office, and misrepresent their character: their office was to convey to the children of Israel the commands, the promises, the threatenings of almighty God; and their character was that of men sustaining, with fortitude, persecution in the discharge of their duty" (59). He insists on the accuracy of the gospels' reports of the crucifixion and in the eighth letter defends as veracity the accounts of the resurrection, including St. Paul's account. He criticizes, as he does elsewhere, Paine's competence as a Biblical scholar. He has no doubt that Jesus ascended to heaven.

The ninth letter is mainly a defense of Paul's reporting, denying against Paine that Paul preached the resurrection of the natural body. Before proceeding to the tenth letter, he summarizes: "You have barbed anew the blunted arrows of former adversaries; you have feathered them with blasphemy and ridicule; dipped then in your deadliest poison; aim them with your utmost skill; but, like the feeble javelin of aged *Priam*, they will scarcely reach the mark, will fall to the ground without a stroke" (105). This is a characteristic piece of Watson's rhetoric.

Though Watson speaks favorably of Deism's ideas of nature and a creator God, he nevertheless finds reason entirely inadequate to answer theological questions and writes sarcastically of it: "The exercise of our reason in the investigation of truths respecting the nature of God, and the future expectations of human kind, is highly useful; but I hope I shall be pardoned by the metaphysicians in saying, that the chief utility of such disquisitions consists in this—that they bring us acquainted with the weakness of our intellectual faculties" (43). He asserts that exhaustion caused by the failure of that route and desire for certainty motivated him to embrace revealed religion: "With a mind weary of conjecture, fatigued by doubt, sick of disputation, eager for knowledge, anxious for certainty, and unable to attain it by the best use of my reason in matters of the utmost importance, I have long ago turned my thoughts to an impartial examination of the proofs on which revealed religion is grounded, and I am convinced of its truth" (43). One can imagine what Paine might have said in response to this. He would have seen it as a confession of weakness.

In the tenth letter, Watson insists that too many questions remain beyond what reason can answer and that only revelation can supply the desired answers. Blake's comment written on the last page of the book sums up his response to the whole:

> It appears to me Now that Tom Paine is a better Christian than the Bishop I have read this Book with attention & find that the Bishop has only hurt Paines heel while Paine has broken his head the Bishop has not answerd one of Paines grand objections [E620].

The ground for this appears to be mainly Watson's dependence almost entirely on evidence internal to the Bible; he simply asserts its historical genuineness and authenticity and tries to explain away various internal contradictions and inconsistencies. For Blake, suspicious of historical accounts and official records, a defense on the basis of historical accuracy is simply irrelevant; properly seen, the Bible is an authentic expression of the imagination, not a historical document.

Blake's Annotations

Most of Blake's annotations are to Watson's first three letters, after which his interest seems to have flagged or he felt his arguments against Watson had been substantially made. On the back of the title page appear several assertions obviously written after he had read the whole book. He seems to have gone through at least part of it more than once.

Blake thinks himself a defender of the Bible, but on grounds very different from Watson's. This difference makes it possible for him to support Paine, even though his attitude toward the Bible differs from Paine's. We can read his first remark as implying what a really effective defense of the Bible might lead to: "To defend the Bible in this year 1798 would cost a man his life" (back of title page, E611). Why? Because "The Beast & the Whore rule without controls." This sounds like an anti–Catholic rant, but it covers for Blake the whole array of churches as well as the alliance in England of church and state. Blake obviously hates Watson's arrogance and tone of self-confidence, and he comments with sarcasm, "It is an easy matter for a Bishop to triumph over Paine's attack [after all, the power of purse and politics is ranged entirely in the Bishop's favor] but it is not so easy for one who loves the Bible" (E610). Blake implies that a real defense would have to attack Watson's and "The Perversions of Christs words & acts are attacked by Paine & also the perversions of the Bible" (E611). He asks, "Who dare defend either the Acts of Christ or the Bible Unperverted?" (E611), meaning not only that one would have to defend against an array of those who have perverted the words of the Bible, but also the terrible examples of human depravity that frequently happen in it.

Blake identifies the effort as duty to his country, insists that Watson should be read carefully, assuming, as he frequently does, that error comes to light if confronted and given shape. But he also writes that he has been commanded not to print any of this, because enemies would want it out, presumably to make it the object of accusation in a dangerous time for political dissent. (The publisher Joseph Johnson spent six months in prison in 1798 for seditious publications [see Paley, 41–2].) Perhaps Blake is thinking of

Paine's having had to flee England even before *The Age of Reason* was written. Would the governing powers come for Blake? They did in 1804. Blake returns to the language of *The Marriage of Heaven and Hell* when he says that the command not to print his comments on Watson's book has come from Hell, the place of energy in *The Marriage*.

Blake does not criticize Paine's Deism in any of his annotations. The reason is partly that Blake had agreed politically with Paine and was more than suspicious of the politics of Watson, who had written, "I cannot agree with those who, in asserting that natural equality of men, spurn the instituted distinctions attending power, rank, and riches" (112). Blake associates such distinctions with what he calls "State Religion" (E613), responsible in his eyes for the "English Crusade against France" (E613). On the surface, he sees Paine's attack as principally against religious oppression, but it is also against political oppression. He does not agree with Paine about how to read the Bible, nor does he with Watson. He takes a third position, which he does not press here. For him, the Bible is an inspired fiction like Milton's or his own poems. This does not mean that certain events did not happen. It means that their meaning does not depend on whether they actually occurred.

The First Letter

In the annotation to the first letter, Blake challenges Watson's notion of conscience. This is an important difference, from which follow others. I quote Watson at length:

> What is conscience? Is it, as has been thought, an internal monitor implanted in us by the *Supreme Being*, and dictating to us on all occasions, what is *right or wrong*? *Or is it merely* our own judgment of the moral rectitude or turpitude of our own actions? I *take the word* (with Mr. Locke) in the latter, *as in the only intelligible* sense. Now who sees not that our judgments of virtue and vice, right and wrong are not always formed from an enlightened and dispassionate use of our reason, in the investigation of truth? They are more generally formed from the nature of the religion we profess; from the quality of the civil government under which we live; from the general manners of the age, or the particular manners of the persons with whom we associate; from the education we have had in our youth; from the books we have read at a more advanced period; and from other accidental causes. Who sees not that, on this account, conscience may be conformable or repugnant to the law of nature?—maybe certain, or doubtful?—and that it can be no criterion of moral rectitude, even when it is certain, because the certainty of an opinion is no proof of its being a right opinion? [2].

Blake makes a series of comments here that express profound disagreement. Underneath all this is his rejection of any authority external to the individual — church, priest, or moral code — that would dictate the content of conscience. Watson believes that there must be an external authority that dictates the law, which overcomes the relativity inevitable in fallibly individual judgment. That authority is for him the doctrine of revealed religion in the Church of England. But, for Blake, the Church imposes an official revelation. He remarks, "Conscience in those who have it is unequivocal, it is the voice of God Our judgment of right & wrong is Reason" (E613). This distinction between conscience and judgment is not only a religious one for Blake. It is also political. Blake was writing at a time when he saw political power imposing its will and claiming the right to decide moral questions. He adds, "If Conscience is not a Criterion of Moral Rectitude What is it?" Plato's Socrates distinguished between thought and mere opinion, and Blake seems also to do so. He remarks, "Virtue is not Opinion" (E613). Above all, he thinks that Watson is preaching submission of the imagination to those forces that control church and state. In this, he sides with Paine, recognizing Paine's freedom of mind:

> Paine is either a Devil or an Inspired man. Men who give themselves to their Energetic Genius in the manner that Paine does are no examiners.... [Watson has written of examining the claims of revealed religion] The man who pretends to be a modest enquirer into the truth of a self evident thing is a Knave [E613].

Thus Blake argues that the knave is Watson, for whom the official version of revealed religion is self-evident merely because it is official. Though Blake identifies Paine with the revolutionary energy he praised without ambiguity in *The Marriage of Heaven and Hell*, later his notion of energy, as Paley points out,* is identified with Orc, whose violence is viewed with ambiguity, especially following later events in France, and whose energy falls into cyclic occurrence with authoritarianism.

The next important disagreement with Watson is based on the question of how to read the many accounts of violence that the Bible contains. Paine declares, "The character of Moses, as stated in the Bible, is the most horrid that can be imagined. If those accounts be true, he was the wretch that first began and carried out wars on the score or on the pretense of religion" (91). Not only is Moses a man of "horrid" character (91), he is a "detestable villain" (92). The example Paine gives is Moses's order to the Israelites to slaugh-

---

*Morton D. Paley, *Energy and the Imagination: A Study of the Development of Blake's Thought*, Oxford at the Clarendon Press, 1970, esp. 77–8.

ter the Midianites (Numbers 31:1–18). Watson pretends that Paine rejects the Bible's veracity as the word of God because God ordered the killing of the Canaanites, but this was for Paine but one piece of evidence of the Bible's falsity. It is not that this didn't happen; it is, for Paine, unthinkable that God would have ordered such a thing.

Watson responds by rejecting entirely Paine's view:

> You hold it impossible that the Bible can be the Word of God, because it is therein said, that the Israelites destroyed the Canaanites by the express command of God: and to believe the Bible to be true, we must, you affirm, unbelieve all our belief of the moral justice of God, for wherein, you ask, could crying or smiling infants offend?—I am astonished that so acute a reasoner should attempt to disparage the Bible, by bringing forward this exploded objection of Morgan, Tindal, and Bolingbroke.... The Word of God is in perfect harmony with his work; crying or smiling infants are subjected to death in both [4–5].

Blake rejects Watson's acceptance that God ordered the Canaanite destruction, but not for the same reason that Paine does. Blake holds that the Bible's intention in this case is to describe the wickedness of the Israelites and show that they used a pretense for their act. He objects to Watson's view of the Israelites as a chosen people and argues that the Jews assumed that right, which "will be a lasting witness against them. & the same will it be against Christians" (E615). In short, the slaughter was ordered by a false god, a massive mental illusion. Blake then introduces Jesus as a revolutionary who preached against that false god:

> To me who believe the Bible & profess myself a Christian a defence of the Wickedness of the Israelites in murdering so many thousands under pretence of a command from God is altogether Abominable & Blasphemous. Wherefore did Christ come was it not to abolish the Jewish Imposture Was not Christ murderd because he taught that God loved all Men & was their father & forbad all contention for Worldly prosperity in opposition to the Jewish Scriptures which are only an Example of the wickedness and deceit of the Jews & were written as a Example of the possibility of Human Beastliness in all its branches. Christ died as an Unbeliever. & if the Bishops had their will so would Paine. see page 1 but he who speaks a word against the Son of man shall be forgiven let the Bishop prove that he has not spoken against the Holy Ghost who in Paine strives with Christendom as in Christ he strove with the Jews [E614]

Blake goes so far here as to claim that in *The Age of Reason* the Holy Ghost spoke through Paine. Blake thinks that Watson has forgotten that "there is a God of This World. A God Worshipd in this World as God & Set above all that is calld God" (E618). This god is a sort of demiurge, creator of the natural, material order, that is, the illusion of it as a reality apart from man. This demiurge appears in Blake's work sometimes as Urizen and sometimes as

If Christ could not do miracles because of Unbelief the reason alledged by Priests for miracles is false for those who believe want not to be confounded by miracles Christ & his prophets & Apostles were not Arbitrary miracle mongers

Moses is not the author of the Pentateuch, is not exclusively your's. *Le Clerc*, indeed, you must not boast of. When his judgment was matured by age, he was ashamed of what he had written on the subject in his younger years; he made a public recantation of his error, by annexing to his commentary on Genesis, a Latin dissertation—concerning Moses, the author of the Pentateuch, and his design in composing it. If in your future life you should chance to change your opinion on the subject, it will be an honour to your character to emulate the integrity, and to imitate the example of *Le Clerc*. The Bible is not the only book which has undergone the fate of being reprobated as spurious, after it had been received as genuine and authentic for many ages. It has been maintained that the history of *Herodotus* was written in the time of *Constantine*; and that the Classics are forgeries of the thirteenth or fourteenth century. These extravagant reveries amused the world at the time of their publication, and have long since sunk into oblivion. You esteem all prophets to be such lying rascals, that I dare not venture to predict the fate of your book.

Before you produce your main objections to the genuineness of the books of Moses, you assert—" that there is no affirmative evidence that Moses is the author of them."—What! no affirmative evidence! In the eleventh century *Maimonides* drew up a confession of faith for the jews, which all of them at this day admit; it consists of only thirteen articles; and two of them have respect to Moses; one affirming the authenticity, the other the genuineness of his books.—The doctrine and prophecy of Moses is true—The law that we have was given by Moses.—This is the faith of the jews at present, and has been their faith ever since the destruction of their city and temple; it was their faith in the time when the authors of the New Testament wrote; it was their faith during their captivity in Babylon; in the time of their kings and judges; and no period can be shewn, from the age of Moses to the present hour, in which it was not their faith.—Is this no affirmative evidence? I cannot desire a stronger. *Josephus*, in his book against *Appion*, writes thus—" We have only two and twenty books which are to be believed as of divine authority, and which comprehend

Prophets in the modern sense of the word have never existed Jonah was no prophet in the modern sense for his prophecy of Nineveh failed Every honest man is a Prophet he utters his opinion both of private & public matters Thus If you go on So the result is So He never says such a thing shall happen let you do what you will. a Prophet is a Seer not an Arbitrary Dictator. It is mans fault if God is not able to do him good. for he gives to the just & to the unjust but the unjust reject his gift

Blake challenges Watson on miracles and prophets.

Satan. For Paine, the Old Testament is a false history. For Blake, it is an imaginative vision of the humanly perverted order of nature after the Fall, "since which time the Elements are filld with the Prince of Evil who has the power of the air" (E614). This is the reason that Blake says, "Natural religion is the voice of God and not the result of reasoning on the powers of Satan" (E614). It is surprising, given Blake's disparagement of natural religion, certainly, for him, synonymous with Deism. But it appears that here both natural religion and Deism in the world are God's voice proclaiming error. This makes sense if we consider Paine's claim that external nature is the only word of God. However, there is another possible reading. Blake says in a letter written in 1799, "... to the Eyes of the Man of Imagination Nature is Imagination itself" (E702), denying the opposition of an objective nature to a perceiving subject but still allowing nature as a projection of imagination. On the other hand, as Paley has argued, "... many of the attitudes that we think of as characteristic of Blake were not yet his in 1798" (38), and that his opposition to Deism was perhaps not so pronounced as it later became. He points out that after the early tract *There Is No Natural Religion* the phrase "natural religion" does not appear until *Vala*, the exception being the Watson annotations (38). I think that, in saying what he did, Blake may have been trying to support Paine even as he disagreed with him on most aspects of religion. As Paley points out, Blake concentrates in his annotations on his political agreements with Paine, not their differences (38). Blake goes on to distinguish between natural and humanly caused disasters, declaring natural ones the result of the fall.

Blake's notion of conscience is connected to a matter that next comes up. Watson thinks it "incredible to many that God Almighty should have had colloquial intercourse with our first parents" (7–8), since it has not been known to occur in later ages. He believes that God did converse with Adam and Eve in order to give, "in the earliest ages, sensible and extraordinary proofs of his existence and attributes..." (9). Blake responds that God still does speak to man as conscience and always has, that Watson is mistaken to assume that there has been mental improvement since the time of the Ancients and that early men were savages: "Read the Edda of Iceland the Songs of Fingal the accounts of North American Savages (as they are calld) Likewise Read Homers Iliad. he was certainly a Savage. in the Bishop's sense. He knew nothing of God. in the Bishops sense of the word & yet he was no fool" (E615). For Blake, the word of Watson's and the Israelites' God as expressed in the Old Testament is "Exclusive of Conscience" (E615).

Throughout the annotations to the first letter and, indeed, throughout all of the annotations Blake comments on the tone of Watson's response to Paine. His prefatory comment on the first letter accuses Watson, in effect, of the same scurrility and illiberality that Watson accuses Paine of, and it does so with a straightforward rhetoric that surpasses the "serpentine" violence of Watson:

> If this first Letter is written without Railing & Illiberality I have never read one that is. To me it is all Daggers & Poison. the sting of the serpent is in every Sentence as well as the glittering Dissimulation Achilles' wrath is blunt abuse Thersites' sly insinuation Such is the Bishops If such is the characteristic of a modern polite gentleman we may hope to see Christ's discourse Expung'd
>
> I have not the Charity for the Bishop that he pretends to have for Paine. I believe him to be a State trickster [E612].

Watson, he complains, is dishonest, he misrepresents, he is full of "Priestly Impudence" (E612), he practices "Contemptible Falsehood & Detraction" (E612), and employs "Serpentine Dissimulation" (E614).

Before the letter ends, Watson says to Paine, "I will not imitate the example you set me; but examine what you shall produce, with as much coolness and respect, as if you had given the priests no provocation; as if you were a man of the most unblemished character, subject to no prejudices, activated by no bad designs..."(9). Blake expresses again his hatred of what he regards as a false and arrogant tone: "Is not this Illiberal has not the Bishop given himself the lie in the moment the first words were out of his mouth Can any man who writes so pretend that he is in a good humour. Is not this the Bishop's cloven foot. has he not spoiled the hasty pudding" (E616).

The Second Letter

In his preface to the second letter, Blake declares that Watson doesn't answer Paine's objections that the Bible is, in Blake's words "a State trick" (E616), that it has been imposed by subtle force, and that its commentators have been sycophants following the approved line. Blake doesn't actually assert that he agrees with Paine on all of these points. Indeed, Blake has already written that he believes the Bible (and Paine, of course, does not), but we know he does not believe it in Watson's sense of belief, nor does he always interpret the events described in the same way. Blake's annotations that follow are concerned with questions of veracity and belief.

The matter of the Bible's veracity goes back to the question of who actually wrote the Pentateuch and whether the books are authentic history. Here Blake sides, for the most part, with Paine again. The question of miracles recounted in the Bible arises. Blake is not much interested in Watson's argument that the evidence for those in the Bible is much superior to the evidence for those told about by Livy and Tacitus. Blake holds, as he says the Bible does, that Jesus could not perform miracles when there was no belief. In asserting this (E616–17), he has some fun at Watson's expense: "Is it a greater miracle to feed five thousand men with five loaves than to overthrow all the armies of Europe with a small pamphlet" (E 617). He argues that we all can perform miracles and have actually done so. But, of course, Blake has referred to something that most people would consider quite different from a biblical miracle. Blake's attack is on Watson's notion of a miracle as "an arbitrary act of the agent upon an unbelieving patient" (E617). He adds that Jesus and his apostles were not "ambitious miracle mongers" (E617).

The last matter regarding belief has to do with prophecy, and here Blake seems to have been impressed by Paine's remark in *The Age of Reason*:

> There is not, throughout the whole book calld the Bible, any word that describes to us what we call a poet, nor any word that describes what we call poetry. The case is, that the word *prophet*, to which latter times have affixed a new idea, was the Bible word for poet, and the word *prophesying* meant the art of making poetry [22].

Paine believes that we have lost the original meaning and that predicting events was not the prophets' purpose. In passing, Paine notes that Jonah's prophecy of Nineveh (3:4) was wrong (68). Watson, seeming deliberately to misunderstand Paine's argument, accuses Paine of saying that all prophets are "lying rascals" (14). Blake echoes Paine but enlarges prophecy beyond the bounds of poetry: "Prophets in the modern sense of the word have never existed Jonah was no prophet in the modern sense for his prophecy of Nineveh failed Every honest man is a Prophet he utters his opinion both of private & public matters/Thus/If you go on So/the result is So He never says such a thing shall happen let you do what you will. a Prophet is a Seer not an Arbitrary Dictator" (E617).

Blake's remarks here reflect his suspicion of a so-called truth dictated to someone by external power or so-called authority. He responds with scorn even to Watson's invocation of public records: "Nothing can be more contemptible than to suppose Public RECORDS to be True" (E 617). Blake returns to Paine's identification of prophecy with poetry, but in a somewhat different key. Still concerned with the question of Moses's authorship, he observes that the facts claimed by the author were ones only he could have known about unless the books are inspired poetry (E617). But then there would be no difference between them and Milton's inspired *Paradise Lost* (E617). In any case, Blake is suspicious of historians, who rarely write at first hand; also they confuse opinion with history. The view he offers here is no different from his remark in *A Descriptive Catalogue* of 1809: "Reasons and

78 Blake's Margins

opinions concerning acts, are not history. Acts themselves alone are history, and these are neither the exclusive property of Hume, Gibbon nor Voltaire, Echard, Rapin, Plutarch, nor Herodotus. Tell me the Acts, O historian, and leave me to reason on them as I please" (E544).

The Third Letter

Here Blake makes his most important distinction between the Bible as history and the Bible as a work of inspired poetry. What does it mean to believe a poem? Whether the events in the Bible are historically true and empirically verifiable or whether they happened at all are irrelevant to Blake's reading:

> "I cannot conceive the Divinity of the books in the Bible to consist either in who they were written by or at what time or in the historical evidence which may be all false in the eyes of one man & true in the eyes of another but in the Sentiments & Examples which whether true or Parabolic are Equally useful as Examples given to us of the perverseness of some & its consequent evil & the honesty of others & its consequent good This sense of the Bible is equally true to all & equally plain to all... [E 618].

Later, Watson again argues that Moses acted under God's command. Blake counters with the claim that all penal laws, including those alleged by some power (in this case the laws of the Jews), to be directly from God, "court Transgression & therefore are cruelty & Murder" (E618). Blake seems to agree with Paine that punishment sets in motion a cycle of revenge. He states that Jesus opposed Jewish law as "The Abomination that maketh desolation" (E618), and he held this to be true when in his notebook he wrote the various lines that, when collected together, make up his poem "The Everlasting Gospel." The laws were an example for Blake of the state religion that for both moral and political reasons he hated. These laws were created under the rule of the "God of this World," as Blake calls him in an annotation to the fourth letter.

The Later Letters

Blake made substantially fewer annotations to Letters Three to Ten (none to Six, Seven, and Eight), and I will discuss everything after Letter Three together in this section.

The question of the law comes up again in the tenth letter, where Watson refers to the "moral precepts of the gospel" and Blake responds, "The Gospel is Forgiveness of Sins & has No Moral Precepts these belong to Plato & Seneca & Nero" (E619). I assume that he means: no moral precept other than those belonging to the Greeks and Romans. For Blake, the forgiveness of sins is fundamental. Blake judges Watson a hypocrite in his response to Paine's argument. Paine writes:

> As to the fragments of morality that are irregularly and thinly scattered in these books, they make no part of this pretended thing, revealed religion. They are the natural dictates of conscience, and the bonds by which society is held together, and without which it cannot exist, and are nearly the same in all religions and in all societies. The Testament teaches nothing new upon this subject, and where it attempts to exceed, it becomes mean and ridiculous. The doctrine of not retaliating injuries is much better expressed in Proverbs, which is a collection as well from the Gentiles as the Jews, than it is in the Testament. It is there said, Proverbs xxv. ver. 21, "*If thine enemy be hungry, give him bread to eat; and if he be thirsty, give him water to drink*"; but when it is said, as in the Testament, "*If a man smite thee on the right cheek, turn to him the other also*"; it is assassinating the dignity of forbearance, and sinking a man into a spaniel.
>
> *Loving enemies* is another dogma of feigned morality, and has besides no meaning. It is incumbent on man, as a moralist, that he does not revenge an injury; and it is equally as good in a political sense, for there is no end to retaliation, each retaliates on the other, and calls it justice; but to love in proportion to the injury, if it could be done, would be to offer a premium for crime [181–2].

Watson rejects Paine's argument, and Blake replies, "Well done Paine" (E 619), but Blake did believe that Jesus's preaching the forgiveness of sins was unique and central to his message. When Watson scorns Paine for treating literally Jesus's words about turning the other cheek, and seems to doubt that Jesus actually did that when the officer of the high priest smote him, Blake comments, "Yes I have no doubt he did" (E619). He goes on to call Watson, "Fool Slight Hypocrite & Villain," when Watson writes, "It is evident, that a patient acquiescence under slight personal injuries is here enjoined; and that a proneness to revenge, which instigates men to savage acts of brutality for every trifling offense, is forbidden" (E619). The hypocrisy Blake sees involves, first, the Bishop's reading allegorically when in a tight spot and literally when it suits him.

Finally, another matter that irritates Blake is Watson's barely concealed snobbishness. In response to the following passage, Blake wonders who the so-called bad men really are:

> — Now, "that thing called Christianity" as you scoffingly speak — that last best gift of Almighty God, as I esteem it, the gospel of Jesus Christ, has given us the most clear and satisfactory information on both these points. It tells us,

> what deism never could have told us, that we certainly shall be raised from the dead — that, whatever be the nature of the soul, we shall certainly live for ever — and that, whilst we live here it is possible for us to do much towards the rendering that everlasting life an happy one — These are tremendous truths to bad men; they cannot be received and reflected on with indifference by the best; and they suggest to all such a cogent motive to virtuous action, as deism could not furnish... [118].

Blake wonders whether the bad men are the publicans and sinners whom he says Christ "loved to associate with" (E619). Just before the passage above, Watson has argued, "The importance of revelation is by nothing rendered more apparent, than by the discordant sentiments of learned and good men (for I speak not of the <u>ignorant and immoral</u>) on this point. They shew the insufficiency of human reason" (117). Blake also thought reason insufficient, especially when given full sway, but he is more interested here in responding that Jesus did not come in order to call the "Virtuous," and he identifies the righteous with pretension (E619) to superiority.

In the prefatory note of his annotations to Reynolds's *Discourses*, Blake speaks with his characteristic honesty of the notes that follow as "Nothing but Indignation and Resentment" (back of title page, E636). In the Watson annotations, he has expressed similar feelings against someone who, in his view has defended not so much the Bible itself as the worst in both church and state and has in addition misunderstood the message of Jesus. That indignation causes him to defend the Deist Paine, with whom he differs on religious and philosophical issues but admires on political ones.

4

Annotations to Sir Francis Bacon's *Essays Moral, Economical, and Political*

Blake annotated Bacon's *Essays* shortly after publication of the edition of 1798.* He writes in an annotation to Sir Joshua Reynolds' *Discourses* (see below p. 133, E660) that he had annotated Bacon's *Advancement of Learning* "when very Young," but the volume has not been found. His annotation expresses deep dislike of Bacon (1561–1626) as well as of Edmund Burke and John Locke, both of whom he read at about the same age. However, in a letter of 1799 to the Reverend Dr. Trusler, in which he defends his way of drawing figures, he quotes Bacon in his support: "Sense sends over to imagination before Reason have judged & Reason sends over to Imagination before the Decree can be acted."† In this letter, well-known to scholars, Blake identifies what is called nature with human imagination and identifies imagination with "spiritual sensation."

Bacon's first publication of essays, ten in number, appeared in 1597 along with *Colours of Good and Evil* and *Religious Meditations*. By 1612, the essays had increased in number to fifty-eight, some revised and many in longer versions. The edition that Blake annotated included an additional essay "Of a King."

Blake's contempt for Bacon has been commented on by critics all the

---

***Essays Moral, Economical, and Political* by Francis Bacon, Baron of Verulam, and Viscount St. Albans, London: Printed by T. Bensley, for J. Edwards, Pall Mall, and T. Payne, News Gate, 1798. The copy that Blake annotated is in the Keynes collection of the Cambridge University Library.

†August 23, 1789, E703. See "The Advancement of Learning, Book Two," *Francis Bacon: The Major Works*, ed. Brian Vickers, Oxford: Oxford University Press, 1996, 217. Blake makes three trivial changes.

way back to Alexander Gilchrist, who observed that the annotations are written in a "very characteristic if very unreasonable fashion." He finds in them "none of that leaven of real sense and acumen which tempers the violence of those on Reynolds."* Nowhere in his annotations to the essays has he a good word for anything Bacon says. His attacks are often *ad hominem,* and they are vehemently expressed. Bacon is often not merely wrong; he is a liar and a hypocrite. The fundamental reasons for Blake's disagreements with Bacon are not often on the surface of his notes, but they certainly lurk beneath. They cover a range of issues including the political, economical, religious, and philosophical. It is possible that his philosophical disagreements were more openly expressed in his annotations to *The Advancement of Learning.* If Blake had read and annotated *Novum Organum* he undoubtedly would have expressed his criticism of Bacon's commitment to induction with even greater vigor.

There is the question also of how much Blake knew about Bacon's political career and the reasons for his eventual downfall. Nieves Mathews, in a thorough effort to rescue Bacon from attacks on his character, writes,

> In general terms the seventeenth century praised and imitated him, the eighteenth century idolized him (for Leibniz he soared to the heavens, while Descartes grovelled on earth), and the nineteenth and early twentieth centuries devoted a large part of their energies to debunking him; so that the Secretary of Nature and all Learning, as his own time saw him, came to be despised as a charlatan and a quack, and was labeled the worst enemy science has ever known.†

Mathews blames mainly Thomas Babington Macauley's prejudiced and inaccurate article "Francis Bacon" in the *Edinburgh Review* of July 1837 for the collapse of Bacon's reputation. This was published a decade after Blake's death, but there were earlier disparagements from anti–Stuart "libellers," including Sir Anthony Weldon in his *Court and Character of King James* (1651), where Bacon is called a "malicious scurrilous liar," and Arthur Wilson in *The Annals of King James I* (1653). Simonds D'Ewes also maligned Bacon in his autobiography and personal journal. These statements may not have been known to Blake, though they certainly influenced views of Bacon in Blake's time. However, Blake would surely have known of Alexander Pope's notorious couplet on Bacon in his *Essay on Man* (1734):

> If parts allure thee, think how Bacon shin'd
> The wisest brightest, meanest of mankind [ll.231–32].

---

*Alexander Gilchrist, *Life of William Blake* (1863), London: J. M. Dent & Sons Ltd.; New York: E. P. Dutton and Co. Inc., 1945. 276.
†Nieves Mathews, *Francis Bacon: The History of a Character Assassination,* New Haven, CT and London: Yale University Press, 1996. 4.

"Meanest" was misunderstood by a series of writers, according to Mathews (332–36); for Pope it implied that Bacon was "modest, unassuming, lowly."*

All of Pope's other remarks about Bacon, Mathews writes, are very favorable, and in *The Dunciad* Pope wrote, addressing dunces,

> 'Tis yours, a Bacon or a Locke to Blame.
> A Newton's genius or a Milton's flame [III, ll. 215–16].

Further, Bacon had many notable and respected friends, among them Ben Jonson, and later admirers, including Abraham Cowley and Joseph Addison. Thomas Carte's *A General History of England from the Earliest Times* (1747–55) treated him favorably.

Blake was certainly swayed by his knowledge of Bacon's 1621 impeachment for corruption (Mathews makes a case for Bacon's innocence or at least naiveté), and it may have encouraged Blake's strong disagreement with Bacon on fundamental issues. The result is a series of annotations in which Bacon is villain, fool, liar, and knave. His writings contain foolishness, trifling nonsense, and blasphemy. They are absurd, stupid, contemptible, and pernicious. Bacon, Blake warns the reader on the title page, gives the Devil's advice: "Good Advice for Satans Kingdom" (E620).

Politics

To a great extent, Bacon's essays are written to offer advice to kings, courtiers, and politicians. Since Blake is more than suspicious of the motivations and morals of all of these, it is not surprising that he refuses to acknowledge that Bacon's advice, coming from a courtier and based on practical experience with intrigue, is often prudent with respect to circumstances remote from Blake's own experience. Such advice seems to Blake only "Wisdom of this World," a world the product of a false philosophy and erroneously believed to be reality. This wisdom is, from God's point of view, "Foolishness." Blake marks a clear line between Christ and Caesar (half-title page, E620), but he insists that a single ethic, drawn from his interpretation of Christianity, should govern both realms with no compromise.

It is difficult to believe, however, that Bacon is wrong or Satanic when, for example, he warns against talking too much, being a "blab" or a "babbler": "In a few words, mysteries are due to secrecy. Besides (to say truth) *nakedness is uncomely*, as well in mind as body; and it addeth no small rever-

---

*Mathews depends on H. Kendra Baker's "Pope and Bacon: The Meaning of the Meanest," *Baconiana* 85 (January 1937).

ence to man's manners and actions, if they be not altogether open" (22). Blake does not leap, as he could, on Bacon's having to imply that he is here actually speaking the truth (as if he often did not), but he certainly dislikes the example Bacon uses to criticize openness. Further, Blake had a deep aversion to mystery, which he thought those in power used to their own ends. At the same time, one has to admit that there must often be silence, prudent in affairs of state. Blake judges it always wrong: "This is Folly Itself" (E623). He is silent when Bacon comes to "simulation," which is the pretense of being what one is not. This, Bacon declares, is more "culpable and less politic; except it be in great and rare matters." He has been discussing secrecy and dissimulation, and he admits that dissimulation often follows by necessity on secrecy. That Blake says nothing in response to Bacon on simulation may only indicate that he considers his earlier annotation quite sufficient. Bacon does not rule rigorously against it. Blake would think that with the use of "politic" Bacon rejects any fixed ethical principle in affairs of state.

Blake was, of course, a republican and opposed to monarchy. His hatred of kings exceeds even his contempt for Bacon, but not by much. "Every Body hates a King," he writes (38, E623), and he thinks that monarchy breeds the very sort of simulation and sedition that Bacon apparently writes against. Blake: "It was a Common opinion in the Court of Queen Elizabeth that Knavery Is Wisdom: Cunning Plotters were considerd as wise Machiavels" (blank page xii, E620).

The essay "Of a King," not published in *Essays* in Bacon's lifetime, generates a strong response from Blake from the start. That response is expressed in a marginal drawing (now only partly visible, but copied by Geoffrey Keynes into another copy of *Essays*.* It shows the Devil's arse dropping excrement on the words "A King" (55). When Bacon calls a king "a mortal god on earth, unto whom the living God hath lent his own name as a great honour" (56), Blake shouts "O Contemptible & Abject Slave" (E624). Implying that Bacon's every thought makes him a slave. He passes by Bacon's further remark, which qualifies the preceding one: "... [a king] should die like a man, lest he should be proud, and flatter himself that God hath with his name imparted to him his nature also." Blake is not often friendly to such qualifications. He also does not comment when Bacon remarks of kings that "of all kind of men God is the least beholding unto them; for he doth most for them, and they do ordinarily least for him" (56).

---

*On this, including reproductions of the original page and Keynes' copying, see Robert W. Rix, "Blake, Bacon and 'The Devils Arse,'" *Blake, An Illustrated Quarterly* 37: (Spring 2004), 137–144. Rix reproduces several examples of cartoons by others, similar in content to Blake's sketch.

Though Blake passes over the following, it is possible that he thinks his earlier outburst is enough to cover this also: "...it is better that the evil event of good advice lie rather imported to a subject than a sovereign" (57). Blake must surely have thought this hypocrisy in action.

On a number of points, however, Blake must have had to agree with Bacon, who writes, "A king that setteth to sale seats of justice oppresseth the people; for he teacheth his judges to sell justice" (58), and "A prodigal king is nearer a tyrant than a parsimonious," and "His greatest enemies are his flatterers; for though they ever speak on his side, yet their words still make against him" (59). This last must have appealed to Blake's hatred of sycophancy. However, it was preceded by the remark, "That king which is not feared is not loved; and he that is well seen in his craft must as well study to be feared as loved; yet not loved for fear, but feared for love" (58). Blake's answer to this is, "Fear cannot Love" (E624). When Bacon resorts to realpolitik, as he frequently does, Blake dissents, usually more violently than here.

The last annotation to "Of a King" comes with Bacon's concluding remarks. Blake responds with "Blasphemy" to "He then that honoureth him [the King] not is next an atheist, wanting the fear of God in his heart" (60, E624). Here again Bacon riles Blake by seeming to deify kings and by indicating that God should be feared.

It is important to recognize that Blake makes no response to Bacon's explicit advice to kings. He offers no agreement; neither does he complain, perhaps because he has no use for the recipient of this advice:

> He must have a special care of five things, if he would not have his crown to be but to him "*infelix felicitas*" [unlucky happiness]:
> first, that "*simulata sanctitas*" [pretense to sanctity] be not in the church; for that is "*duplex iniquitas*" [twofold impropriety]:
> secondly, that "*inutilis aequitas*" [useless calmness] sit not in the chancery; for that is "*inepta misericordia*" [absurd sympathy]:
> thirdly, that "*utilis iniquitas*" [expedient injustice] keep not the exchequer; for that is "*crudele latrocinium*" [crude piracy]:
> fourthly, that "*fidelis temeritas*" [certain rashness] be not his general; for that will bring but "*feram poenitentiam*" [savage punishment]:
> fifthly, that "*infidelis prudential*" [unfaithful discretion] be not his secretary; for that is "*anguis sub viridi herba*" [a serpent under a green plant] [59].

"Of a King" is followed by the essays "Of Nobility" and "Of Seditions and Troubles." In the first of these, Bacon attempts first to show the value of a nobility. He argues that in the state nobles "attemper" sovereignty and thus prevent an "absolute tyranny" (60). He goes on, rather surprisingly, to observe that democracies have no need of a nobility, and he regards the democracies of Switzerland and the Low Countries with so much respect that one concludes he favors them, at least here, over monarchy. This implied reservation about monarchy and nobility he somewhat tempers in his discussion of "nobility in particular persons," which he admires if it belongs to "an ancient noble family." However, even here he observes that "nobility of birth commonly abateth industry" (62), and he thinks that a numerous nobility causes poverty and inconvenience.

Blake jumps immediately on Bacon's first words in "Of Nobility": "We will speak of Nobility first as a portion of an estate [state]" (60). Here Blake questions whether there is a nobility in a state, which word he interprets here, though not elsewhere, as a republic; and he accuses Bacon of self-contradiction (E624) when Bacon proceeds to his mention of democracies. Bacon speaks of nobles as "commonly more virtuous, but less innocent than their descendants; for there is rarely any rising but by a commixture of good and evil arts" (62). Blake answers, "Virtuous I supposed to be Innocents was I Mistaken or is Bacon a Liar" (E624). Here Bacon and Blake use "innocent" in different senses. In his commentary on Bacon's words (732), Brian Vickers connects his use of "virtuous" with the Italian *virtu,* strength and resourcefulness. Blake identifies it here with blamelessness, as in the innocence of children in his *Songs of Innocence.*

Finally, with respect to nobility, Blake views as "Nonsense" Bacon's observation, "Nobility extinguisheth the passive envy from others towards them, because they are in possession of honour" (62, E624). For Bacon, a person of honor is one of superior standing, requiring in a class society respect. For Blake, however, honor is to be identified with integrity.

"Of Sedition and Troubles" is one of the longest of the essays, and it evokes more comments from Blake than any of the others. Here his attack is not merely against reverence for kings and nobles, but also against reverence for government itself, presumably of any kind whatever. Bacon remarks, "When discords, and quarrels, and factions are carried openly and audaciously it is a sign the reverence of government is lost" (63). Blake answers, "When the Reverence of Government is Lost it is better than when it is found Reverence is all For Reverence" (E624). This statement stands very well for Blake's political views, at least at this time, and expresses his suspicion of reverence as really sycophancy toward external power, a failing he certainly attributes to Bacon. At the beginning of this essay Blake has written, "This Section contradicts the Preceding" (63, E624), for Bacon claims at the outset that in the State things become tempestuous as "things grow to *equality,*" even though he has observed order in the democracies known to him. There is no doubt that Bacon, like most people of his time, deeply feared social unrest.

Bacon calls religion, justice, counsel (to the monarch), and treasure the "four pillars of government" (66), and Blake observes that these pillars are all of "different heights and sizes" (E624). The essay does not discuss each of these. Rather, it turns to the material and secondary causes (in Aristotle, efficient causes) of sedition. For Bacon, there are two such specific causes, "much poverty and much discontentment" (65). For Blake, "These are one Kind Only" (E625), and indeed Bacon nearly reduces them to one in the rest of the essay. However, before turning to the subject of economics, it is well to consider Bacon's advice to kings not to regard the seeking of counsel as weakness but instead strength. Blake is clearly sarcastic when Bacon suggests that the king would better choose for committees "indifferent [impartial] persons, than to make an indifferency by putting in those that are strong on both sides" (101). Blake's response: "better choose Fools at once" (E628). The response is characteristic, and Blake indulges in the same sort when in a later essay "Of Faction" Bacon warns kings against factionalism, for it militates against their authority, and it reveals their weakness when it is carried to heights: "The motions of factions under Kings ought to be like the motions, (as the astronomers speak,) of the inferior orbs; which may have their proper motions, but yet still are quietly carried by the higher motion of 'primum mobile'" (236). Blake no doubt hated this simile and responded: "King James was Bacons Primum Mobile" (E632).

Blake is also sarcastic in his response to the following: "... neither was there ever prince bereaved of his dependances by his council, except where there hath been either an over-greatness in one counselor, or an over-strict combination in divers, which are things soon found and holpen [remedied]"(98). Blake brackets this and responds, "Did he mean to Ridicule a King & his Council," implying that either Bacon admits weakness in the king and villainy in the counselors or he has not succeeded in saying exactly what he meant (90, E627).

It seems that, for Bacon, a king must be cunning. But in the essay "Of Cunning" Bacon appears ambivalent about the cunning of courtiers. He offers some examples of deceptive acts that were successful. His tendency toward seeking the mean between extremes seems to frustrate him here. Blake responds with contempt, cunning being a quality he despises, certainly in politicians; however, he does not pause to castigate Bacon for approving of the acts he mentions, if indeed Bacon has approved of them. They are merely "absurd" or acts of a "Fool" (104–5, E628). In one instance Blake thinks something Bacon has reported "too stupid to have been True" (108, E628). All are examples of successful manipulation, and if Bacon may not admire them, he clearly thinks that they work, in spite of his opening statement, "We take cunning for a sinister or crooked wisdom" and "There is a great difference between a cunning man and a wise one" (104).

Blake resists here the distinctions Bacon makes between practical and intellectual abilities. The matter comes up again in "Of the True Greatness of Kingdoms and Estates," where Bacon thinks of true greatness (grandeur) as neither "over-measuring" one's forces nor "undervaluing" them. Blake comments only, "Princes Powers" and "Powers of darkness" (136, E629). The subject here is war, conquest, and empire (137–8). Blake, strongly opposed to these, observes, "The Kingdom of Heaven is the direct Negation of Earthly domination," and he goes on to observe dryly, "Bacon knows the wisdom of War if it is Wisdom" (E629).

Bacon, who was steeped in the classics, takes Ancient Rome as his model for war and empire. Its policy was to grant citizenship to those it conquered. This increased population and kept a proper balance between nobility and commoners, preventing the growth of the nobility out of proportion to the population as a whole. Most important in Roman policy was the profession of arms: "But above all, for empire and greatness, it importeth most that a nation do profess arms as their principal honour, study, and occupation" (143). Blake lets this pass, but when Bacon claims that a political body requires exercise of arms and that a "just and honourable war is the true exercise" (147), Blake responds, "Is not this the Greatest Folly" (E630). He proceeds to declare Bacon foolish to advocate not just the few things done to honor soldiers but more the honors bestowed in ancient times. Bacon has written,

> There be now, for martial encouragement, some degrees and orders of chivalry; which nevertheless are conferred promiscuously upon soldiers and no soldiers; and some remembrance perhaps upon the scutcheon; and some hospitals for maimed soldiers; and such like things. But in ancient times the trophies erected upon the place of the victory; the funeral laudatives and monuments for those that died in the wars; the crowns and garlands personal; the style of Emperor, which the great kings of the world after borrowed; the triumphs of the generals upon their return; the great donatives and largesses upon the disbanding of the armies; were things able to inflame all men's courages. But above all, that of the Triumph, amongst the Romans, was not pageantry or gaudery, but one of the wisest and noblest institutions that ever was [149].

Blake hates this glorification of war: "what can be worse than this or more foolish" (E630).

Blake regards his quarrel with Bacon as one of spirit and intellect against materialism and utilitarian interests. In an annotation to "Of Seditions and Troubles," he writes, "The Increase of a State as of a Man is from Internal Improvement or Intellectual Acquirement. Man is not Improved by the hurt of another States are not Improved at the Expense of Foreigners. Bacon has

4. Bacon's Essays Moral, Economical, and Political 89

no notion of any thing but Mammon" (70, E625). Behind this is Blake's suspicion of empire-building, which in England might dilute the nation's Christian tradition (142, E629).

But deeper than this is Blake's commitment to "Intellectual Arts." Bacon writes,

> It is certain, that sedentary and within-doors arts, and delicate manufactures (that require rather the finger than the arm,) have in their nature a contrariety to a military disposition. And generally, all warlike people are a little idle, and love danger better than travail. Neither must they be too much broken of it, if they shall be preserved in vigour. Therefore it was great advantage in the ancient states of Sparta, Athens, Rome, and others, that they had the use of slaves, which commonly did rid those manufactures. But that is abolished in greatest part, by the Christian law. That which comest nearest to it, is to leave those arts chiefly to strangers (which are the more easily to be received), and to contain the principal bulk of the vulgar natives within those three kinds,—tillers of the ground; free servants; and handicraftsmen of strong and manly arts, as smiths, masons, carpenters, &c: not reckoning professed soldiers [143].

Blake's response clearly expresses a fundamental difference of opinion and predicts the eventual triumph of intellect over war and empire ("The Kingdom of Heaven is the direct Negation of Earthly domination" [E629]): "Bacon calls Intellectual Arts Unmanly Poetry Painting Music are in his opinion Useless & so they are for Kings & Wars & shall in the End Annihilate them" (E629).

Throughout the annotations Blake shows no willingness to grant Bacon the right to offer practical advice pertinent to the real problems of state that kings and counselors face. Indeed, he simply rejects kingship itself so that the whole edifice Bacon acknowledges is negated. Bacon's political consistency was his effort to defend the sovereignty of the king while at the same time keeping it in balance with the liberty of the commons. It is at best a neat trick, and Bacon's strategy was to avoid ideological issues as much as possible and choose realpolitik over political theorizing. His writings indicate his skepticism that there could be a science of politics, for political success and survival involves a balancing act. As a result, Bacon put forward the notion that the monarch had absolute prerogative, some prerogatives directly from God. Nevertheless, the king must follow the law and rules by virtue of the law. Bacon straddles the line between monarchical absolutism and opposition to complete royal authority. At the same time he places much emphasis on the king's responsibility for sustaining traditions, and yet he considers tyranny worse than sedition.*

---

*On Bacon's political views, see especially, Markku Peltonen, "Bacon's Political Philosophy," *The Cambridge Companion to Bacon,* ed. Peltonen, Cambridge: Cambridge University Press, 1996, 283–310.

For these reasons, Blake refuses to accept or even recognize Bacon's tendency toward republicanism when it appears. Bacon's own political life made that impure, and Blake saw that as hypocrisy.

Economics

What Blake says about Bacon and money we might consider in the light of Henry Crabb Robinson's report: "[Blake] spoke of his horror of money,— of his having turned pale when money was offered him."* We have already seen that Blake accuses Bacon of having "no notion of any thing but Mammon" (E625). He also calls him a usurer. There is no evidence that Bacon loaned money at interest. Blake must be referring to the essay "Of Usury," where Bacon defends the practice from the many complaints made against it:

> I say this only, that usury is a "concessum propter duritiem cordis" [concession to the hardness of the heart]: for since there must be borrowing and lending, and men are so hard of heart as they will not lend freely, usury must be permitted [190].

Blake quarrels with Bacon's description of the values and economic "discommodities" of usury and summarizes by declaring, "Bacon is in his Element on Usury it is himself & his Philosophy" (193, E631). Beyond these remarks, when Bacon offers ways to prevent sedition, generated in his view by poverty and discontent, Blake opposes one of his remedies, the regulation of the price of necessities. Blake rejects Bacon's observation, "Certainly, if a man will keep but of even hand, his ordinary expenses ought to be but to half of his receipts; and if he thinks to wax rich, but to the third part" (133). This reveals, in Blake's view, Bacon's ignorance of the condition of the poor. He calls "Nonsense" Bacon's advice, "He that can look into his estate but seldom, it behoveth him to turn all to certainties" (134, E629). In short, Blake thinks Bacon is no one to give advice on matters of money: "Bacon was always a poor Devil if History says true how should one so foolish know about Riches Except Pretence to be Rich if that is it" (169, E631). In any case, "Bacons Business is not Intellect or Art" (197, E631).

Writing on usury, Bacon is interested in finding practical solutions to social and economic problems. He understands that usury will not go away. Therefore, the question is how to control it for the public good. For Blake, the issue is strictly a moral one allowing for no compromise. When Bacon

---

*Henry Crabb Robinson, *Diary, Reminiscences, and Correspondence*, selected and edited by Thomas Sadler, Ph.D., London: Macmillan and Co. 1869, I: 318.

writes the essay "Of Expense," Blake comments, "If this is advice to the Poor, it is mocking them — If to the Rich, it is worse still it is The Miser If to the Middle Class it is the direct Contrary to Christs advice" (133, E629).

Religion

Blake accuses Bacon not only of usury but also of atheism. His attack on Bacon as a usurer seems to be based on guilt by association. If you defend usury, you are yourself a usurer. The attack with regard to atheism is more complicated, since Bacon nowhere explicitly attacks religion. Indeed, he writes about it in many places as a practicing Anglican. Nevertheless, Blake calls him a "Contemplative Atheist" (77, E626), suggesting some distance between Bacon's practice and what Blake thinks his true belief is. For Blake, this is at least self-contradiction and probably hypocrisy.

On the surface, Blake's attack, sprinkled with personal invective, seems to fly in the face of Bacon's writings having to do with religion, and it can be understood by seeing what Blake meant by atheism, a matter to which I will eventually come. In his late twenties, probably between 1589 and 1591, Bacon entered religious controversy with his "An Advertisement touching the Controversies of the Church of England." He entered characteristically as a mediator and was critical both of extremism in the Church establishment and of certain Puritan excesses. It is as if he were arguing that the Church's government should be more like a secular one. Brian Vickers comments on Bacon's *Certain Considerations touching the better Pacification and Edification of the Church of England* (1604): "In it he reviews the present state of the Church, expressing surprise that 'the civil state' should make laws every three or four years to keep itself healthy while 'contrariwise the ecclesiastical state should still continue upon the dregs of time, and receive no alteration now for these five and forty years and more.'"* There is no doubt that Bacon, though an Anglican, was sympathetic to some Puritan views; here, as often, he takes a middle course. It is likely, had Blake known these documents, he would have agreed with many of Bacon's criticisms of both sides, but in religious matters Blake did not like mediation; it revealed to him a weakness of commitment and character.

Certainly, from Bacon's other writings it would be difficult to accuse Bacon of atheism unless one were to define the term eccentrically. In *A Confession of Faith*, first printed in 1641, fifteen years after Bacon's death, he begins,

---

*Bacon: The Major Works, 500.

"I believe that nothing is without beginning but God; no nature, no matter, no spirit, but only one and the same God. That God as he is eternally almighty, only wise, only good, in his nature, so he is eternally Father, Son, and Spirit, in persons."* In *Religious Meditations*, Bacon wrote on miracles, charity, and types of religious imposture. He wrote on atheism not only there but also in *Essays*. In the latter, Bacon offers the following: "It is true, that a little philosophy inclineth man's mind to atheism; but depth in philosophy bringeth men's minds about to religion" (75). This has a parallel in the former work's argument that it is the fool without judgment who makes the argument for atheism: "... it is out of the corruption of his heart and will, and not out of the natural apprehension of his brain and conceit that he doth set down his opinion."†

Blake's complaint about the remark above in *Essays* begins with a criticism of Bacon's notion of "second causes," as Bacon calls them. He refers, I think, to Aristotle's efficient cause, that is, Blake identifies these with natural causation and denies their existence. Indeed, he denies the existence of first causes as well. In this he follows Hume, but passes beyond him, for Hume argued only that we could not ever demonstrate the existence of a causal relation: causality cannot be proved any more than we can prove that because something has happened in a certain way, it will inevitably happen in that way again. For Blake everything *is* its own cause, generated out of itself. This arises out of his rejection of any distinction between so-called nature and mind; causes pertain only to things of material nature. As he remarks in the first of several annotations to Bacon's "Of Atheism," "The Devil is the Mind of the Natural Frame" (75, E625); that is, it is the alienated part of a mental reality when the mind assumes the separate existence of nature. By the same token, Blake rejects the distinction between reason and emotion. Thus atheism cannot be the result of an absence of reason and a presence of heart and will.

Blake rejects Bacon's list of mundane causes of atheism (77). When Bacon argues that primitive people have gods and thus can be placed on the side of those who reject atheism, Blake distinguishes between paganism and the "New Birth" that was and is, in his view, Christianity: "A lie," he writes, "Few [savages] believe it is a New Birth. Bacon was a Contemplative Atheist [Bacon's own phrase] Evidently an Epicurean Lucian [mentioned as an example by Bacon] disbelievd Heathen Gods he did not perhaps disbelieve for all that Bacon did" (E626).

---

*Bacon: The Major Works, 107.
†Bacon: The Major Works, 95.

For Blake, Bacon is not just a disbeliever, he contradicts himself. When Bacon indicates that there are worse things than atheism, Blake says that Bacon is praising it (E626). Bacon's words in his essay "Of Superstition" are as follows: "Atheism leaves a man to sense, to philosophy, to natural piety, to laws, to reputation; all which may be guides to an outward moral virtue, though religion were not [did not exist]; but superstition dismounts all these, and erecteth an absolute monarchy in the minds of men. Therefore atheism did never perturb states; for it makes men wary of themselves, as looking no further: and we see the times inclined to atheism (as the time of Augustus Caesar) were civil times" (80). Bacon is contrasting atheism with superstition and declaring the latter worse: "But superstition hath been the confusion of many states, and bringeth in a new *primum mobile*, that ravisheth all the spheres of government. The master of superstition is the people; and in all superstition wise men follow fools; and arguments are fitted to practice, in a reversed order" (80).

Blake has taken two opposed views of superstition. In his annotations to Watson's *Apology for the Bible*, he defends Thomas Paine for attacking superstition (E612), but in the annotations to Lavater's *Aphorisms on Man* he defends "true superstition" as "ignorant honesty" (E591), referring, I think, to the poor who are prevented from gaining true knowledge. At the same time, he calls superstition among the more privileged merely self-deception and thus hypocrisy (E591).

Blake's complaint against Bacon is grounded on his rejection of Deism and natural religion, which to his mind amounts to atheism. Blake's objection to Deism was that it rejected revealed religion, that is, it claimed that reason provides the basis of everything necessary to religious belief, thereby discounting revelation, which for Blake meant the rejection of imaginative vision. Blake assumed, as he wrote in the annotations to Reynolds's *Discourses on Art* that Bacon's "first princip is unbelief" (E648). He objects to what he sees as a fundamental skepticism in Bacon's method for obtaining knowledge. It proceeds, in his view, from universal doubt: "Bacon put and End to Faith" (E621).

Philosophy

Blake's complaint about Bacon is philosophical as well as religious. He denies distinctions between true philosophy, religion, and poetry. "Philosophy" and "philosopher" are words that do not frequently occur in Blake's writings. They do appear, however, along with "metaphysics" in *The Marriage of Heaven and Hell*. In that work, the prophet Ezekiel, conversing with Blake, declares that the ancient philosophers taught that "the Poetic genius (as you now call it) with the first principle [of human perception] and all the others merely derivative" (E39). This notion stands at the base of Blake's epistemology and opposes what he regards as Bacon's. For Blake, Bacon's experimentalism is based on a view that all knowledge begins with doubt and proceeds to develop the idea of an alien natural world. Blake comments at the very beginning of "Of Truth," "Self Evident Truth is one Thing and Truth the result of Reasoning is another Thing Rational Truth is not the Truth of Christ but of Pilate It is the Tree of the Knowledge of Good & Evil" (E621). The reference is, of course, to Pilate's skeptical remark to Jesus, "What is truth?" Self-evident truth is produced by imagination. What imagination grasps and shapes is the real, which is not produced by impingement on the eye of something called nature. A separate nature is really a product of a false distinction between subject and object. For Bacon, nature is such an object; it has to be something apart and only deducible as a series of abstract ideas. Blake sees Bacon as the precursor of John Locke and his distinction between primary and secondary qualities of experience and of Newton's science. Reality becomes, falsely, the product of but general knowledge, abstraction away from a series of acts of vision. Further, it separates God from his creation and creation from the perceiving human mind. It is, thus, the truth of Pilate. Nature, then, becomes the work of a human mind, which, engaged in that activity, can be properly called the Devil, as it is by Blake (E625).

For Blake, the problem with Bacon's induction is that it begins with the hypothesis that what is known is unchanging and that inductive acts based on this belief are imprisoned by the premise. In an important article, Harry White describes Blake's view:

> By claiming that knowledge of the unknown could reasonably be arrived at on the basis of already acquired knowledge, the new philosophy put itself in the wholly illogical position of supposing it could deduce knowledge of all existence before it had experienced all of existence. Blake contended to the contrary that from "already acquired knowledge Man could not acquire more" (*All Religions Are One*, E1). If science is to progress, the ratio of what we know must not be established so as to fix, circumscribe and limit all future knowledge. Scientific knowledge cannot be based, as Bacon claimed, on past experience. The acquisition of new knowledge comes through new experience.*

Blake also finds Newton guilty of the same limitation.†

---

*Harry White, "Blake's Resolution of the War Between Science and Religion," *Blake: An Illustrated Quarterly*, 39: 3 (Winter 2005–06), 116.
†Harry White," Blake and the Mills of Induction," *Blake Newsletter* 10, 4 (Spring 1977), 110.

Finally, Blake's view that Bacon was an atheist follows from these criticisms. As Henry Crabb Robinson reported, Blake declared, "Bacon, Locke, and Newton are the three great teachers of Atheism or of Satan's doctrine. Every thing is Atheism which assumes the reality of the natural and unspiritual world."* An atheist is one who, if he has any belief, thinks wrongly that the natural world of causes, matter, and abstract generalizations is the real world and that it is God's creation.

Little of Blake's argument against Bacon, Newton, and Locke appears explicitly in his annotations to Bacon, but it is present beneath everything he came to believe and write.

Of Art and Artists

When in his essay "Of Travel" Bacon gives advice to travelers and does not specifically recommend the viewing of works of art or the seeking out of artists or learned men, Blake attacks: "The Things worthy to be seen are all the Trumpery he could rake together Nothing of Arts or Artists or Learned Men or of Agriculture or any Useful Thing His Business & Bosom was to be Lord Chancellor" (E627). Bacon does recommend visiting libraries, antiquities, "eminent persons in all kinds" and "whatsoever is memorable" in the places where "the better sort of persons" go (83–4). But he is quite interested in princes, courts, and places of armament. The bit of snobbery Blake must have detected probably offended him as much as the failure to mention explicitly art or artists. The annotation goes along with Blake's accusation that with respect to the arts Bacon was a crass utilitarian. Blake meets him on his own ground above by noting that "Useful Thing[s]" are absent from Bacon's list, connecting art to usefulness. Blake accuses Bacon, partly on these grounds, of being an Epicurean. Blake says of the whole book of essays, "Every Body Knows that this is Epicurus and Lucretius" (E260). But Bacon disliked the Epicureans and Stoics for not valuing involvement in public affairs, and he criticized philosophers generally not just for their clinging to old fashioned ways of thought, but also for their distance from public life. Blake's disagreement here is based on his feeling that Bacon

---

[continued] It is true, however, as White points out in comparing Newton to Blake's Urizen, that "Urizen does not follow Newton's advice of proceeding 'upon the Evidence' and stopping where 'Evidence is wanting.' ...Yet Blake realized that despite his warnings to stick to phenomena, Newton himself was mistaken if he thought his theories actually did proceed upon the evidence" ("Blake's Resolution ...," 114). Blake thought that Hume's critique of causation supported his view.

*Henry Crabb Robinson, *Diary, Reminiscences, and Correspondence*, II: 306.

drew a false line between morality and civil action that Jesus never did: "Christianity is Civil Business Only There is & can Be No Other to Man what Else Can Be Civil is Christianity or Religion or whatever is Humane" (E621). For Blake, "Thought is Act. Christs Acts were Nothing to Caesars if this is not so" (E623).

5

Annotations to Henry Boyd's *A Translation of the* Inferno *of Dante Alighieri*

It is uncertain just when Blake annotated Boyd's two preliminary essays to his translation of Dante's *Inferno*.* Blake's reading of Henry Francis Cary's translation came later, near the end of his life. Later still was his study of Italian before executing his illustrations to the *Commedia*. Boyd's "historical notes" are sandwiched between Thomas Warton's essay on Dante and a brief life of Dante by Leonardo Bruni.

Boyd's translation was preceded in 1782 by Charles Rogers's blank-verse rendition of the *Inferno*. Boyd later translated the *Purgatorio* and the *Paradiso*, published with the *Inferno* in 1802. However, the work Blake seems to have depended on most was Cary's *The Inferno of Dante* (1805–6), which was followed by all three books in three volumes in 1814. Critics have not been kind either to Rogers or to Boyd. C. P. Brand wrote harshly in 1957, "The versions of Rogers, Boyd, and Hume hardly deserve the name of translations, being neither faithful to the original nor of any worth as poetry in their own right.† He declared Cary's blank-verse translation "an immense improvement" (57). William J. De Sua agreed and elaborated: "Boyd takes it upon himself to expand, condense, alter, prune, and bowdlerize in order to conform to his idea of neoclassical stylistic demands. The translation in pentameters, is arranged into six-line stanzas rhyming aabccb, but with no particular correspondence to Dante's tercets"§ He

---

***A Translation of the Inferno of Dante Alighieri in English Verse with Historical Notes, and the Life of Dante, to which is added, a Specimen of a New Translation of the Orlando Furioso of Ariosto* by Henry Boyd, A. M., Dublin: Printed by P. Byrne, 1785. The copy that Blake annotated is in the Keynes collection of the Cambridge University Library.
†C. P. Brand, *Italy and the English Romantics: The Italianate Fashion in Early Nineteenth Century England*, Cambridge: Cambridge University Press, 1957, 57.
§William J. De Sua, *Dante into English: A Study of the Translations of the Divine Comedy in Britain and America*, Chapel Hill, NC: University of North Carolina Press, 1964, 14.

97

further noted, "On the whole, Boyd's verse is stilted and ponderous, prone to inversions, periphrasis, the use of obvious or decorative epithets ('streaming' blood, 'piercing' cries, 'furious' haste, 'deadly' fangs), and literary borrowings" (16). Like Brand, De Sua saw Cary's work as the first translation of merit (26).

Blake makes no annotations to Boyd's translation. His notes are entirely to the preliminary essays. One of his remarks may possibly refer to the quality of the translation: "It appears to Me that Men are hired to Run down Men of Genius under the Mask of Translators" (E634). However, this more likely refers to Boyd's treatment of Dante's political career.

The First Essay and Blake's Annotations

The first of the two essays is "A Comparative View of the Inferno, with some other Poems relative to the Original Principles of Human Nature, on which they are founded and to which they appeal." Boyd's aim in this essay is to defend Dante's poem by showing where it is superior to the classical works of Homer and Virgil, admitting after criticizing them the greatness of these writers:

> I have been obliged to cast a veil on the venerable Father of *Grecian* Poetry, yet, I hope it will not be thought owing to want of either Respect or Love.—It is in some sort necessary to shew Dante in his proper light, HOMER and VIRGIL have all the advantages of Nature and Art, they may easily allow to DANTE that single one of appealing to Sentiments and Principles more general, and more permanent than their Poems refer to [71–2].

Boyd, a clergyman of the Church of Ireland, proceeds to make a Christian defense of the *Inferno* by emphasizing its morality and qualities that he thinks the classical writers lacked. He recognizes at the outset that Dante had not always been appreciated, though he was "a favourite with such as were possest of true taste and dared to think for themselves" (27). He points out that both Homer's and Dante's poems are epics, but that Homer received his subject from tradition and Dante had to invent his. That subject is, "*The conversion of a sinner by a spiritual guide, displaying in a series of terrible visions the secrets of Divine Justice* [unknown to Homer], *and whose interposition had been procured by the supplication of a saint in Paradise, deeply interested in his eternal welfare*" (30). Dante offers a "nearer and more inward view of the *man*," particularly as he appears "in the eye of an offended and omniscient justice" (35).

In addition to providing a greater variety of characters, it is this inwardness or spirituality that Dante's poem has in contrast especially to the *Iliad*. Boyd allows that in the *Odyssey* an inward view of Ulysses is present, making it possible for us to share his sentiments in a way that we do not with Achilles or Agamemnon:

> We feel the injuries of Ulysses; we enter thoroughly into his resentment against men, who had treated him with the highest injustice, ingratitude and perfidy; men who had taken advantage of his long absence to invade his property and attempt to injure him in the tenderest point. We are not only interested for the Father, but we seem to feel the generous indignation of the young Telemachus. And we tremble at the dangers of the fair Penelope. We do not think any punishment too severe for such a complication of cruelty, effeminacy, and injustice, as appears in the character of the suitors of Penelope: we can go along with the resentment of Ulysses, because it is just, but our feelings must tell us that Achilles carries his resentment to a savage length, a length where we cannot follow him [38–9].

By contrast, the *Inferno* appeals to the "original principles of our nature" and the "sentiments to which they appeal" (42). The *Iliad* would be interesting to a Greek only as an expression of national glory, the *Aeneid* likewise to a Roman. Dante appeals to our natural feelings upon which Christian morality is based.

Boyd's real aim is to show that Dante's poem is superior on the ground that its Christian morality has a universal appeal rooted in nature, as does the belief in an afterlife. The rest of his essay is devoted to "how these sentiments rise in the mind" (43). The argument is based on the following Christian and supposedly natural principles:

> ...wherever the abhorrence of vice, the natural love of virtue, and justice, and the notion of a moral Governor of the Universe prevails; wherever the notion of Providence is found; wherever the persuasion of immortality of the soul and divine justice predominates; wherever the power of conscience, and the idea of right and wrong and of future rewards and punishments governs the human breast; there the poem of the *Inferno* can never fail to interest. These notions to us have all the appearances of innate principles, of ideas born with us, because they are by instruction introduced so early in the mind that we do not recollect their origin; because they are familiar they are too little considered; and by want of consideration, their effect is lessened [42–3].

In spite of his emphasis here on instruction in morality, for Boyd, it is neither instruction nor reasoning finely and disputatiously on the nature of things, as did the classical philosophers, that lead to these notion of morality. They come from the "light of nature" (51). It provides that which is found an all men: "some common and uncontroverted maxim of reason" (51).

Beyond all this and prior to the disputes of the philosophers is the belief in immortality and divine judgment. That belief arose as the "opinion of the multitude" from the "common sense that men have of the differences of good and evil" (53) and the inevitability of judgment:

> ...it is not the expectation of *Living* that makes him infer the necessity of a Judgment to come, but it is that noblest principle of his nature, the Love of Virtue, and the Abhorrence of Vice and Injustice, which makes him see the reasonableness of a *Judgment* to come, and from thence he infers that there must be a *Life* to come [55].

By contrast to the *Inferno*, the passions appealed to in the *Iliad* and the *Aeneid* are but "transitory and variable," and thus we cannot feel for the characters in them as we do for Dante's.

It is surprising that Blake makes no response until page 57 to Boyd's emphasis on nature as a source of morality. He must have considered Boyd's Christianity tainted by Deism or what he thought of as "natural" religion. Boyd writes:

> As to those who thought that the notion of a future Life arose from the descriptions and inventions of the Poets, they may just as well suppose that eating and drinking had the same original, and that man had never thought of sustaining nature, but for the fine feasts and entertainments described in such writers. The Poets indeed altered the genuine sentiments of nature, and tinged the Light of Reason by introducing the wild conceits of Fancy, and when once they had grafted such scions on the stock of nature they throve so fast, and grew so rank, that the natural branches were deprived of their nourishment; by the luxuriance of this wild Olive. But still the root was natural, though the fruit was wild. All that *nature teaches* is, that there is a future life, distinguished into different states of happiness and misery [56–7].

Blake writes, "False" and follows with "Nature Teaches nothing of Spiritual Life but only of Natural Life" (E634). He must think that Boyd has things reversed. For Blake, because nature teaches nothing of spiritual value, notions of an afterlife must have been an inspired creation of the human spirit that he called the "poetic genius" (E1–2), represented in *The Marriage of Heaven and Hell* as the "ancient poets," the original namers of things (E38). (This visionary creativity became corrupted by system and priesthood.) For Blake, nature itself is a figment of human reason; it is not prior to thought. Nor is there a nature prior to the allegedly corrupting "wild conceits of Fancy" produced by poets.

Blake's deepest philosophical disagreement with Boyd is over what is meant by "nature," but he expends more annotations on his disagreement over poetry and its relation to morality. Boyd's tendency to see in a poem only its moral implications irritates Blake from the beginning and leads to a certain amount of hyperbole. He edits Boyd's words and reverses the meaning (deletions by Blake follow in brackets): "[But] the most daring flights of fancy, the most accurate delineations of character, and the most artful conduct of fable, are [not, even] when combined together, sufficient of themselves to make a poem interesting" (35, E633). The poem, for Boyd, must appeal to our immediate feelings dictated by our innate Christian sense of right and wrong. Thus, though we can sympathize with Ulysses because in his long absence he has been treated unjustly by the suitors of Penelope, the "discord of Achilles and Agamemnon" leaves us cold. We can sympathize with neither. Tasso's crusaders do not interest us despite "the exploded machinery of Demons and Magicians." There must be something to "interest the heart" (36): Likewise, "we cannot sympathise with Achilles for the loss of his Mistress, when we feel that he gained her by the massacre of her family:—and when, in the very middle of his complaint, he owns that he brought destruction upon the Trojans without any manner of provocation" (36). Blake refuses to accept Boyd's identification of moral judgment with sympathy: "nobody considers these things when they read Homer or Shakespear or Dante" (E633). Boyd goes on to observe of Achilles and others, "When a man, where no interest is concerned, no provocation given, lays a whole nation in blood merely for his *glory*; we to whom his glory is indifferent, cannot enter into his resentment" (37). The annotation which follows marks Blake's fundamental disagreement with Boyd about poetry: "false All poetry gives the lie to this" (E633). He proceeds to claim that "If Homers merit was only in these Historical combinations & Moral sentiments he would be no better than [Richardson's] Clarissa" (E633). It is not that Blake fails to recognize that poetry deals with moral questions. It is that he thinks Boyd lets issues of right and wrong override all other consideration, and as a result Boyd misses the subtlety with which Homer treats them. We might in passing note that Boyd seems to have allowed that there might be moral reasons for laying "a whole nation in blood." Boyd writes "*Iliacos extra muros peccatur, et intra*" [The Trojans are at fault both outside and within the wall] [The *Iliad*] is a contest between barbarians, equally guilty of injustice, rapine, and bloodshed; and we are not sorry to see the vengeance of Heaven equally inflicted on both parties" (39–40). Blake thinks that Boyd does not understand Homer's irony here and considers it a fault that in the *Iliad* there is no right to prevail over wrong. Blake observes only, "Homer meant this" (E633).

But Blake goes beyond this criticism to observe that a simple opposition of right and wrong is inane. Boyd seems to think that Virgil made a mistake in his treatment of Aeneas: "Aeneas indeed is a more amiable personage than Achilles; he seems meant for a perfect character." But then Boyd notices that

Aeneas is not perfect after all, suggesting that Virgil has failed in this matter":

> But compare his conduct with respect to Dido with the self-denial of Dryden's Cleomenes, or with the conduct of Titus in the Berenice of Racine, we will then see what is meant by making the character interesting. Aeneas, by the connivance of the Gods, leads the hospitable queen of Carthage into guilt and, by the command of the Gods, *piously* leaves her to ruin and despair [40].

Blake's response to this is not to observe that Aeneas turns out to be imperfect but that he is presumed to be perfect and that is the problem. There is something suspicious about perfection, as there is about goodness: "Every body naturally hates a perfect character because they are all greater Villains than the imperfect as Eneas is here shewn a worse man than Achilles leaving Dido" (E633). Blake's attitude goes back again to *The Marriage of Heaven and Hell* and his rejection there of the distinction between good and evil as selfishly imposed by powerful political and religious interests. The annotation is excessive, but it is effective because it recalls for us the self-congratulation of some people and the sycophancy of others.

Blake does not leave the matter there, nor does Boyd, who proceeds to speak generally about morality:

> Antecedent to and independent of all laws, a man may learn to argue on the nature of moral obligation, and the duty of universal benevolence, from Cumberland, Wollaston, Shaftesbury, Hutcheson; he may learn from them the balance of the passions, and the difference between those of the social and unsocial kind;—but, would he *feel* what vice is in itself; would he learn the genuine sentiments of nature upon it; would he see the best natural comment upon the Decalogue; let him enter into the passions of *Lear*, when he feels the ingratitude of his children; of *Hamlet*, when he learns the story of his father's murder; of *Othello*, when he shudders at *Iago's* tale, of *Charmont*, when he burns with honourable indignation at a sister's wrongs; let him feel what *Hermione* or *Edgar* felt, when sinking under the weight of a false accusation; let him reflect on the sentiments of those, who suffered by the ambition of *Richard*, the avarice of *Shyloc*, or the cruelty and lust of *Bajazet*; and he will know the difference of right and wrong much more clearly than from all the moralists that ever wrote [45–6].

His argument continues to be that the moral sense is both natural (innate) and based on Scripture. In reading the literary texts he mentions, one's moral sense is aroused by sympathetic identification with those wronged. Blake may well have agreed with this, but he is concerned with something else, the question of the morality of poetry itself. For him, the poet is identified with intellectual and imaginative freedom, the moral philosopher with passive obedience to power. Blake answers Boyd's catalogue of deeply wronged characters with his own of those who were wicked (Othello makes both lists), and he suggests that something else causes our interest, perhaps the wickedness itself: "the grandest Poetry is Immoral the Grandest characters Wicked. Very Satan, Capanius Othello a murderer. Prometheus. Jupiter. Jehovah." Blake seeks to humanize Jesus: "Jesus a wine bibber," a statement deliberately designed to be offensive (E634). It is not merely the characters in the poem that are immoral; it is poetry itself that commits offense: "Cunning and Morality are not Poetry but Philosophy the Poet is Independent & Wicked the Philosopher is Dependent & Good" (E634). With his use of "wicked" here, Blake offers a bold irony.

There follows an interesting statement that reveals his recourse to a higher ethic than that of imposed morality: "Poetry is to excuse Vice & shew its reason & necessary purgation" (E634). The statement seems to recall Aristotle's notion of the catharsis of emotions, usually interpreted to refer to the emotions of the play's audience. Blake excuses the vice because it has been present in order to move the plot toward that cleansing which the audience or reader witnesses.

Indeed, Blake seems to reject not only Boyd's moralistic view, but also his sense of natural justice and injustice. Boyd writes,

> The industrious knave cultivates the soil; the indolent good man leaves it uncultivated. Who ought to reap the harvest? Who ought to starve? Who live in plenty? The natural course of things decides in favour of the villain; the natural sentiments of men in favour of the man of virtue [49].

Blake's comment is, "False" (E634). As elsewhere, Blake's view of politics and class comes out here. Boyd refers to a farmer who is, apparently by virtue of his position, a knave (in the older sense of that word: someone of humble birth or at least position in life), a villain, an uncouth person. (It is interesting to see how these terms, over time, have taken on moralistic meanings, though they arose out of social ones to which Blake was sensitive.) Blake seems to reject not only the way these men are characterized but also the distinction itself, which identifies the knave with industry and goodness with indolence.

The Second Essay and Blake's Annotations

Boyd's second essay is titled, "HISTORICAL ESSAY OF THE STATE OF AFFAIRS IN THE THIRTEENTH AND FOURTEENTH CENTURIES: *With Respect to the* HISTORY OF FLORENCE, *With a* VIEW *of their* INFLUENCE *on the succeeding* AGES." Boyd's aim here is to make it easier for his reader to recognize the many historical characters and events alluded to in the *Inferno*. His historical account takes up almost half of the essay. It is concise and clear about a complex period of turmoil.* Boyd begins with an account of the papal-imperial feud and the dispute between the houses of Anjou and Swabia. He proceeds to the strife between the Guelphs, who sided with the Pope, and the Ghibellines, who took the secular side and supported the emperor. He discusses the opposition in Florence of populace to nobility that resulted in the creation of the priors (or praetors), of which Dante was one when a dispute over a thrown snowball became the pretext for civil strife between the so-called Whites and Blacks. Dante was caught in the middle of this, which led to his long exile from Florence, lasting for the rest of his life. Boyd's history is concluded with a very brief discussion of science and art in the period. There then follows an account of religion, with much editorial comment and judgment. It is this and the relation of religion to politics that occupies Blake in most of his annotations.

First, however, Blake responds at some length to Boyd's statement that as Prior of Florence "Dante gave the advice, <u>ruinous to himself</u>, and <u>pernicious to his native country</u>, of calling in the heads of the two factions to Florence" (118). The first part of Blake's annotation is curious: "Dante was a Fool or his Translator was Not That is Dante was Hired or Tr was Not" (E634). Blake used "hired" and "hireling" elsewhere in a pejorative sense. A "hireling" is for him one who follows not only the orders of power but also the perceived wishes. The statement is difficult to interpret. I read it with some misgivings to mean: You can say that Dante was a fool and a hireling to have acted as he did *and* Boyd was not a fool and not a hireling but instead accurate in his description of Dante's behavior and its results. The statement, read this way, is not then judgmental but rather interpretive of what Boyd has written. It is difficult to make sense of the reading that "or" usually leads us to make, since the two statements do not seem to be relatable by "or" in its sense that only one of them can be true. I wonder whether Blake miswrote here and meant to say that you had to decide who was the fool and hireling, Dante or Boyd.

On the other hand, Blake goes on to declare that both were in different ways hirelings:

> It appears to Me that Men are hired to Run down Men of Genius under the Mask of Translators, but Dante gives too much [to?] Caesar he is not a Republican

---

*Useful clarifying studies are Ferdinand Schevill, *A History of Florence, from the founding of the city through the Renaissance*, New York: F. Ungar Publishing Co., 1961, and Francisco Guiccardi, *The History of Florence*, tr. Mario Domandi, New York: Harper and Row, 1970.

> Dante was an Emperors a Caesars Man Luther also left the Priest & joind the Soldier [E634]

Here Blake acknowledges Dante's genius and yet does not like his political actions. Boyd does not come off as well.

The rest of Boyd's essay turns to discussion of religion, as did the first one, and in much the same way. Blake has nothing good to say about it. Boyd's argument concludes as follows:

> Thus I have endeavoured to shew, that religion, under its most unfavourable aspect, and attended with the most untoward circumstances, was yet eminently beneficial to the best interests of society; that, when polluted, it threw off the contamination; when perverted, it recovered its rectitude; and when traduced, it triumphed over calumny [148].

Blake is contemptuous in his five remaining annotations. Boyd, he thinks, is foolish, hypocritical, and irrational in his defense of the behavior of those he called in his poem *Milton* the "religious"; it is a word he came to use pejoratively to describe bigotry. Boyd tries to excuse religious excess as understandable: "The fervours of religion have often actuated the passions to deeds of the wildest fanaticism.—The *booted Apostles* of Germany, and the *Crusards* of Florence, carried their zeal to a very guilty degree." Blake would no doubt agree that this was so, but Boyd proceeds defensively:

> But that passion for any thing laudable will hardly carry men to a *proper* pitch, unless it be so strong as sometimes to push them beyond the golden mean.— The enthusiasm of *English* valour has often pushed our countrymen to acts of the wildest desperation, but with *less*, perhaps, Britons had not been heroes [129–30].

Blake, no doubt noticing the recourse to patriotic chauvinism, remarks, "How very Foolish all this Is" (E634). I think he objects principally to the kind of defense Boyd mounts, which seems a desperate effort to excuse acts of violence as inevitable. A little later, Boyd writes, "The wildest extravagancies of mistaken zeal tend to work its own cure," and he adds that religious disputes inflame the passions, but "nothing so much opens the mind and enlarges the understanding," and nothing is more important (130).

Boyd then describes acts in Florence that bred intolerance and attempts to show in what degree intolerance is acceptable. He seems to treat religion and politics here as inseparable, which they certainly were in Florence:

> Such were the effects of intolerance even in the extreme. In a more moderate degree, every well-regulated government, both ancient and modern, were <u>so far</u> intolerant as not to admit the pollutions of every superstition and <u>every pernicious opinion</u>. It was from a regard to the morals of the people, that the

> Roman Magistrates expelled the Priest of Bacchus, in the first and most virtuous ages of the republic. It was on this principle that the <u>Persians</u> destroyed the <u>temples of Greece wherever they came</u> [131].

Blake accuses Boyd of hypocrisy here: "If Well regulated Governments act so who can tell so well as the hireling writer whose praise is contrary to what he Knows to be true Persians destroy the Temples & are praised for it" (E635). For a moment, at least, he seems to allow that Boyd really knows better, but the example of the Persians destroying the Greek temples is preposterous to him and leads to the implication once again that Boyd is a hireling who will go to any length to protect regulation by the powerful. Blake is impelled to ask rhetorically, "What is Liberty without Universal Toleration" (E635), when Boyd seems to identify acceptable religious and political intolerance with piety and belief in immortality. Calling Polybius in support, Boyd laments their decline in Roman life and defends opposition to Papal power in Florence on the ground that it was supported by "foreign influence." For Blake, this was a case of both sides expressing intolerance. Boyd writes,

> The dread of popery in the last age was not an unmeaning antipathy to certain *speculative* opinions, but a well-grounded fear of the influence of such opinions on society. It was a design well becoming any government, to abridge the power of a body of men confessedly under foreign influence [133].

Apparently, for Boyd, speculative opinions are tolerable when they have no social consequences. But when they do, government is right to suppress them if they present a challenge to authority.

Boyd continues to defend one form of oppression against another:

> The Athenians and Romans kept a watchful eye, not only over the grosser superstitions, but over impiety; because they knew, that impiety and infidelity dissolved the sanctions of morality, and brought on both public and private corruption. *Polybius* plainly attributes the fall of freedom in Greece to the prevalence of atheism.* In Rome, Epicurean philosophy and political corruption went hand in hand. It was not till the republic was verging to its fall, that Caesar dared in open senate to laugh at the *speculative* opinion of a future state. These were the times of universal toleration, when every pollution, from every clime, flowed to Rome, whence they had carefully been kept out before [133–4].

Blake does not enter into a discussion of piety or the belief in immortality. His interest is in political liberty, and for him that requires universal toleration. He views religious controversies as struggles over the effort to impose competing political power. Boyd's interest is in the maintenance of

---

*Boyd describes atheism in a footnote: It "attributes the formation of the world to chance, and denies a providence" (133).

morality. He castigates the critics of revealed religion, those who attack it either for what they allege is its origin or for its consequences. Moreover, revealed religion is rational.

> ...when they meet with the sober censure of reason, they declaim against it as the clamour of ecclesiastical tyranny; and they will not allow that religion can be favorable to the light of knowledge or the cause of liberty, when it censures them for the propagation of their opinions; but there are certain *bounds*, even to *liberty*, beyond this it takes the name of licentiousness. The liberty of loosening the bands of society, and deriding the solemn functions of virtue, is the liberty of a lunatick, and it was to prevent such wanton mischief, that the true principles of freedom were first laid down [147–8].

As for the "bounds" to liberty, Blake responds, "If it is thus the extreme of black is white & of sweet sower & of good Evil & Nothing Something" (E635). That is, if one treats liberty in this way, one can turn it into its opposite even as it is still called liberty.

In many ways, Boyd's defense of religion returns us to the arguments of the latter part of the first essay, but he does not refer in this second essay to the moral sense as natural. However, it is so implied. His view is that great nations have declined and fallen for "loss" of a general standard of morality and the pernicious influence of disputatious philosophers (135–6). Blake challenges what lies behind this history by going to the ground of Boyd's theory of natural morality; it does not seem to him likely ever to have existed in the light of what he sees around him. It requires belief in a so-called state of nature: "Yet simple country Hinds are Moral Enthusiasts Indignant against Knavery without a Moral criterion other than Native Honesty untaught while other country Hinds are as indignant against honesty and [are?] Enthusiasts for Cunning & Artifice" (E635). "Enthusiasts" is an interesting word here, for it implies something deeper than reason. Boyd argued that the moral sense was natural, innate, Christian, and grounded in reason. For Blake, simple honesty is something different from the usual socially created oppositions of good and evil, morality and immorality, reason and irrationality, and so on. These oppositions are what he called negations, tools of suppression.

On a blank page (74) between the two essays, Blake harshly summarizes his view of Boyd's essays:

> Every Sentiment & Opinion as well as Every Principle in Dante is in these Preliminary Essays Controverted & proved Foolish by his Translator If I have any Judgment in Such Things as Sentiments Opinions & Principles [E634]

This statement is, of course, ironic. It is also hyperbolic. It is based on Blake's belief that Dante put poetry before all that Boyd emphasizes. Blake had his serious differences with Dante, as his later illustrations show. Nevertheless, he thought that Dante was a great poet, and poetry is "of the Devils party" (E35), as was Milton without knowing it. Boyd's Dante is a moralist, no more. That morality is based on a concept of nature and reason, grafted on to his view of Christianity, that he thinks generates sympathetic feelings. Blake refuses to see a relation of reason to sympathy and nature as the basis for anything.

6

Annotations to Sir Joshua Reynolds's *Discourses on Art*

Blake's annotations to the first eight *Discourses* of Reynolds and to Edmond Malone's essay prefatory to Reynolds's *Works*, which immediately precedes the eight *Discourses* in Volume 1, range from angry accusations and denunciations to occasional agreement.* These are interspersed with important statements reflecting not only Blake's taste but also his philosophical presuppositions. On the back of the title page to Volume I, in a note probably written after he had made most of his marginal comments, Blake states that he has expressed, as he says, "Indignation & Resentment," indeed "Nothing but" (E636). In addition, he refers to the readers of these annotations, revealing that he expects his words to be read and remembered and to exert some influence in the world of thought about art.

Lawrence Lipking argues well that Blake takes over Reynolds's book.† Certainly, Blake inserts his remarks at critical moments with the confidence that they will be read by others. He even provides his own brief prefaces to some of the discourses. Indeed, not a few of those who have written on the

---

The Works of Sir Joshua Reynolds, Knight; Late President of the Royal Academy: Containing His Discourses, Idlers, A Journey To Flanders And Holland, And His Commentary On Du Fresnoy's Art Of Painting; printed from his revised copies (with his latest corrections and additions,) In Three Volumes to which is prefixed An Account Of The Life And Writings Of The Author, By Edmond Malone, Esq. One of His Executors, the second edition corrected, Volume The First. London: Printed for T. Cadell, Jun. and W. Davies, in the Strand, 1798. The copy that Blake annotated is in the British Library. Almost everyone who has written on Blake has had occasion at least to mention Blake's notes on the *Discourses*. The fullest and best work on Blake's theory of art is Morris Eaves, *Blake's Theory of Art*. Princeton, NJ: Princeton University Press, 1982.

†Lawrence Lipking, *The Ordering of the Arts in Eighteenth-Century England*, Princeton, NJ: Princeton University Press, 1970, 164–5. He preceded H. J. Jackson in making this point in her *Romantic Readers: The Evidence of Marginalia*, New Haven and London: Yale University Press, 2005, 169.

Discourses have discussed or mentioned Blake's responses. Lipking is right that Blake managed to change the book into a dialogue with Reynolds, and Blake has the first word on the title page facing Reynolds's portrait, saying as if pointing to it, "This Man was Hired to Depress Art This is the opinion of Will Blake my Proofs of this Opinion are given in the following Notes" (back of title page, E635). It is clear that Reynolds is seen as one of "Satans Hirelings" (blank page facing dedication, E637), mentioned in his comment on the book's dedication to King George III. Blake thought that Reynolds had hirelings of his own by virtue of his important position as president of the Royal Academy.*

Blake is well aware of what he is doing. This does not prevent him from occasional bitter accusations based on little but his own self-acknowledged resentment. An example is a comment on Reynolds's account of his responses to Raphael, a painter who is on the whole much revered in the *Discourses*. Reynolds confesses that, like that of others of whom he knew, his first response to Raphael was one of disappointment. At the same time, however, he recognizes that the defect was in himself:

> I did not for a moment conceive or suppose that the name of Raffaelle, and those admirable paintings in particular, owed their reputation to the ignorance and prejudice of mankind; on the contrary, my not relishing them as I was conscious I ought to have done, was one of the most humiliating circumstances that ever happened to me. I found myself in the midst of works executed upon principles with which I was unacquainted: I felt my ignorance and stood abashed [quoted by Malone, xv].

Blake responds to this sharply: "A Liar he was never Abashed in his Life & never felt his Ignorance" (E638). There is no evidence for this other, perhaps, than Blake's awareness of Reynolds's well-known even temper and diplomatic demeanor. Reynolds is said to have admitted his hatred for only one person, the painter James Barry, and they were reconciled before Reynolds's death.

Blake hates what he regards as control, self-satisfaction, complacency, and the hypocrisy of the social climber. To a great extent this was, to Blake, a matter of class difference and class arrogance. But Reynolds was not of the privileged upper classes, though as a portrait painter he came to hobnob with many who were. He was the son of a scholarly clergyman who made his living as a school-teacher in Plympton, Devonshire. In the introduction to his

---

*On Blake's relation to Reynolds and to the Royal Academy, see Aileen Ward's excellent article in *The Huntington Library Quarterly* 52 (1989): 75–95. She reminds us that Blake agreed with Reynolds on the value of copying the old masters and of history painting. In a letter to Thomas Butts (November 22, 1802) Blake expresses agreement with Reynolds on the opposition of picturesque style to "grandeur" (E718–9).

edition of the *Discourses*, Pat Rogers remarks, "It is so easy to imagine that he was always Sir Joshua Reynolds, PRA, and could never have been anything less," but his position and the esteem in which he was held were earned by persistence, hard work, and possession of an agreeable personality.* He was the third of eleven children. At age seventeen he was made a pupil of the painter Thomas Hudson, his somewhat unworldly father having recognized that the expected profession of apothecary was not suited to him. The father died in 1746 when Reynolds was twenty-three. He had been painting in Devonshire and London on his own, left, as Edmond Malone wrote, "to raise, as he could, the fabrick of his own fortune" (xi). He seemed to have a capacity to meet and become friendly with helpful people, some of whom became patrons. This was the case with Lord Edgcumbe and Captain Augustus Keppel, later Commodore and Viscount, whom he accompanied on a voyage in the Mediterranean. That voyage enabled him to visit Italy, where he stayed through 1752.

Reynolds seems to have gotten to know and to have painted portraits of everyone of social importance in England. His remarkable rise, patronage by the king, position of power in the world of art, and acquaintance with members of the so-called "Club" that he himself formed must have contributed to Blake's resentment. Johnson, Boswell, Burke, Goldsmith, Percy, Garrick, Warton, Gibbon, and Sheridan were among the members. Malone was elected member in 1782.

Front Matter

On the back of the title page of Volume One of Reynolds's *Works*, Blake complains of oppression by "Sr Joshua & his Gang of Cunning Hired Knaves" (E636). While Reynolds was "rolling in Riches Barry was Poor & Unemployed except by his own Energy Mortimer was calld a Madman & only Portrait Painting applauded & rewarded by the Rich & Great" (E636). Blake's friend Fuseli "Indignant almost hid himself—I am hid" (E636).

The remaining notes on the back of the title page and on the contents pages emphasize the cultural and political importance of art, which, Blake declares, opposes tyranny and is often as a result suppressed. Blake asks why good government should try to "Depress What is its Chief & only Support" (E636).

---

*Sir Joshua Reynolds, *Discourses*, edited with an introduction and notes by Pat Rogers, London: Penguin Books, 1992, 24. On Reynolds's writings see Frederick W. Hilles, *The Literary Career of Sir Joshua Reynolds*, Cambridge at the University Press, 1936. On Reynolds as a painter see *Reynolds*, the catalogue of the great Reynolds exhibition of 1986 at the Royal Academy, London, edited by Nicholas Penny, published by the Academy in association with Weidenfeld and Nicolson.

Blake took the trouble to copy in the original French a passage from Voltaire in which a churchman later elevated to Cardinal praised Pope Leon X for encouraging science, but warned him that it was dangerous to render men too learned. Blake later remarks that fortunately the Pope did not take that advice (E642). He then asks why Englishmen are "of this foolish Cardinals opinion?" (contents pages [not numbered], E636). The passage and remark extend a vein of sarcasm begun on the title page with a quatrain expressing Blake's view of the advice given by the Popes who came after Raphael:

> Degrade first the Arts if you'd Mankind degrade,
> Hire Idiots to Paint with cold light & hot shade:
> Give high Price for the worst, leave the best in disgrace,
> And with Labours of Ignorance fill every place [E635].

Blake is particularly bitter at the treatment of Barry and even of Fuseli. Both were certainly eccentric, Barry difficult and probably paranoid; but without question they were important painters. Unlike Reynolds, they did few portraits, Barry's surviving ones being mainly of himself.

Dedication to the King

Blake was probably unaware that Samuel Johnson wrote for Reynolds, who signed it, the book's dedication to King George III; but had he known, it would not have prevented him from the comments he made. Blake wrote of Johnson only once. In the unfinished manuscript called by Blake's editors *An Island in the Moon,* Johnson is the object of an obscene lyric by the Epicurean philosopher Suction, who is joined by Quid the Cynic:

> Lo the Bat with Leathern wing
> Winking & blinking
> Winking & blinking
> Winking & blinking
> Like Doctor Johnson
> Quid — O ho Said Dr. Johnson
> To Scipio Africanus
> If you don't own me a Philosopher
> Ill kick your Roman Anus
> Suction — A ha To Dr Johnson
> Said Scipio Africanus
> Lift up my Roman Petticoatt
> And kiss my Roman Anus [E458]

Suction begins to say something uncomplimentary about Sir Joshua, but he is interrupted by Quid (E456). Suction is not necessarily a mouthpiece for Blake; almost everything and everyone mentioned is satirized in this work, including Voltaire, Locke, and Newton, among Blake's favorite *bêtes noires*. Johnson, no doubt, belonged to this group, as did Johnson's good friend Reynolds.

Johnson begins the dedication with this remark: "The regular progress of cultivated life is from necessaries to accommodations, from accommodations to ornaments" (i). He proceeds to observe that it has been left to the king to found the Royal Academy for the "arts of elegance." Blake reverses Johnson's history: Cultivated life existed first. It was not that Satan first took away ornament, then necessaries, and finally accommodation. "Uncultivated Life. comes afterwards from Satans Hirelings" (E637), among whom he seems to include Reynolds and his followers, "Sir Joshua and his Gang of Cunning Hired Knaves" (back of title page), with Reynolds in the Satanic role. "Ornament" Blake seems here to use not in the sense of embellishment or bauble but rather in the more general sense, as the *Oxford English Dictionary* says, of "a quality or circumstance that confers beauty, grace, or honour." Blake's remark is consistent with his notion that art does not improve. Johnson implies that it does, though he may mean only that conditions for artists have improved.

Blake is also irritated by what he must have thought groveling before the king. He attacks Johnson's reference to "royal liberality" (ii, E637) and implies that in the present state of uncultivated life there is no fair price offered for the work of artists, nor is there a "General Demand for Art." Just how the king is to bring about a change is not clear, nor is it clear whether Blake thought an academy could contribute to these ends, though in a note to *Discourse One* (misnumbered iv, end of foreword, E642) he wrote, "The Rich men of England form themselves into a Society. to Sell & Not to Buy Pictures." For him, the nation does not properly reward its artists, though art is "the First in Intellectuals" (ii, E637), meaning the first in thought or in possession of intellectual faculties. This is a view that he shared with Reynolds to the extent that both believed the activity of the artist an intellectual one. He has just claimed supreme importance for art in any nation, even to the extent of identifying it along with science as "The Foundation of Empire" (contents pages, E636), though the notion of empire is one that Blake elsewhere is vehemently opposed to. His remark above this is more characteristic: "The Arts & Sciences are the Destruction of Tyrannies or Bad Governments."

Malone's "Some Account of the Life and Writings of Sir Joshua Reynolds"

Blake not only annotated Reynolds; he also commented on Edmond Malone's long introduction to Reynolds's *Works* in Volume One, which contained the eight discourses Blake is known to have annotated. Some of Blake's comments on the introduction are on what Reynolds wrote, for Malone quoted from Reynolds at length.

Malone, born in Dublin, son of an Irish MP, graduate of Trinity College, Dublin, and one of Reynolds's executors, was well known in his time and later for his edition of Shakespeare, his work on determining the order in which Shakespeare's plays were written, and his attack on the antiquity of Chatterton's Rowley poems.* He also wrote lives of Shakespeare and Dryden. The posthumous *Works* of Reynolds came out first in 1797, the second edition with the introduction in 1798. Malone was a friend of Reynolds and associated with him in the "Club."

At the top of the title page, clearly in the position of emphasis where he wanted it, Blake offers an idea he expresses elsewhere: "Invention depends Altogether upon Execution or Organization. as that is right or wrong so is the Invention perfect or imperfect" (E637). This statement is important in two respects. First, it implies a distinction between what is innate and what is learned. In his discussion of his first response to Raphael's work, quoted at length by Malone (xiv–xvi), Reynolds remarks that he was not initially impressed, but learned to appreciate Raphael's value, and claims that "a relish for the higher excellencies of art is an acquired taste" (xvii). Blake comments that, as for himself, Raphael was never, even in childhood, "hidden" from him, and he complains, "All this Concession is to prove that Genius is Acquired" (E638). Blake carries all of this over to the artist's activity, not limiting the idea to a viewer's capacity for appreciation, but declaring artistic genius innate as well.

Second, if we identify Blake's "invention" with Benedetto Croce's "intuition," we find him anticipating Croce's insistence on the identity of intuition and expression, that is, the idea that there is no intuition without expression of it, the artist finding the complete intuion in the act of expression. Croce thought of expression as an internal formation and added the notion of externalization to it.† Blake goes further. In his so-called *Public*

---

*On Malone, see Peter Martin, *Edmond Malone, Shakespearean Scholar: A Literary Biography*, Cambridge: Cambridge University Press, 1995.

†Benedetto Croce, *Aesthetic, as a Science of Expression and General Linguistic* (1909), New York: The Noonday Press, 1963, esp. 1–12.

Address (c. 1809–10), Blake emphasizes what elsewhere he calls the language of art as properly an identity of idea and finished design:

> I have heard many People say Give me the Ideas. It is no matter what Words you put them into & others say Give me the Design it is no matter for the Execution. These People know Enough of Artifice but Nothing Of Art. Ideas cannot be Given but in their minutely Appropriate Words nor Can a Design be made without its minutely Appropriate Execution [E576].

The power of invention is for Blake innate, as was his appreciation of Raphael, while Reynolds's remark about his response to Raphael shows that Reynolds did not have the power that Blake identifies with imagination.

If, indeed, taste and artistic ability are acquired, the contradictions Blake claims to detect in Reynolds, he says, are inevitable:

> The Contradictions in Reynolds's Discourses are Strong Presumptions that they are the Work of Several Hands But this is no Proof that Reynolds did not Write them. The Man Either Painter or Philosopher who Learns or Acquires all he Knows from Others. Must be full of Contradictions [xlv, note 28; E639]

Blake seems to allude here to the rumors that the *Discourses* were actually written by Johnson or Burke, but the main point is Reynolds's inconsistencies. In a long footnote stretching over four pages, Malone convincingly refutes these rumors, which he describes as "ridiculous and absurd" (xlv). From time to time in his annotations, Blake accuses Reynolds of contradictions, as we shall see.

A further statement of particular importance involves Blake's criticism of generalization from sense data in the work of Locke and his follower Burke. In a footnote, Malone notes that Burke attributes Reynolds's "disposition to generalize" (xcvii) to the influence of Zacharia Mudge of Exeter, a friend of Reynolds's father. Burke wrote, and Reynolds quotes, the following: "[Mudge] was a great generalizer, and was fond of reducing every thing to one system, more perhaps than the variety of principles which operate in the human mind and in every human work, will probably endure" (note 54, xcvii). This tendency violates Blake's notion that the artist's knowledge is based on intensity of imagination and vision (for Blake synonymous) of what one sees with the mind through the eyes: "To Generalize is to be an Idiot. To particularize is the Alone Distinction of Merit — General Knowledges are those that Idiots possess" (note 54, xcviii, E641). Blake's impulse here is to extend the critique of generalization in a work of art to a critique of generalization in all thought.

Most of Malone's "Account" is factual, and Blake's comments on it are usually on matters having to do with Reynolds's career and his views. However, there is one important instance where Malone speaks for himself in support of Burke's views in *Reflections on the Revolution in France* (1790) and goes on to praise Reynolds for "the rectitude of his judgment concerning those pernicious doctrines, that were made the basis of that Revolution which took place in France not long before his death" (cii). Reynolds had read Burke's manuscript and, according to Malone, was "lavish in his encomiums upon it" (cii). Indeed, Malone reports that Reynolds "frequently avowed his contempt of those 'Adamwits,' who set at nought the accumulated wisdom of ages, and on all occasions are desirous of beginning the world anew" (ciii). Not long after this, Malone is compelled to wander away from his main subject, fulminating in a lengthy sentence:

> I still cherish a hope that the cloud which hangs over us will be dispersed, and that we have *stamina* sufficiently strong to resist the pestilential contagion suspended in our atmosphere: and my confidence is founded on the good sense of my countrymen; of whom far the greater part, justly valuing the blessings which they enjoy, will not lightly hazard their loss; and rather than suffer the smallest part of their inestimable Constitution to be changed, or any one of those detestable principles to take root in this soil, which our domestick and foreign enemies with such mischievous industry have endeavoured to propagate, will, I trust, risk every thing that is most dear to man [cv].

At this point, Blake is aroused to verse utterance:

> When France got free Europe 'twixt Fools & Knaves
> Were Savage first to France, & after; Slaves [ciii, E641]

And in response to a footnote describing England's "unparalleled state of wealth and prosperity" Blake remarks, "This Whole Book was Written to Serve Political Purposes," having written and erased "First to Serve Nobility & Fashionable Taste & Sr Joshua" (note 59, civ, E641). Blake had already complained bitterly (blank page facing title page of *Works*) about the treatment of Barry. Again here (cxx, E641) Barry comes up. Burke apparently denigrated a picture by Barry for which he had paid twenty guineas.

Blake's resentments were based in part not only on his sense of rejection because of his class, but also, to some extent, on his profession of engraver. In Blake's view, Reynolds climbed socially and professionally by behaving hypocritically, that is, falsely, with others, or at the very least in a way that Blake, with stubborn honesty, could not. He says nothing about Reynolds's paintings.

Discourse One

Blake wrote his most violent attack on Reynolds on the back of the title page to the *Discourses* proper (after Malone's "Account"). Here Reynolds's

"Softness & [appearance of] Candour" are those of a smiling hypocrite. The *Discourses* are an insult to "True Art & True Artists" (E642). Blake then makes an interesting remark: "Whether Reynolds. knew what he was doing. is nothing to me; the Mischief is just the same, whether a Man does it Ignorantly or Knowingly" (E 642). After his attack on Reynolds's character, Blake concerns himself with the effect of the *Discourses* on artists. Certainly he thought the *Discourses* would have a bad influence, but his remarks are an attack on the man, no matter what he says here. We are not to forget that Reynolds is one of "Satan's hirelings," even a stand-in for Satan in the world of art.

Two major points that Blake makes in *Discourse One* have to do with his criticism of the notion that genius may be taught and that "minute discrimination" should be avoided. He also considers the question of imitation. Blake's remarks about genius continue the argument he makes in his annotations to Malone's quotation from Reynolds. Involved here is Blake's critique of memory as against inspiration. At the very outset of the *Discourse*, Blake notes that the Ancient Greeks were responsible for calling the Muses the "Daughters of Memory" (E642), and they were wrong to have done so. Blake seems to identify memory in all his writings with Lockean and Hartleyan building blocks, abstraction from direct visionary experience, which is not necessarily of external objects and their combinations, but is always a creative act of imagination. This view is connected with Blake's emphasis on outline, which discriminates and clarifies objects of vision. Blake thinks Reynolds's emphasis on Lockean memory implies collecting a store of sense impressions combined and abstracted from what we usually call "nature," not the creative act of innate genius. Blake finds that this hidden assumption in Reynolds's emphasis on deliberate effort suggests he believes genius can be acquired by slow, methodical study. Blake clearly thinks that Reynolds is really advancing a position that surreptitiously defends his own lack of genius. Blake even acknowledges and implicitly defends dissipation and wildness among artists when Reynolds emphasizes the necessity of hard work and claims that the great painters did not spend any part of their time in dissipation. Whether Reynolds means profligacy or simply idleness is not clear, but Blake chooses to assume the former and at the same time to distinguish the two. He remarks, taking a crack at Reynolds: "The Lives of Painters say that Rafael died of Dissipation Idleness is one Thing & Dissipation Another He who has Nothing to Dissipate Cannot Dissipate the Weak man may be Virtuous Enough but will Never be an Artist Painters are noted for being Dissipated & Wild" (15, E643–44).

Blake's remarks on memory, learning, and genius include an insistence that copying the work of other artists is a necessary part of the painter's education and that imitation of other artists is a form of criticism (E643). The remark is elicited by Reynolds's statement, "...models, which have passed through the approbation of ages, should be considered by them as perfect and infallible guides; as subjects for their imitation, not their criticism" (11). It is obvious that Reynolds here means negative criticism only, while Blake insists on the larger sense. Although Reynolds sometimes speaks of imitation as the copying of nature, which Blake rejects on anti–Lockean grounds, for the most part he means attention to and emulation of the tradition of art in the "grand style."

The second major point in the annotations to *Discourse One* has to do with Blake's defense of what both he and Reynolds call "minute discrimination," which Blake further discusses in *Discourse Three*. Reynolds explicitly warns students against "minute accidental [in Aristotle's sense of a property that a thing can but need not have] discriminations of particular and individual objects" (9). Blake answers, "Minute Discrimination is Not Accidental All Sublimity is founded on Minute Discrimination" (E643). (Indeed, elsewhere Blake insists on the sublimity of small things.) Reynolds, as his later remarks show, wants to eliminate all oddity in the object and treat the result as something like a generalization or Platonic idea. Blake's response is about a vision that constitutes an object, not something passively observed as treated by Locke. However, Reynolds is really attacking a servile imitation that Blake, too, dislikes — a sort of objectifying photographic accuracy, such as he finds in Flemish painting. Blake might more properly have objected to what Reynolds would substitute: "that grand style of painting, which improves the partial representation by the general and invariable ideas of nature" (9). Blake would deny that such a program could express any reality: the more general the less real. His view is connected to his emphasis on outline, which he identifies with minute discrimination, though it is clear that Reynolds also advocates clarity based on clear outline.

Another of Blake's complaints is based on a quibble. Where Reynolds attacks what he calls a "facility in composing," meaning a certain flashy superficiality, Blake carps: "Why this Sentence should be begun by the Words A Facility in Composing I cannot tell unless it is to cast a stigma upon Real facility in Composition by Assimilating it with a Pretence to & Imitation of Facility in Execution or are we to understand him to mean that Facility in Composing is a Frivolous pursuit" (13, E643). Blake insists on "Real facility" as "the Greatest Power of Art," but, of course, that is not what Reynolds is talking about. We are in a semantic thicket. Blake also objects to Reynolds's attack on "mechanical felicity" (14), changing the phrase to "Mechanical Excellence" and defending it (E643). We can make the same observation here.

Reynolds is warning against superficiality of technique at the expense of thoughtful work. Blake continues to detect in the line of Reynolds's argument the hidden, self-defensive notion that genius is learned by slow methodical study. For Blake, "This is All Self-Contradictory! Truth & Falsehood Jumbled Together" (E643).

But Blake's last annotations call three of Reynolds's remarks "excellent." Those remarks praise "correct out-line," "drawing correctly what we imagine" (we shall see that Blake and Reynolds, however, do not mean the same thing by "imagination"), and exactness and precision. Blake observes, "This is Admirably Said," but he adds, "Why does he not always allow as much" (17–18, E644). He is reminded of Reynolds's attack on "minute discrimination" and acceptance of the notion of general nature, and thus he is satisfied that his accusation of self-contradiction is sustained.

It is interesting and not surprising, for we know of Blake's republican attitudes, that he is silent when in conclusion Reynolds praises the king. By this time, Blake, who had stood trial for sedition, had learned the danger of criticizing George III.

Discourse Two

Blake begins his annotations (22, back of title page, E644) with an attack on Venetian journeyman artists and later complains that "They could not Draw" (43, E646). Reynolds writes that in the second stage of the young artist's study (after gaining facility of drawing, tolerable management of colors, and acquaintance with the "most simple and obvious rules of composition" [24]) he should "endeavour to collect subjects for expression; to amass a stock of ideas, to be combined and varied as occasion may require" (25). Blake does not like this because it means that he puts the ideas of others to his own use. He might have added that the remark is Locke all over again, Reynolds recommending a combining of pieces of sense data into generalized forms. Reynolds's most definite statement of this matter is as follows, and could have come directly from Burke or Locke:

> Invention, strictly speaking, is little more than a new combination of those images which have been previously gathered and deposited in the memory; nothing can come of nothing; he who has laid up no materials, can produce no combinations [28].

Burke puts it as follows:

> Besides the ideas [by ideas Burke, following Locke, means sense perceptions], with their annexed pains and pleasures, which are presented by the sense; the

mind of man possesses a sort of creative power of its own; either in representing at pleasure the images of things in the order and manner in which they were received by the senses, or in combining those images in a new manner, and according to a different order.*

Blake connects these views with the venerable idea of copying nature, but he believes that nature is, in Locke's and Burke's epistemology, an outer world of the primary qualities of experience, devoid of sound, scent, color, and taste. Blake rarely employs "nature" in any other sense than a pejorative one. He believes that what Reynolds decries as "ideas equally remote from nature and from art" (34) are no different from the Lockean nature that he embraces. It is a generalized nature: combinations of sense data with all individuality and immediacy of vision drained out. There would ultimately be, for Reynolds, if he understood the implications of his position, only one ideal true painting combining the common quality present in all painting. Reynolds remarks, "you cannot do better than have recourse to nature herself, who is always at hand" (34). Blake's response is, "Nonsense — Every Eye Sees differently As the Eye — Such the Object" (E645). This is not, as it may appear, an example of a solipsistic relativism, for Blake also thinks that everything that is individual is connected to everything else by metaphorical identity. It is mildly surprising that Blake does not write even one word in the margin when Reynolds apes Burke; he saves his comment for five pages later, where he complains, "General Principle Again!" (35, E645).

In the meantime, he returns to criticism of Reynolds for complaining about spending time on "finished copies" (32, E645), but he refuses to recognize that Reynolds is not talking about a student but a professional artist addicted to making copies. Blake ended his comments in *Discourse One* by calling excellent Reynolds's advocacy of copying for learners (18, E644).

Though Blake does not say this anywhere, he must have thought that Reynolds's emphasis on effort, learning, and emulation of the masters through strict training reflects his own lack of genius, his want of true inspiration. When Reynolds writes of the artist's fatigue in learning his art, Blake responds that there is no fatigue in the accomplishment of a work of clear and determinate vision. He means that such accomplishment is exhilarating and that softness in art is a sign of weakness: "The man who asserts that there is no Such Thing as Softness in Art & that every thing in Art is Definite & Determinate has not been told this by Practise but by Inspiration & Vision because Vision is Determinate & Perfect & he Copies That without Fatigue" (48, E646).

---

*Edmund Burke, *A Philosophical Enquiry into the Origin of Our Ideas of the Sublime and the Beautiful* (rev. ed. 1759), J. T. Boulton, ed., London: Routledge and Kegan Paul, 1958, 16.

Toward the end of *Discourse Two*, Reynolds criticizes "mere" enthusiasm, which was connected in the minds of many with irrational religiosity in some forms of Protestant Christianity. That is not what Reynolds means, but the word suffered with this aura attributed to it. In any case, Reynolds declares that enthusiasm alone will carry the artist "but a little way" (35). Blake connects Reynolds's attack on enthusiasm with what he considers an attack on inspiration and genius: "Meer Enthusiasm is the All in All!— Bacons Philosophy has Ruined England Bacon is only Epicurus over again" (E645). He credits Bacon for Reynolds's thought here. Whether, as it appears, he identifies Bacon with Epicurus's adoption of Democritus's atomic materialism or his view that all ideas arise out of sensation or both is not clear to me.

As in *Discourse One*, Blake announces his agreement with some things Reynolds says: "We all must have experienced how lazily, and consequently how ineffectually, instruction is received when forced upon the mind by others. Few have been taught to any purpose, who have not been their own teachers" (37). Blake's response: "True!" (E645).

Discourse Three

This *Discourse* evokes perhaps the most important annotations by Blake in that they express some of his fundamental philosophical and critical notions. He begins by making use of Milton to argue in behalf of inspiration:

> A Work of genius is a Work "Not to be obtained by the Invocation of Memory & her Syren Daughters. But by Devout prayer to that Eternal Spirit. Who can enrich with all utterance & knowledge & sends out his Seraphim with the hallowed fire of his Altar to touch & purify the lips of whom he pleases." Milton [50, back of title page, E646].*

Once again he has posed, in what amounts to his own preface to the discourse, inspiration, which he identifies with enthusiasm and innate genius, against Reynolds's emphasis on deliberate and systematic learning.

Reynolds has indicated that he is now proceeding beyond discussion of the "rudiments," that is, "attainment of manual dexterity" and "imitation of the object" (51). He will now warn against too closely copying nature. Blake makes no comment here, for he certainly would have agreed (though Reynolds and Blake do not mean the same thing by "nature"). However, after this preface Blake repeats a disagreement that he had with Reynolds in *Discourse One*.

---

*"The Reason of Church-Government Urg'd Against Prelaty," *Complete Works of John Milton*, Don M. Wolfe, ed., New Haven: Yale University Press, 1953, I, 820–1. Blake omits "Dame" before "Memory."

It is fundamental and generates many of the annotations to this discourse. Indeed, it is arguably an expression of the most important of Blake's ideas about art, having to do with the relation between particulars and universals, and is developed with greater intensity here than before.

Reynolds's view is that the painter must rise above the copying of nature:

> The wish of the genuine painter must be more extensive: instead of endeavouring to amuse mankind with the minute neatness of his imitations, he must endeavour to improve them by the grandeur of his ideas; instead of seeking praise, by deceiving the superficial sense of the spectator, he must strive for fame, by captivating the imagination [52–3].

Here again is exhibited Reynolds's mixture of Platonic idea with Lockean generalization, the real located in one or the other. Both idea and generalization are detached from an experienced or constituted image and are thus at best an arbitrary allegorical representation and at worst a pure imageless abstraction. This is the reason that Blake always objects when Reynolds attacks the representation of minute particulars, although Blake himself was not much of a copier of such things. Blake is taking a philosophical position that opposes the Platonized empiricism that Reynolds, not philosophically sophisticated, embraces.

For Blake, inspiration (or vision) is an innate power to see into things, and its expression is based on intensity of concentration and "minute neatness of execution" (52, E646). Blake identifies expression of vision with clarity of outline. Actually, Reynolds and Blake agree on the importance of outline, though Blake thinks him inconsistent on the matter. On the other hand, Reynolds is objecting not to what Blake calls the "wirey ... bounding line" (E550), but to excess of detail. Blake thinks Reynolds inconsistent because of his recourse to the ideal, which has to be vague because it is imageless. He also faults Reynolds for his praise of Rubens and others who, in his view, "blot and blur" (E576) and produce insipidity of coloring.

Blake's annotations to Reynolds's remarks on pages 60 and 61 (E648) are central to this disagreement and to his own views. Reynolds has been discussing his notion of ideal beauty. The argument is that everything in nature has defects. He recommends long, laborious study and comparison of like objects. The artist thus

> acquires a just idea of beautiful forms; he corrects nature by herself, her imperfect state by her more perfect. His eye being enabled to distinguish the accidental deficiencies, excrescences, and deformities of things, from their general figures, he makes out an abstract idea of their forms more perfect than any one original; and what may seem a paradox, he learns to design naturally by drawing his figures unlike to any one object. This idea of the perfect state of nature,

which the artist calls the Ideal Beauty, is the great leading principle by which works of genius are conducted [58–9].

Here Blake gets caught up in Reynolds's language, repeating the phrase "ideal beauty" in his comment (E648). "Beauty" is not a word Blake often uses, nor is "ideal," for it implies imagelessness, despite Reynolds's calling on the support of Proclus's remark that when Phidias sculpted Jupiter he "contemplated only that image which he had conceived in his mind from Homer's description" (54). Blake's comment, closer to Proclus's, is, "All Forms are Perfect in the Poets Mind. but these are not Abstracted nor Compounded from Nature but are from Imagination" (60, E648). Reynolds discards from the individuality of the object all that is not common to all of the type, working to one "central form," as he calls it. All deviations from this form are deformity. In opposition, Blake preserves the idea of direct individual vision of individual things, properly delineated by the "hard and wirey line of rectitude and certainty," as he calls it in his *Descriptive Catalogue* (E550).

Reynolds has spoken of the Phidian ideal as divine and goes on to describe how the artist is to come to it: "Thus it is from a reiterated experience, and a close comparison of the objects in nature that an artist becomes possessed of the idea of that central form, if I may so express it, from which every deviation is deformity" (60). He discards from the individuality of the object all that is not common to all of the type. Blake's response is very important as an expression of his view: "One Central Form Composed of all other Forms being Granted it does not therefore follow that all other Forms are Deformity" (E648). When Blake grants that there is a central form he has to be alluding to the sort of imageless Platonic or empirical form that Reynolds's position implies. For Blake, it has to be a fiction, that is, a rationally constituted abstract idea that has nothing to do with art. Blake is saying that, all right, there can be such an abstract idea, but he goes on to argue, as we have seen above, that a poetic image is always individual. What remains is to show that it is also universal. This Blake does not demonstrate in the annotations. The missing link in his argument is assertion of the logic of metaphor, in this case the synecdoche, where an individual thing is identified with some larger thing that it is a part of.* Blake's notion is that intense vision into a particular thing reveals its metaphorical identity with the larger thing, indeed with all things. Small things as well as supposedly overwhelming (according to Burke) large things are sublime. Looked into, they reveal themselves as infinite.

*On this point, see my "Synecdoche and Method," *Critical Paths: Blake and the Argument of Method*, Don Miller, Mark Bracher, and Donald Ault, eds.: Durham, NC: Duke University Press, 1988, 41–71. Reprinted in my *Antithetical Essays in Literary Criticism and Liberal Education*, Tallahassee, FL: Florida State University Press, 1990, 21–51.

When Reynolds, following Burke, speaks of obscurity as a quality of the sublime, Blake answers in *Discourse Seven*, "Obscurity is Neither the Source of the Sublime nor of any Thing else" (188, back of title page, E 658). In *Discourse Three*, Blake remarks: "Without Minute Neatness of Execution. The. Sublime cannot Exist! Grandeur of Ideas is founded on Precision of Ideas" (52, E 646). The principle of metaphorical identity, especially the synecdoche, is more than simply a matter of artifice for Blake. It is a spiritual matter that binds everything together in the imagination, and imagination is always of particulars, as finally is knowledge. One cannot know anything without the image of something: "What is General Nature is there Such a Thing what is General Knowledge is there such a Thing All Knowledge is Particular" (61, E648). Blake has erased "strictly speaking" before "All," probably in the name of emphasis; but "strictly speaking" would have been better, for Blake is speaking strictly in line with his epistemological position.

As Reynolds proceeds in his discourse he speaks not of one central form but of several:

> To the principle I have laid down, that the idea of beauty in each species of beings is an invariable one, it may be objected, that in every particular species there are various central forms, which are separate and distinct from each other, and yet are undeniably beautiful; that in the human figure, for instance, the beauty of Hercules is one, of the Gladiator another, of the Apollo another; which makes so many different ideas of beauty.
>
> It is true, indeed, that these figures are each perfect in their kind, though of different characters and proportions; but still none of them is the representation of an individual but of a class. And as there is one general form, which, as I have said, belongs to the human kind at large, so in each of these classes there is one common idea and central form, which is the abstract of the various individual forms belonging to that class [62–3].

Blake's response, "Every Class is Individual" (E648), comes directly to the point that to paint something representative of a class — for example, the figures in Blake's painting of the Canterbury pilgrims — one must create an individual. Blake saw his Canterbury figures as representative of certain classes of men and women, but there is nothing of the attempt to abstract common aspects of, say, all pardoners, and paint only those. That would be absurd. Soon Reynolds is in greater trouble, admitting, "There is ... a kind of symmetry, or proportion, which may properly be said to belong to deformity" (64). This is his way of recognizing that some painters of minute particulars have been talented (Hogarth, for example), but their achievement has been of a low level. This makes Durer, for Reynolds, someone who might have been great had he known and followed the rules Reynolds has set forth. Blake is incredulous: "What does this mean 'Would have been' one of the first Painters of his Age Albert Durer Is! (65, E649).

The name of Bacon appears in this discourse, with Reynolds quoting Bacon to oppose his "treat[ing] with ridicule the idea of confining proportion to rules, or of producing beauty by selection" (61). This leads Blake to note that when Bacon says this he contradicts his own principle that "Every Thing must be done by Experiment" (E648). Blake identifies Baconian experiment with the process of generalization that gets Reynolds into so much trouble.

But on the last page Blake declares that Reynolds has written "A Noble Sentence" (E649). It is: "A firm and determined outline is one of the characteristics of the great style in painting; and, let me add, that he who possesses the knowledge of the exact form which every part of nature ought to have, will be fond of expressing that knowledge with correctness and precision in all his works" (75). However, Blake must add, "Here is a Sentence Which overthrows all his Book" (E 649). Not quite, for Reynolds's remark remains based on the notion of an ideal nature abstracted from its "accidents."

Discourse Four

Blake tells us that this discourse and the next one are "Particularly Calculated for the Setting Ignorant & Vulgar Artists as Models of Execution in Art" (78, back of title page, E 649). However, Reynolds begins with a remark praising "mental labour" (79) and makes such labor characteristic of the Roman against the Venetian school. Yet Reynolds goes on to criticize once more any emphasis on "minuteness" and argues again for

> leaving out particularities, and retaining only general ideas: I shall now endeavour to shew that this principle, which I have proved to be metaphysically just, extends itself to every part of the Art; that it gives what is called the *grand style*, to Invention, to composition, to Expression, and even to Colouring and Drapery [80].

He proceeds to distinguish between portrait painters, who should retain the individual likeness, and history painters, who show the man only by showing his actions. Blake objects to this division, declaring that individuality should be shown in both cases.

Blake also quarrels with Reynolds's notion of invention. He disagrees that invention in history painting does not imply invention of the subject, insisting on his own meaning for "invention," that is, the conception and execution of the work as a whole. He objects to Reynolds's view that the less significant parts should be sacrificed for the sake of the whole: "Sacrifice the Parts. What becomes of the Whole" (83, E650). When Reynolds says that a history painter should show "the man by shewing his actions," Blake objects. He should show the whole man (86, E650).

The rest of the discourse and annotations deals with matters of technique, especially coloring. Except for their disagreement over generality, Reynolds's and Blake's views are not far apart. Both are critical of the Venetians, but Blake more absolutely and vociferously, as in the following:

> Reynolds: "...the principal attention of the Venetian painters, in the opinion of Michael Angelo, seemed to be engrossed by the study of colours, to the neglect of the *ideal beauty of form*, or propriety of expression."
>
> Blake: "Venetian Attention is to a Contempt & Neglect of Form Itself & to the Destruction of all Form or Outline Purposely & Intentionally" [98, E651].

It is significant that Blake omits the phrase "ideal beauty" in his response. He certainly did not like Reynolds's notion of the ideal, and, for that matter, "beauty" is not a word to which Blake gives much importance. Generally, he subsumes beauty under the sublime.

Blake has just criticized Reynolds for self-contradiction even as he agrees with him. Reynolds has remarked that the styles of Raphael and Veronese or Tintoretto could not be blended together. Blake says: "What can be better Said. on this Subject? but Reynolds contradicts what he says Continually He makes little Concessions, that he may take Great Advantages" (95, E651). Nevertheless, Blake's anger is directed in the annotations more at the Venetians than at Reynolds. When Reynolds calls the Venetian school (principally in his mind Veronese and Tintoretto, not Titian) "the most splendid of the schools of elegance," Blake comments, "Vulgarity & not Elegance" (101, E652) and refuses to attach the phrase "ornamental style" to the school, which is one of "Gross Vulgarity" (103, E652). This is for Blake one of Reynolds' concessions, another being application of the phrase "mechanical power" to the Dutch; Blake thinks Reynolds has "prostituted" the phrase (104, E652). As for Reynolds's attribution of the "composite style" to Correggio, Blake simply says that there is no such thing (109, E652).

Blake always insists on the individuality of a painter's style, even to the extent of denying that genius can err when Reynolds says that the errors of genius are pardonable (111, E652). By "genius" Blake means something different. It is a power or quality of a certain artistic act, not a term describing someone. No one *is* a genius; some works and their creators *have* it.

Discourse Five

This discourse is devoted principally to comparison of the exemplary styles of Raphael and Michelangelo. Nevertheless, Blake writes on the back of the title page this caustic comment;

> Gainsborough told a Gentleman of Rank & Fortune that the Worst Painters always chose the Grandest Subjects. I desired the Gentleman to Set Gainsborough about one of Rafaels Grandest Subjects Namely Christ delivering the Keys to St Peter. & he would find that in Gainsboroughs hands it would be a Vulgar Subject of Poor Fishermen & a Journeyman Carpenter.
> The following Discourse is written with the same End in View. that Gainsborough had in making the Above assertion Namely to Represent Vulgar Artists as the Models of Executive Merit [114, E652].*

Again the issue of minute discrimination comes up, and again Reynolds here eschews all "accidents" of appearance. He argues that if you are trying to "preserve the most perfect beauty *in its most perfect state*, you cannot express the passions," because they produce "distortion and deformity" (117–8).† Blake does not think much of this: "Passion & Expression is Beauty Itself— The Face that is Incapable of Passion & Expression is Deformity Itself" (E653). Reynolds offers Raphael as an example, and Blake contradicts him by insisting on variety of character in Raphael and the Ancients. Reynolds's view here is that you cannot successfully unite "stately dignity, youthful elegance, and stern valour" (120), but then he goes on to say, "The summit of excellence seems to be an assemblage of contrary qualities, but mixed, in such proportions, that no one part is found to counteract the other" (120). Blake doesn't note the contradiction as such but does accuse Reynolds of making "A Fine Jumble" (E653).

Reynolds, who, as did Blake, revered both Michelangelo and Raphael, contrasts them: Raphael is not nearly as accomplished in oils as in fresco. Michelangelo did not have as many excellencies as Raphael. Reynolds believes he thought more as a sculptor, and he rejected all specious ornaments. Reynolds then summarizes: "Raffaelle had more taste and Fancy, Michael Angelo more Genius and imagination" (128). Blake will hear no criticism of

---

*Raimonda Modiano has reminded me that a convention of the aesthetics of the picturesque landscape was to depict rustic or indigent people. But Gainsborough's later landscapes displayed Arcadian figures as if he were following Reynolds's strictures on what constitutes a lofty subject. It does not seem that in his comment Blake was aware of this, nor does his remark indicate what seems to be characteristic of Gainsborough's work at any time.

†This remark recalls Winckelmann's argument in *Gedanken über die Nachahmung der griechischen Werke in der Malerei und Bildhauerkunst* (1754) and Lessing's comment on it at the beginning of his *Laocoön* (1766).

either. Such comparisons are always odious to him, for in his view painters should be judged on their own. Actually, Reynolds agrees to some extent, there being for him another meritorious style different from the "great style":

> ...though inferior to the former, [it] has still great merit, because it shews that those who cultivated it were men of lively and vigorous imagination. This, which may be called the original or characteristical style, being less referred to any true archetype existing either in general or particular nature, must be supported by the painter's consistency in the principles which he has assumed, and in the union and harmony of his whole design [131].

Blake cannot but agree with this, except for the presumption that the style is of secondary worth, for he sees *it* as the true "Great Style," a style that is "always Novel or New in all its Operations" (E654).

Though Blake does not want to make a hierarchy of styles with respect to ornament, he is quite willing to make judgments with respect to coloring and, of course, to distinctness of outline. On both scores Rubens fails, as he does for Reynolds. Blake, indeed, finds nothing good in Rubens, while Reynolds allows a certain skill, faculty of invention, richness of composition, and harmony and brilliance of coloring.

Against Rubens Reynolds places Poussin, "simple, careful, pure, and correct" (135). Blake agrees with this, but nevertheless he faults Reynolds for not opposing to Rubens "All Men of Genius who ever Painted" (E655).

All told, it is hardly true that in his choice of artists to be praised Reynolds has "Represent[ed] Vulgar Artists as the Models of Executive Merit" (E652), as Blake complains in his "preface" to the discourse. Reynolds is even willing to find some good in Salvator Rosa, though he severely criticizes him for being "void of all grace, elegance, and simplicity" (132–3).

In short, Reynolds always seeks the mean of criticism, balancing strengths and weaknesses among lesser painters and even among the greatest. This is clearly not Blake's practice.

Discourse Six

In this discourse, Reynolds indicates that he has two purposes: first, to lay down principles for the "formation of a sound taste" (145); second, to "intercept and suppress those prejudices which particularly prevail when the mechanism of painting is come to its perfection" (146), that is, when the student has mastered fundamentals. The specific subject will be imitation, and by that he means the following of masterly predecessors (146–7). In his view, painting is "intrinsically imitative" (148), in the sense of imitating objects of nature. He launches a criticism of inspiration as the source of heightened ability or genius; it has, in his opinion, been given too much importance, and for this reason both ancients and moderns have wrongly inveighed against imitation. On this point, Blake wholly rejects Reynolds, though he does say elsewhere that painters do and should copy a lot (E 645). His complaint is specifically against what he considers the denigration of inspiration. For this kind of view he blames the experimental philosophy of Bacon, which has "Destroyd all Art & Science The Man who says that genius is not Born. but Taught.— Is a Knave" (147, E 656). Reynolds regards genius as the "child of imitation" (151). It is fair to say that Blake would reverse this and claim that imitation is the child of genius, part of the artist's education certainly, but not the source of excellence.

For Reynolds, genius is different in different times and places. Blake denies this. Reynolds believes that art advances and criticism along with it, generating more rules fixing continually the idea of art. The rules will change with time, progressing toward a sort of ideal set. Nevertheless, he asserts, "Genius will still have room enough to expatiate, and keep always at the same distance from narrow comprehension and mechanical performance" (154). Blake rejects all notions of progress in art: "If Art was Progressive We should have had Mich Angelo's & Rafaels to Succeed & to Improve upon each other But it is not so. Genius dies with its Possessor & comes not again until Another is Born with It" (E656).

The disagreement here goes back to the notion, which Reynolds derived from Bacon and Locke, of the mind as a Cartesian *tabula rasa*. It is, in Reynolds's words, "but a barren soil; a soil which is soon exhausted, and will produce no crop, or only one, unless it be continually fertilized and enriched with foreign matter" (157–8). Blake responds, "Reynolds Thinks that Man Learns all that he Knows I say on the Contrary That Man Brings All that he has or Can have Into the World with him" (E656). When Reynolds says, "Nothing can come of nothing," Blake interprets him to mean that the human being is nothing until filled up with sense data. His rhetorical question at this point is, "Is the Mind Nothing?" (159, E657).

As Reynolds proceeds he does give more to genius, but still it is something learned:

> What we now call Genius, begins, not where rules, abstractly taken, end; but where known vulgar and trite rules have no longer any place. It must of necessity be, that even works of Genius, like every other effect, as they must have their cause, must likewise have their rules; it cannot be by chance, that excellencies are produced with any constancy or any certainty, for this is not the nature of chance; but the rules by which men of extraordinary parts, and such

as are called men of Genius, work, are either such as they discover by their own peculiar observations, or of such a nice texture as not easily to admit being expressed in words; especially as artists are not very frequently skilful in that mode of communicating ideas [155].

Although Blake does not annotate the latter part of this passage, he does quarrel with the notion that genius has a material cause. Such a cause would have to be, for Reynolds, a pile of sense data. Blake rejects the idea of genius as a product; it is an identifiable quality, not an effect. Rather than nature being the maker of experience, the mind is, for it is "the most Prolific of All Things & Inexhaustible (157, E656).

Much of the remainder of the discourse repeats ideas we have seen before: peculiarities are warned against; do not ignore nature; study many artists, not just one; revere the ancients; seek beauties beyond the "multitude of defects" (181), that is, nature's accidents; select "both from what is great, and what is little" (181). Blake has no sympathy with any of this. He makes no comments on the last five pages, even where Reynolds repeats the admonition to guard against false belief in "the imaginary powers of native genius, and its sufficiency in great works" (186). Blake has seen this idea offered before.

In his annotations, Blake usually goes to fundamental philosophical issues, but his remarks also indicate that he thinks Reynolds's advice reflects Reynolds's own lack of native genius and the fact that he had to learn everything and thought everyone else did, too. This may be the reason that Blake's last annotation, in response to Reynolds's observation of artists "bound down by the almost invincible powers of early habits," is "He who Can be bound down is No Genius Genius cannot be Bound it may be Renderd Indignant & Outrageous" (180, E658). The latter part of this looks very much like a comment on himself.

However, the discourse may be read as Reynolds's criticism of ignorance and sloth, both of which Blake surely hated.

Discourse Seven

As he did in his prefatory notes to the third, fourth, and fifth discourses, Blake assigns a purpose, as he sees it, to *Discourse Seven*. It is "to Prove That Taste & Genius are not of Heavenly Origin & that all who have Supposed that they Are so. Are to be Considerd as Weak headed Fanatics" (188, back of title page, E658). Reynolds had other purposes, though he does begin by asserting, "As our art is not a divine *gift*, so neither is it a mechanical *trade*" (189). This may have rankled Blake, not just because of its rejection of innate

6. *Reynolds's* Discourses on Art 131

genius as Blake understood it, but also because Blake probably thought that Reynolds regarded engraving as merely a mechanical trade. The Royal Academy did not admit engravers to membership. Taste and genius, introduced in *Discourse Six*, are Reynolds's main topics, but the discourse as a whole touches on fundamental issues taken up already. Thus it can be regarded as one of the most important.

Before introducing taste and genius, Reynolds emphasizes the importance of "industry," not of "the *hands*, but of the *mind*" (189). This precedes reference to the importance of learning in its broadest sense. A great artist cannot be "grossly illiterate," but he need not know everything. He ought to be "tolerably conversant with the poets" and "with that part of philosophy which gives an insight into human nature, and relates to the manners, characters, passions, and affections" (190–1). He needs also to know about the mind and the human body. Blake makes no comment on any of this. Reynolds then proceeds to set up a straw man:

> To speak of genius and taste, as in any way connected with reason or common sense, would be, in the opinion of some towering talkers, to speak like a man who possessed neither; who had never felt that enthusiasm, or, to use their own inflated language, was never warmed by that Promethean fire, which animates the canvas and vivifies the marble [193].

Still no answer from Blake, but when Reynolds goes on to castigate sarcastically those who say, "The wild freedom and liberty of imagination is cramped by attention to established rules," Blake responds, "The Ancients & the wisest of the Moderns were of the opinion that Reynolds Condemns & laughs at" (194, E658), and he proceeds to accuse Reynolds of anxiety to "Disprove & Contemn Spiritual Perception" (196, E658), continuing to express his sense of Reynolds's doubts about his own abilities.

Reynolds sees genius and taste very closely related. In fact, genius is the power of execution added to taste (197), which is the source of right judgment. His complaint is that both are popularly supposed to be entirely exempted from the "restraint of rules" (197). Blake wonders if there was ever anyone who actually said this (E658).

The whole disagreement is played out in Blake's comments on pages 198–202 (E659). Reynolds's argument is probably influenced by David Hume's "Of the Standard of Taste" in his *Four Dissertations* (1757), but, if so, it is a simplistic extension. Blake identifies Reynolds's argument as "Epicurean" in that Reynolds calls all opinions not materially grounded, as Blake says, "Unsolid & Unsubstantial" (198, E 659). He adds that his disagreements with Reynolds are not simply semantic ones. Reynolds has presented a strictly

Lockean view of the defects of language. He has complained that we use the word "taste" in two incompatible ways:

> Our judgment upon an airy nothing, a fancy which has no foundation, is called by the same name which we give to our determination concerning those truths which refer to the most general and most unalterable principles of human nature; to the works which are only to be produced by the greatest efforts of the human understanding. However inconvenient this may be, we are obliged to take words as we find them; all we can do is distinguish the THINGS to which they are applied [199].

Reynolds's argument begins with a two-fold definition of "truth." There is fixed truth, and there is also "apparent truth, or opinion, or prejudice." This second kind of truth is subject to change over time: "truth upon sufferance, or truth by courtesy ... not fixed, but variable" (201). It is this second kind that, in Blake's view, gets Reynolds into difficulty. Indeed, Reynolds himself helps to foment trouble for himself by calling the first kind "real," leaving the second kind apparently unreal, a truth that is not true. Further, it appears that much art, "whose office it is to please the mind, as well as instruct it, must direct itself according to opinion, or it will not attain its end" (201), which is to please. Indeed, it is to please at once (208). Reynolds has forgotten that Raphael did not immediately please him, though he takes the responsibility for this. Still, Reynolds, who wants a fixed principle, seems to have lost it both in the art work and in the viewer. What he is trying to preserve is a sense of the importance of a tradition of taste: Opinions of long standing should be considered as "really true" (202), because they have approached "nearer to certainty, and to a sort of resemblance to real science" (201).

Blake distorts Reynolds's view when he claims that for Reynolds all truth is prejudice, forgetting Reynolds's first type of truth; but Reynolds has very nearly forgotten, himself. Blake sees that Reynolds has contempt for "spiritual perception" (E658) and condemns immediate insight to a position of inferiority.

Meanwhile, Reynolds's preferred type of truth, the only real truth, is identified by him with "mathematical demonstration" (201). Blake remarks, "God forbid that Truth should be Confined to Mathematical Demonstration" (E659), and he does not think of opinion and prejudice as truth. He *does* think there is such a thing as "Truth at Sight" (E269).

We have seen that despite what he has said, or maybe because of some of what he has said, Reynolds thinks that age brings truth to some prejudices and advocates the artist's following those that are deeply ingrained. He has been caught in a tangle of his own definitions, and Blake must certainly think that Reynolds's giving in to what amounts to popular pressure is an example of hypocrisy.

Some of the difference between Blake and Reynolds has to do with what "reason" means. Reynolds sees reason as the source of "settled principles," even though he has admitted that some of these are grounded only in prejudice or opinion that has gained the venerability of age. For Blake, even reason can lead to change its content: "Reason or A Ratio of All We have Known is not the Same it shall be when we know More. he [Reynolds] therefore takes a Falshood for granted to set out with" (202, E659). By "ratio" here Blake must mean something like an essential ground or principle, and he turns here to remind of Reynolds's empirical views.

Finally, Reynolds returns to the idea of "general nature," and he identifies "universal opinion" with it:

> The beginning, the middle, and the end of every thing that is valuable in taste, is comprised in the knowledge of what is truly nature; for whatever notions are not conformable to those of nature, or universal opinion, must be considered as more or less capricious.
>
> My notion of nature comprehends not only the forms which nature produces, but also the nature and internal fabrick and organization, as I may call it, of the human mind and imagination [204].

Mind and imagination are here subject to rules of reason that go back to the materialist and empiricist notions of how the mind works, combining sense data into new wholes. Reynolds, though with some self-contradictions along the way, does not give up his debt to Bacon, Newton, Locke, and Burke. Blake attacks with a summary judgment: "Here is a Plain Confession that he Thinks Mind & Imagination not to be above the Mortal & Perishing Nature. Such is the End of Epicurean or Newtonian Philosophy it is Atheism" (204, E660).

Discourse Eight

On the back of the title page of *Discourse Eight*, apparently written after reading that discourse, Blake summarizes his response to the discourses he has read:

> Burke's Treatise on the Sublime & Beautiful is founded on the Opinions of Newton & Locke on this Treatise Reynolds has grounded many of his assertions. in all his Discourses I read Burkes Treatise when very Young at the same time I read Locke on Human Understanding & Bacons Advancement of Learning on Every one of these Books I wrote my Opinions & on looking them over find that my Notes on Reynolds in this Book are exactly Similar. I felt the Same Contempt & Abhorrence then; that I do now. They mock Inspiration & Vision

> Inspiration & Vision was then & now is & I hope will always Remain my Element my Eternal Dwelling place. how can I then hear it Contemnd without returning Scorn for Scorn — [244, E660]

Though Reynolds did not always agree with Burke on some aspects of art, it is clear that the epistemology Burke, following Locke, implies in his work on the sublime and the beautiful is Reynolds's also. In any case, Reynolds rarely criticized his friends and often praised them. In *Discourse Eight* he says, "A complete essay or enquiry into the connection between the rules of Art, and the eternal and immutable dispositions of our passions, would be indeed going at once to the foundation of criticism." Then he adds a footnote: "This was inadvertently said. I did not recollect the admirable treatise *On the Sublime and the Beautiful*" (282). Reynolds quickly moved to correct what might have been regarded as a snub. He typically avoided extremes of thought and utterance, being quite self-protective; while Blake, of course, spoke his mind without reluctance, sometimes not only to a fault, but also to his disadvantage. (Exceptions here are his letters to William Hayley, in which a certain resentment is suppressed.)

Having pointed out the source of his philosophical disagreement with Reynolds, Blake seems uninterested in repeating complaints based on it. However, he does not tire of accusing Reynolds of inconsistency, which, I think, he believes goes along with Reynolds's tendency to compromise in the hope of pleasing or at least not offending anyone: "If you Endeavour to Please the Worst you will never Please the Best To please All Is Impossible" (264, E661). One of the inconsistencies Blake claims to detect has to do with Reynolds's earlier rejection of mixing Florentine and Venetian styles and his statement at the beginning of *Discourse Eight*: "Artists should learn their profession by endeavouring to form an idea of perfection from the different excellencies which lie dispersed in the various schools of painting" (245). However, Reynolds is talking about young student artists here and not mature artists, as he had earlier. Reynolds also invokes the "indispensable rule" (285) of careful and distinct expression, which Blake thinks an excellent notion but "Contrary to his usual Opinions" (285, E662). But Blake overlooks or doesn't comment on what precedes Reynolds's statement. There, Reynolds opposes "leaving any thing to the imagination" (285). The idea of perfection gives him trouble, because he identifies it with the result of a process of generalization, which Blake thinks always makes a jumble. If Blake were to use "perfection" he would claim that every artist creates his own idea of it and that the problem with rules of art past a certain point in one's training is that they become a hindrance because they are externally imposed.

Reynolds, however, does argue in *Discourse Eight* that rules should be understood but finally not slavishly followed, for rules can be of a "perplexed variety" and the artist should direct "his attention to an intimate acquaintance with the passions and affections of the mind, from which all rules arise, and to which they all are referable" (281). Blake makes no response to this, though I can imagine him thinking that Reynolds is trying once again to have it both ways. Later, when Reynolds introduces the notion of imagination into his discourse, he refers to a preliminary drawing and remarks of it,

> From a slight undetermined drawing, where the ideas of the composition and character are, as I may say, only just touched upon, the imagination supplies more than the painter himself, probably, could produce; and we accordingly often find that the finished work disappoints the expectation that was raised from the sketch; and this power of imagination is one of the causes of the great pleasure we have in viewing a collection of drawings by great painters" [284].

Blake replies, "What Falshood" (E662). I doubt that Blake objects to the notion of the viewer's imagination going beyond the sketch, but it appears that he sees the sketch and the completed work as two different things and thinks that the viewer's imaginative action with respect to the sketch is irrelevant and, perhaps, even a hindrance to imaginative response to the finished work. As for the phrase "could produce," it suggests that somehow the painter should anticipate that surplus in the viewer's mind, and if he does not, he reveals a weakness. Blake is probably also objecting to this.

In any case, Reynolds's meaning for "imagination" is not Blake's, being an act of combining sense data like building blocks into abstract ideas.

What Would Blake Have Thought of the Later Discourses?

We don't know for sure whether Blake read the later discourses or whether if he did he annotated them. It is likely that he had read at least the fifteenth and last, the ending of which probably inspired him to ridicule Reynolds in verse. Reynolds concludes his last discourse with the remark: "...I should desire that the last words which I should pronounce in this Academy, and from this place, might be the name of— Michael Angelo" (II, 217–18). Blake's notebook verses, titled "A Pitiful Case," comment:

> The Villain at the Gallows tree
> When he is doomed to die
> To assuage his misery
> In Virtues praise does cry

> So Reynolds when he came to die
> To assuage his bitter woe:
> Thus aloud did howl & cry
> Michael Angelo Michael Angelo [E 504]

Blake here treats Reynolds's final remark and perhaps the whole panegyric on Michelangelo, which takes up much of *Discourse Fifteen*, as a hypocritical act of contrition generated by fear and misery. Is it possible to declare that the later discourses ought to have softened Blake's view of Reynolds in any way or merely enforced his sense of the great gulf between them? It may be that by the time he had annotated eight discourses Blake felt that he had fully enough expressed his indignation at and his fundamental differences with Reynolds.

There has not been entire agreement about whether or to what extent Reynolds's views changed in the later discourses. There is somewhat more agreement about Reynolds's alleged contradictions and inconsistencies. Robert R. Wark observes, "Many apparent shifts in opinion and inconsistencies in the *Discourses* dissolve at once when the passages are read in context, with due attention to the level of the student to whom they are addressed."* Earlier, Walter J. Hipple argued that the supposed inconsistencies in Reynolds are often caused by the reader's "overlooking or confounding the several stages Reynolds prescribes for the education of artists" and "juxtaposing passages without regard to the 'level' of their argumentative contexts."† Though Wark sees very little change in point of view or emphasis, an earlier critic, Wilson O. Clough, detects "something like a mellowing, almost a conversion."§

If there is a change that would have strongly affected Blake's attitude, it would have occurred in Reynolds's fundamental tenets. If such a change is detectable in the later discourses, it is likely to have occurred in connection with Reynolds's exposition of "genius" in *Discourse Eleven* and "imagination" in *Discourse Thirteen*.

It is in *Discourse Eleven* that Reynolds attempts an extended treatment of genius. He continues to claim that genius can err and that a work can be faultless and exhibit no genius. Blake would, of course, continue to disagree, the difference being over the nature of beauty, Reynolds treating beauty under the classical theory of harmony and proportion and Blake subsuming beauty

---

*Robert R. Wark, ed. *Discourses on Art by Sir Joshua Reynolds*, San Marino CA: Huntington Library, 1959, xvii.

†Walter J. Hipple, "General and Particular in the Discourses of Sir Joshua Reynolds: A Study in Method," *Journal of Aesthetics and Art* Criticism, 11 (1953): 232. But see Morris Eaves's conclusions in *Blake's Theory of Art*, 95fn.

§Wilson O. Clough, "Reason and Genius," *Philological Quarterly*, 23 (1944): 45–50.

under the sublime. Reynolds continues to talk about "the Genius of mechanical performance" (XI, 43), implying that there can be such genius apart from a content. Blake would reject the separation.

However, Reynolds does seem to soften his strictures against minute particulars. He concedes, "A Painter must have the power of contracting as well as dilating his sight; because, he that does not at all express particulars, expresses nothing" (XI, 43). But this turns out to be no more than a slight softening, because Reynolds immediately adds that expression of detail alone does not prove genius and any detail that does not contribute to the expression of the "main characteristic" is "worse than useless" (XI, 44), since it draws attention from the principal point. The word "express" is employed a number of times and gives a somewhat new tone to the argument. It is joined by reference to the "pleasure" of the viewer. The use of the former suggests a slight movement in a direction Blake might have welcomed. The latter, however, reveals maintenance of the values Reynolds has held all along, for pleasure is defined as a result not of the artist's power of imagination but of his expression of the general idea.

The fundamental question to ask about Reynolds's *Discourse Thirteen* is whether he comes to define "imagination" as an independent, creative mental power or merely as a special operation of the reason. If the former, Blake could possibly come to agreement with him; if the latter, their disagreement would remain as wide as ever. From Blake's point of view, Reynolds starts out in a rather encouraging way. He states that whether the imagination is affected is the only test of art (XIII, 114), all other principles being tested by this one. But at once he implies that the imagination depends on memory (XIII, 114–15). He is talking about the viewer here, but he goes on to described the artist's imagination as follows: the artist's "animated thoughts" proceed from "the fullness of his mind, enriched with the copious stores of all the various inventions which he had ever seen, or had ever passed in his mind. These ideas are infused into his design, without any conscious effort" (XIII, 116). They should not, Reynolds warns, be overly considered and corrected or they will become commonplace. Here again is the familiar associationist theory of memory and knowledge, derived from Locke and Hartley, in which no radically creative act can be attributed to the mind. What occurs is only the moving about of the elements of memory into new combinations by a sort of spontaneous working, rather than a deliberate act, of the reason. It is finally a matter of unconscious (because radically foreshortened) as against conscious behavior, both operating according to the same laws. It is precisely what Blake calls elsewhere "corporeal understanding" (E730).

For half a sentence, Reynolds seems to go a considerable distance to admit imagination to his system as an independent power. He cautions students to resist "an unfounded distrust of the imagination and feeling, in favor of narrow, partial, confined, argumentative theories; and of principles that seem to apply to the design in hand; without considering those general impressions on the fancy in which real principles of *sound reason*, and of much more weight and importance are involved, and, as it were, lie hid, under the appearance of a sort of vulgar sentiment." He goes on to remark, "reason, without doubt, must ultimately determine every thing; at this minute it is required to inform us when that very reason is to give way to feeling" (XIII, 116–17). One can imagine Blake welcoming the first part of this advice to students only to note that Reynolds had slipped back into his characteristic ways. Blake would have seen immediately that for Reynolds the imagination has no creative power and is merely a species of reason and thus of the corporeal understanding.

In *Discourse Thirteen* Reynolds speaks of artists addressing themselves to "another faculty of the mind" than reason (XIII, 126), but his own presuppositions make that faculty only a special instance of the mind's single faculty: Blake claims that imagination includes reason, which is an outgrowth of it, rather than the other way around. Yet it is possible to imagine Blake concluding that Reynolds, in searching for a way to admit imagination into his system, was also trying to move to a more expansive view of mental powers. It is possible to imagine him also sensing this in the remark that directs the painter and poet to be allowed to "dare every thing" (XIII, 125), and in the attempt in *Discourse Fifteen* to come to terms with the genius of Michelangelo. Even the word "visionary" appears with the word "enthusiasm" in honorific contexts in *Discourse Fourteen* (XIV, 169), and Blake might have remembered a remark of his own about the mind seeing "through the eye" when he discovered Reynolds distinguishing "that which addresses itself to the imagination from that which is solely addressed to the eye (XV, 188). At the same time, Blake was not likely to forget that for Reynolds "imagination" is never emancipated from the control of the reason and that Reynolds's complaint about the eye may come out of his old complaint about minute particulars. In the end, Reynolds returns to his distinction between the "narrow idea of Nature" and the "grandeur of the general ideas" (XV, 192). It is a distinction that for Blake has no meaning. Blake's "Indignation & Resentment" (back of title page) would have remained through to the end even though Reynolds profusely praised Michelangelo in his final pages.

7

Annotations to J. C. Spurzheim's *Observations on the Deranged Manifestations of the Mind, or Insanity*

Blake made only two annotations to Spurzheim's study of insanity,* but they are both interesting, and they require interpretation, which will follow after brief discussion of Spurzheim's career, that of his mentor Franz Joseph Gall, phrenology as practiced by them, and the contents of Spurzheim's book. It and the annotations are of interest if only because some people in his day thought that Blake was insane. He had been described as an "unfortunate lunatic" in Robert Hunt's *Examiner* review of his one exhibition, and others who did not know him had said nearly the same. Some acquaintances saw a touch of madness in him at times. Blake was aware of this and may have read Spurzheim in part because he was curious about what a scientist thought insanity was. On the other hand, Spurzheim was the chief advocate of phrenology, at least in England; and the so-called visionary heads that Blake drew were influenced by the theory.† It should come as no surprise that a painter and poet would be interested in a theory that made external appearance an

---

*J. G. Spurzheim, *Observations on the Deranged Manifestations of the Mind, or Insanity*, London, 1817. There was an American edition in 1833, and there is a facsimile of that edition (Gainesville: Scholars' Facsimiles & Reprints, 1970). In publication, Spurzheim has gone by various given names: Johann Gaspar, Johann Christophe (in the facsimile), Johann Fridericke or Friedrich, Jean Gaspar Christophe, Gaspard F., J. G. (as in the 1817and American editions), J. C., and G. The usage today is Johann Christophe.
†For a helpful discussion of phrenology and three of Blake's visionary heads, based on it, see Anne K. Mellor, "Physiognomy, Phrenology, and Blake's Visionary Heads," *Blake in His Time*, Robert N. Essick and Donald Pearce, eds., Bloomington, IN: Indiana University Press, 1978, 53–74.

expression of character, since artists do that much of the time. Also, Blake knew of Johann Caspar Lavater's invention of the science of physiognomy, a forerunner of phrenology, and his book on the subject.* He had annotated Lavater's *Aphorisms* (see Chapter 1) with considerable interest and approbation shortly after it had come out. Physiognomy became cranioscopy, and finally phrenology, so named by Thomas I. Forster in 1815 and thence adopted by Spurzheim.

Gall, Spurzheim, and Phrenology

Spurzheim (1776–1832) was the protégé of Franz Joseph Gall (1758–1828), who was a pioneer in the study of the brain. What Gall called cranioscopy was a method meant to determine character by examination of the shape of the skull. He sought to locate the different mental and moral faculties or sources of their functions in areas of the brain. His methods were crude and his assignment of locations completely inaccurate, but his theory that brain functions were localized turned out to be correct. However, his conclusion that the skull's surface reflects the shape of the brain itself was never widely accepted and proved to be false. His views got him in trouble with the Catholic Church, in which he was brought up in Germany, and the government of Austria, where he lived for a time. The religious dogma his theory offended was that the mind or soul was immaterial and had no physical existence either in or as the brain.

Spurzheim became Gall's pupil in 1800 and later his collaborator. In 1809 in Paris, where both he and Gall had settled after the Austrian trouble, he published *Recherche sur le système nerveux en générale et sur celui du cerveau en particulier*. Later there were collaborations with Gall, including the first two volumes of an ambitious work on the same subject. (The latter two volumes were written by Gall alone.) Spurzheim went to England in 1813 and resided thereafter either in London, where phrenology became quite well known and controversial, and Paris. In 1832 he was invited to the United States and in a short time gained there a significant following. He died of a fever in Boston, where his funeral, attended by a large crowd, took place. The *Boston Medical and Surgical Journal* reported his death and described in some detail the examination of his brain, which was found to be unusually large and fifty-seven ounces in weight. The Boston Medical Association declared in a resolution, "We view the decease of Dr. Spurzheim and the termination of his

---

*Johann Caspar Lavater, *Essays on Physiognomy, Designed to Promote the Knowledge and the Love of Mankind*, Henry Hunter, tr., 3 vols., London: John Murray, 1789–1798.

labors as a calamity to mankind, and in an especial manner to this country." From its beginning, however, phrenology was controversial, and those who practiced it were often accused of quackery.

In the phrenological system as it was developed, the outer surface of the skull was divided into forty-three or more areas. The organs of the brain, mapped on to the skull, were thought to be the sources of psychological traits and mental capacities of various kinds. The *Dictionary of Philosophy and Psychology* comments as follows:

> That part of the head which seemed well developed in a quarrelsome young man became the place of the organ of 'combativeness'; a portion which Gall believed was prominent in pickpockets was identified as 'acquisitiveness'; the head of a beggar who excused his poverty on account of his pride served to locate 'self-esteem'; a hesitating ecclesiastic and a vacillating councilor with large parietal eminences indicated these parts to be the organ of 'cautiousness'; and so on with even slighter and more fanciful analogy. The division of the faculties recognized the distinction between the feelings and the intellect; it divided the former into propensities (impulses to action) and sentiments (impulses giving rise to emotions as well as actions), which in turn were higher when peculiar to man and lower when shared by animals. As types of propensities were 'amativeness,' 'philoprogenitiveness,' 'destructiveness,' &c.; of the lower sentiments, 'self-esteem,' 'cautiousness'; of the higher sentiments, 'veneration,' 'hope,' 'wonder,' 'wit.' The intellectual faculties were perceptive, such as 'individuality,' 'size,' 'language,' 'form,' 'number,' 'tune,' 'eventuality'; or reflective, such as 'comparison,' 'causality.'*

The *Dictionary* remarks, "The evidence for the location of the faculties was extremely crude" and then bluntly asserts, "...the system involves on its anatomical side a relation between brain function and cranial formation that does not exist."

Spurzheim on Insanity

Spurzheim's book of 1817 on insanity begins with a criticism of the public attitude toward and the medical treatment of madness. He divides its forms into those that have external and internal causes, the former being the product of physical injury or deformity, the latter by "derangement of internal functions" (11).† He also writes of "disorders of voluntary motion" (12ff.) and "diseases of the five senses" (25–7), as in convulsion, spasm, epilepsy, catalepsy,

---

**Dictionary of Philosophy and Psychology*, James Mark Baldwin, ed., New York: The Macmillan Co., 1911. vol. 2, 299.
†Page numbers refer to the American edition.

and palsy, insisting that symptoms should not be mistaken for causes, as they often were. He writes of "derangements of the internal functions of the mind," as in apoplexy, phrenitis, and hydrocephalus acutus (31–48). Further along, he describes four "general forms" of insanity: idiotism, fatuity, irresistibility, and alienation (129). Mania and melancholia, which very much interested him, are types of alienation. Causes are always corporeal. They can be hereditary. Madness may come with age and even as a result of the weather. The influence of his phrenological views appears in his remark that many who suffer from epilepsy have "small foreheads, and the upper posterior part of the head across the summit or across the midst of both parietal bones, elevated"(15). But he adds, with his usual caution, "This configuration, however, is not observed in all who are subject to this complaint, and it often exists without epilepsy; hence it cannot be considered as a cause" (15). Still, from time to time, he makes remarks that seem to insist on a phrenological interpretation. Citing John Haslam's *Observations on Madness*,* he notes Haslam's report that an insane boy had a "well formed head"(97). Spurzheim seems a little defensive in doubting this: "This expression is vague," he says. He thinks the head was not "sufficiently attended to. I dare say that the upper part of the forehead of this subject, and the whole coronal part of his head, were small in proportion to the basilar intermedial and inial regions" (97fn). Yet he also denies that the shape of the head can be studied to determine insanity. Nevertheless, "in insanity, the configuration of heads is neither to be overlooked, nor to be over-rated" (109). On the whole, the book on insanity is not grounded on phrenology to the extent that most of its views need to be rejected. Spurzheim has, for his time, many important things to say about how insanity and the insane should be treated, as well as grim accounts of how it and the insane *are* treated.

Spurzheim's definition of insanity is as follows:

> Insanity ... is an aberration of any sensation or intellectual power from the healthy state, without being able to distinguish the diseased state; and the aberration of any feeling from the state of health, without being able to distinguish it, or without the influence of the will on the actions of the feeling. In other words, the incapacity of distinguishing the diseased functions of the mind, and the irresistibility of our actions, constitute insanity [53].

Though he is not always clear about it, he rejects a mere mental insanity and considers that all derangements belong to "organic parts." Insanity is, for him, a "corporeal" disease; to consider it otherwise leads to all kinds of

---

*John Haslam, *Observations on Madness and Melancholy*, second edition, London: G. Hayden, 1809, 188–206, is quoted extensively by Spurzheim on this case.

mistakes (202–3). He argues that insanity and its symptoms have as many causes and circumstances as any other disease and that it has no one specific remedy. Each case should be regarded as a special one without necessarily routine treatment.

Blake's First Annotation: Spurzheim and Mind

The first of Blake's two annotations follows a passage on the subject of insanity in children:

> In children idiotism from birth is often observed. There are also numerous cases where children by accidental causes, lose the manifestations of the mind. But it may be asked, whether children suffer mania and insanity. Mr. Haslam [185] describes several cases of insane children. These cases, however, belong to one of the two already noticed sources of idiotism. I have seen several examples of that kind in different countries. They are mostly partial idiots from birth, and I shall detail their history when I treat of the nature of the causes of insanity. The reason that children do not appear as insane, strictly speaking, in my opinion is, because their cerebral organization is too delicate, and does not bear a strong morbid affection without entirely losing its fitness for the mind and endangering life. The disturbances of the organization appear merely as organic diseases, because the functions are entirely suppressed. Later, in proportion as the brain becomes firmer, it bears morbid changes longer without becoming entirely unfit for its function or causing death. Its functions then are only disturbed, and appear under the symptoms called insanity [80].

I have offered this passage at some length. The notes, which Blake made on a separate sheet of paper, are lost. Our only source for them is the three-volume edition of Blake's work edited with commentary by Edwin J. Ellis and W. B. Yeats in 1893. Ellis and Yeats were notoriously inaccurate transcribers. Erdman, in his edition of Blake, used in my transcriptions, believed that Ellis and Yeats must have punctuated Blake's two annotations as they saw fit, for Erdman thought that the punctuation is not characteristic of Blake, and he changed it.*

In any case, Blake's first annotation, as we have it from Erdman, is as follows:

---

*Ellis and Yeats found the sheet in the manuscript of Blake's Vala (*The Four Zoas*), in the possession of John and William Linnell, who inherited it from their father, the painter John Linnell, a friend of Blake. They punctuated as follows: "Corporeal disease, to which I readily agree. Diseases of the mind: I pity him. Denies mental health and perfection. Stick to this, all is right. But see page 152." Edwin J. Ellis and William Butler Yeats, eds, *The Works of William Blake*, 3 vols., London: Bernard Quaritch, I: 155.

> Corporeal disease. to which I readily agree. Diseases of the mind I pity him. Denies mental health and perfection Stick to this all is right. But see page 152 [E662]

One question to ask here is what he and Spurzheim mean by "mind," and whether they agree about it, even though "mind" does not appear in either of the two quotations above. This is not a simple matter. A few pages earlier, Spurzheim seems to equate mind and soul, though with "or" he leaves the possibility of difference: "Certainly the manifestations of the mind may be deranged; but I have no idea of any disease, or of any derangement of an immaterial being itself, such as the mind or soul is. The soul cannot fall sick, any more than it can die" (75). It may be that Spurzheim remembers here Gall's problem with the Church. He goes on to remark, "I consider the mind in this life confined to the body, of which it makes use; that is, the powers of the mind want instruments for their manifestations; or, these manifestations are dependent on the instruments; cannot appear without them; and are modified, diminished, increased, or deranged according to the condition of the instruments or organs" (75–6). Soul and mind, according to these passages, may or may not be two different immaterial entities. Spurzheim gives no characteristics that distinguish the two from each other. Indeed, this is his only mention of soul. The immateriality of the mind is the cause of his referring frequently to the mind's "manifestations" rather than the mind itself constituted as corporeal. The brain is where the incorporeal mind is confined in this life. Spurzheim's acrobatics here cause a problem.

Blake comes to his reading of Spurzheim having early in his career declared the division of soul and body what he came to call a negation. In *The Marriage of Heaven and Hell*, he had written, "Man has no body distinct from his Soul for that calld Body is a portion of the soul discerned by the five Senses. The chief inlets of Soul in this age" (E34). It would appear from this that for Blake the imagination is capable of outstripping the bodily senses and engaging in mental or spiritual perception. It appears that if Blake were to use the word "mind" it would be identical to "soul." Both would be subsumed under imagination or intellect, also usually identical in Blake's writings. Presumably the imagination, if strong enough, would be able to perceive the entire man, or spiritual body, as Blake elsewhere calls it.

Blake accepts Spurzheim's initial assertion that children's insanity lies not in the mind but occurs by "accidental causes" and "corporeal," as Blake would call them, manifestations of the mind. There is a difference, however, in that Spurzheim considers the manifestations material while Blake thinks these manifestations are, like everything else, not really material but what most people (at least circa 1817) are capable of imagining. As Spurzheim's statement proceeds, Blake comes to suspect that Spurzheim has forgotten about the care with which he relegated insanity to manifestations, not to the mind itself; or perhaps Blake has forgotten about the distinction Spurzheim has made. In any case, Blake now suspects that Spurzheim attributes disease directly to the mind. He writes, " Diseases of the mind I pity him." He thinks Spurzheim has, in spite of himself, made mind into a material thing which is itself capable of being diseased. This leads to Blake's next remark: "Denies mental health and perfection" (E662).

But then Blake seems to think that Spurzheim rights himself when toward the end of the passage he declares that the child is not susceptible to a "morbid affection" because of the "delicacy" (the simplicity and undeveloped nature) of its "cerebral organization" or brain, which causes the disturbance to take forms other than those of insanity. Blake comments that if Spurzheim continues to imply, as this apparently does, that the mind itself is not diseased, then all will be well with his argument: "Stick with this all is right." Of course, Blake would reject the materialism present in the argument, but he does not raise that issue here.

However, he does invite the reader to look at page 152 (114, American edition), where Spurzheim remarks, "Whatever occupies the mind too intensely or exclusively is hurtful to the brain, and induces a state favorable to insanity, in diminishing the influence of will." It appears that Blake thinks this again introduces the notion of the mind's materiality, even though Spurzheim seems elsewhere to have kept mind and matter apart. The problem as Blake sees it may be introduction of the term "will," which may be, for Spurzheim, material. But matter for Blake is a product of a weakened imagination, the sort of imagination that in some cases can't get beyond thinking of the material world as a congeries of Locke's primary qualities of perception and all else illusion of the secondary qualities.

My reading of Blake's annotation implies a process of reading by Blake, which as it proceeds directs us to the text's parts.*

Over the nineteenth century, mind came to be identified with changes of consciousness in time, whereas soul remained permanent behind the mind's phenomena. Despite his prudent theological care to keep the mind free of matter and, probably, of temporality, Spurzheim must have thought along these lines. He was a materialist, Blake a special sort of idealist, perhaps the only one of his kind.

---

*For a reading, which does not do this, and comes to a different conclusion, see Mellor, *op. cit.*, 60–1.

Blake's Second Annotation: Cowper and Madness

In the section of his book on the causes of insanity, Spurzheim considers religion:

> Religion is another fertile cause of insanity. Mr. Haslam, though he declares it sinful to consider religion as a cause of insanity, adds, however, that he would be ungrateful, did he not avow his obligation to Methodism for its supply of numerous cases. Hence the primitive feelings of religion may be misled and produce insanity; that is what I contend for, and in that sense religion often leads to insanity. The Domestic Guide for Insanity says, "How often has the preacher of Christianity been stigmatized as the cause of insanity in some darkminded hearer? When at the same time out of a hundred people, all living in the same neighborhood, possessing nearly the same means of information, all reading the same religious books, and receiving the same religious instruction from the same preacher, ninety-nine have felt the cheering influences of religion. Surely, if the cause had been in the preacher or religious instruction, the bad effects would have been more general; but the poor creature had a predisposition to insanity, and religion happened to be the thing by which it was first discovered to the world" [154, American edition, 115].

However, with his usual care to separate the disease from its often alleged causes and its symptoms, Spurzheim proceeds to lay the responsibility elsewhere:

> The same observation might be made with respect to all madmen and their exciting causes; and it shows the error of considering the external impressions alone as sufficient causes. The internal predispositions of the mind, in its state of health and disease are too often overlooked. In my work on Phrenology I have sufficiently detailed the innate dispositions of the mind, which may be diminished, excited, cultivated, and directed in their actions by external circumstances; but their activity is the result of internal innate power and exciting causes together. It is the same in the state of disease or deranged functions. The internal predispositions are often of more consequence than the external impressions [American edition, 115–6].

Blake seems to have made his comment after reading the first of these passages. He writes:

> Methodism &c p. 154. Cowper came to me & said. O that I were insane always I will never rest. Can you not make me truly insane. I will never rest till I am so. O that in the bosom of God I was hid. You retain health & yet are as mad as any of us all — over us all — mad as a refuge from unbelief — from Bacon Newton & Locke* [E663].

*Ellis and Yeats, choosing to use their own punctuation, transcribed as follows: "Methodism, &c. 154. Cowper came to me and said, 'Oh! That I were insane, always. I will never rest.

Cowper suffered three major periods of what was then called madness or insanity, the form of which was in his case called melancholia. Spurzheim observes that melancholia often occurs with mania in the same person. Today we describe such a person as manic-depressive. However, there doesn't seem to be any record of manic behavior by Cowper. Nor does it seem that Methodism played any significant role. His depression occurred before he experienced various influences of Methodism.* He had an unwavering belief that he was irredeemably damned and abandoned by God. The reason for his damnation is not clear; perhaps he thought that his depression was itself proof. Though intermittent, it was severe at times.

"The Cast-Away," a poem of 1799, not long before his death, has been for critics emblematic of his depression. He based it on an actual event that took place in 1741, when in heavy seas on Cape Horn a seaman was washed overboard and lost. From the poem's beginning Cooper is, himself, like the seaman, a "destined wretch" bereft of hope. But at the end of the poem his own lot is declared to be worse:

> ...Mis'ry still delights to trace
> Its semblance in another's case.
>
> No voice divine the storm allay'd,
>   No light propitious shone,
> When snatched from all effectual aid,
>   We perish'd, each, alone;
> But I, beneath a rougher sea,
> And whelm'd in deeper gulphs than he.†

This is a large claim to make for one's own depressed state. The theme, though less bluntly put, is not absent from some of Cowper's other poems.

Blake was an admirer of Cowper's poetry. Though he had never met him, he came to know a great deal about him through his acquaintance with William Hayley, who was writing Cowper's biography.§ Hayley commissioned

---

[continued] Cannot you make me truly insane? I will never rest till I am so. Oh! That in the bosom of God I was hid. You retain health and yet are mad as any of us all-over us all-mad as a refuge from unbelief-from Bacon, Newton, and Locke.'"

*On Cowper's relation to evangelicalism see Charles Ryskamp, *William Cowper of the Inner Temple*, Esq., Cambridge: at the University Press, 1959, especially 158–76 and 213–34, which includes some relevant letters by Cowper.

†My transcription is from *The Poems of William Cowper*, John D. Baird and Charles Ryskamp, eds., Oxford: Clarendon Press, 1995, 3: 216. On the genesis of this poem see James King's fine *William Cowper: A Biography*, Durham, NC: Duke University Press, 1986, 279–80.

§Morton D. Paley has written a thorough and excellent account of Blake's relation to Cowper, to which I am indebted in the remarks that follow. See "Cowper as Blake's Spectre," *Eighteenth-Century Studies*, 1 (1967–8), 236–52. See also G. E. Bentley, Jr., "Blake, Hayley, and Lady Hesketh," *The Review of English Studies*, new series, 7: 27 (July 1956), 264–86.

Blake when Blake was living at Felpham to produce a miniature and later an engraving of Cowper's head based on George Romney's much-admired portrait. Blake also did a tempera portrait of Cowper for Hayley and several other works related to Cowper's poems. Lady Hesketh, Cowper's cousin, ruled strongly against any mention in the biography of Cowper's madness and hated the miniature Blake executed, the eyes suggesting insanity to her. The later engraving she liked.

Blake's work with Hayley and his acquaintance with others who knew the poet put him in a position to know the extent of Cowper's malady, and there is no doubt, as Paley points out, that not only Hayley but also Blake found similarities between them. In one of the three stanzas of his manuscript poem, "William Cowper Esqre," Blake wrote,

> You see him spend his Soul in Prophecy
> Do you believe it a Confounded lie
> Till some Bookseller & the Public Fame
> Proves there is truth in his extravagant claim [E507]

He writes of Cowper here, but Cowper's poetry was broadly admired in his lifetime, Blake's known only to a few, some of whom thought the author mad.* Paley convincingly observes that the characterization of the Spectre early in *Jerusalem* seems based on Cowper, for in a significant speech the Spectre personifies himself as "Despair" (E152). Paley observes also that Blake's Spectre is "a Calvinist who believes himself irrevocably damned by a God of wrath and doomed to suffer forever" (236).

Blake's interest in Cowper's madness was, as Paley points out, probably influenced by three works published in 1814, 1815, and 1816, all of which discuss it. The last was Cowper's own *Memoir*, in which he speaks of his own despair. A controversy developed over whether Cowper's evangelical religious views caused his madness or "whether his severe despondency was simply the expression, in religious terms, of a constitutional insanity" (Paley, 248). As we have seen, Spurzheim raised a similar issue about cause in 1817.

Blake's view expressed in his note, as is often the case, does not fit either of these interpretations. At the outset, Blake takes notice of Methodism, apparently to mark where Spurzheim's discussion of it is, but he makes no comment. Instead, he offers one of his visions: a visitation by Cowper, who pleads for his aid. The ironic turnaround is that Cowper, who he knew had

---

*On attributions of madness to Blake, see G. E. Bentley, Jr., *The Stranger from Paradise: A Biography of William Blake*, New Haven, CT: Yale University Press, 2001, especially 379–82. See also Max Byrd, *Visits to Bedlam: Madness and Literature in the Eighteenth-Century*, Columbia: University of South Carolina Press, 1974, which contains a chapter on Cowper and Blake (145–175), in which Cowper's madness and Blake's are contrasted.

fits of serious depression, implies that he is not always insane or that he is not insane enough and asks that he always be, that Blake make him so. If he were, he would be protected by God, "hidden" in his bosom and thus protected, presumably from the world. He declares Blake to be healthy and yet mad, but it is a madness "over us all," greater and better than that of "any of us."

In an ironic conclusion, Cowper treats Blake's madness as what amounts to a sane refuge from the madness of the prevailing intellectual culture, which is dominated by the experimentalism, empiricism, and materialism of Blake's favorite triumvirate of villains, Bacon, Newton, and Locke. Cowper sees in Blake a higher form of madness, a truly visionary state that he desires. Blake has made him an ironic, though also desperate, voice that explains Blake's own visionary insanity — or profound sanity. The "unbelief," of which Cowper speaks, is the state in which the power of imagination has been swept away in skepticism by the influence of the triumvirate. Blake identified God with Man. Cowper had been tragically mistaken to declare himself bereft of God. In Blake's vision of Cowper he had, when he came to Blake, named error and discovered a truth.

One might recall that in the so-called *Public Address* to the Chalcographic Society, never finished or delivered, Blake said, "It is very true what you have said for these thirty two Years I am Mad or Else you are so both of us cannot be in our right senses Posterity will judge by our Works" [E573].

8

Annotations to Bishop George Berkeley's *Siris*

Certainly Blake was familiar with more of Berkeley's writings than *Siris*.* It is likely that he had read Berkeley's most important work *The Principles of Human Knowledge* (1710), published when Berkeley was twenty-five. I intend to discuss first Blake's epistemological views in relation to Berkeley's, next *Siris*, and finally Blake's annotations to that work, in which he expresses some disagreements.

Berkeley, Blake, and Human Knowledge

Berkeley provides an introduction to his book that sets out what is fundamental to his philosophy, his criticism of the notion of abstract general ideas. Blake would have agreed with his critique and with his attack on John Locke's distinction between primary and secondary qualities of perception as set forth in *An Essay Concerning Human Understanding* (1690). As early as the annotations to Lavater's *Aphorisms* (1788), Blake had taken his stance on Locke's distinction:

> Deduct from a rose its redness. From a lilly its whiteness from a diamond its hardness from a sponge its softness from an oak its heighth from a daisy its lowness & rectify every thing in Nature as the Philosophers do. & then we shall return to Chaos... [532, E 595]

Berkeley devoted the whole introduction of *The Principles* to a criticism of abstractions as general ideas. Strictly speaking, ideas for Berkeley, as for

---

**Siris: A Chain of Philosophical Reflexions and Inquiries Concerning the Virtues of Tar Water, And divers other Subjects connected together and arising from one another*. By G[eorge] B[erkeley] L[ord] B[ishop] O[f] C[loyne]. Dublin, 1744. References to Siris are to the numbers of the paragraphs in the text. The copy that Blake annotated is in the library of Trinity College, Cambridge.

Locke, are sense impressions. For Berkeley, but not for Locke, an abstract idea, such as extension or the general notion of color, is a contradiction in terms because it does not itself refer to something perceptible as such. Only a particular color is. Blake agreed with this, it being the basis of his critique in the annotations to Reynolds's *Discourses*: "All Forms are Perfect in the Poets Mind. but these are not Abstracted nor Compounded from Nature but are from Imagination" (E648), and "what is General Knowledge is there such a Thing All Knowledge is Particular" (E648).

Blake also could have found in *The Principles* an argument for a notion of particulars and universals that begins to approach his own:

> It is, I know a point much insisted on, that all knowledge and demonstration are about universal notions [not "ideas"], to which I fully agree. But then it does not appear to me that those notions are formed by abstraction in the manner premised—*universality*, so far as I can comprehend, not consisting in the absolute, positive nature or conception of anything, but in the relation it bears to the particulars signified or represented by it; by virtue whereof it is that things, names, or notions, being in their own nature *particular*, are *rendered universal* [15].*

Blake's notion is more radical than what follows the remark above:

> Thus, when I demonstrate any proposition concerning triangles, it is supposed that I have in view the universal idea of a triangle: which ought not to be understood as if I could frame an *idea* of a triangle which was neither equilateral, scalenon, nor equicrural; but only that the particular triangle I consider, whether of this or that sort it matters not, doth equally stand for and represent all rectilinear triangles whatsoever, and is in that sense universal [15].

Berkeley's universal is not an idea (in his and Locke's sense) because it cannot be apprehended by sense. Blake's universal exists in a synecdochic relationship with the particular. The particular's identity with the universal is achieved by intensely looking *into* the thing and grasping its infinitude and thus its identity with everything else. In its infinitude it remains an image (or what Berkeley calls an idea). Still, Blake may well have thought Berkeley's remark moved toward his own view. A later statement would come closer:

> The reason ... that any particular body seems to be of a finite magnitude, or exhibits only a finite number of parts to sense, is, not because it contains no more, since in itself it contains an infinite number of parts, but because the sense is not acute enough to discern them. In proportion therefore as the sense is rendered more acute, it perceives a great number of parts in the object, that is, the object appears greater; and its figure varies, those parts in its extremi-

---

*I quote throughout from *The Principles of Human Knowledge* (1710) in *The Works of George Berkeley Bishop of Cloyne*, vol. 5, A. A. Luce and T. E. Jessop, eds., Edinburgh: Thomas Nelson and Sons, 1953. References are to the numbers of the paragraphs in the text.

152   Blake's Margins

> ties which were before unperceivable appearing now to bound it in very different lines and angles from those perceived by an obtuser sense. And at length, after various changes of size and shape, when the sense becomes infinitely acute, the body shall seem infinite. During all which there is no alteration in the body, but only in the sense [47].

We have approached here Blake's "world in a grain of sand," which leads us to his statement "All deities reside in the human breast" (E38) and several others in his extant writings. But Blake would object to "seem" above. For him, the body, being projected by "infinitely acute" senses, would *be* infinite.

Berkeley's Siris

The first half of *Siris* is devoted to an account of the benefits gained by the ingestion of tar-water. This is fortunately not the tar made from petroleum but instead that emerging from certain trees:

> This balsam, weeping or sweating through the bark, hardens into resin; and this most copiously in the several species of pines and firs, whose oil being in greater quantity, and more tenacious of the acid spirit or vegetable soul (as perhaps it may not improperly be called), abides the action of the sun, and, attracting the sunbeams, is thereby exalted and enriched so as to become a most noble medicine: such is the last product of a tree, perfectly maturated by time and sun [38].

Tar-water was prepared for use by infusing it with cold water and allowing the mixture to stand until the oil rises and is then a scum which is removed. The liquid is then drunk.

Berkeley seems to have learned of its use during his time in North America from 1728 to 1731, where it was thought to help prevent smallpox. From his own experience he came to consider it a panacea: either a preventive, a palliative, or a cure. He recommended it for such things as scurvy, pneumonia, dysentery, gout, urinary problems, nervous disorders, hypochondria, and hysteria. It was, he thought, of value in preserving the teeth and gums, and even the voice. He further comments:

> Studious persons also, pent up in narrow holes, breathing bad air, and stooping over their books, are much to be pitied. As they are debarred from the free use of air and exercise, this I will recommend as the best succedaneum to both. Though it were to be wished that modern scholars would, like the ancients, meditate and converse more in walks and gardens and open air, which upon the whole would perhaps be no hindrance to their learning, and a great advantage to their health. My own sedentary course of life had long since thrown me into an ill habit, attended with many ailments, particularly a nervous colic,

which rendered my life a burden, and the more so because my pains were exasperated by exercise. But since the use of tar-water, I find, though not a perfect recovery from my old and rooted illness, yet such a gradual return of health and ease, that I esteem my having taken this medicine the greatest of all temporal blessings, and am convinced that, under Providence, I owe my life to it [119].

However, as Luce, Berkeley's editor, notes, his colic changed to gout and sciatica, "the tar-water having drove it into my limbs and, as I hope, carrying it off by those ailments, which are nothing to the colic" (letter of 16 March 1744 to Gervais).

Luce goes so far as to say that Berkeley's scientific writing in *Siris* is "humiliating, for here one of our ablest and most learned minds is writing things which the most mediocre student of to-day knows to be wrong" (8). Still, tar-water became popular after Berkeley wrote in its favor. Though most of what Berkeley thought about it was indeed wrong, it is still in occasional use as an external skin medicine and has been said to give relief to coughs, diseases of the lungs, and gastric disturbances.

About two-thirds of *Siris* is given over to discussion of the medicinal virtues of tar-water, its natural sources and chemistry. This leads to a discussion of physics and the philosophy of nature, including the role of fire in its history. The book concludes with a discussion of the dependency of the world on a supreme mind, or God. Berkeley hoped that his discussion of tar-water would lead to "farther inquiries, and those on to others, remote perhaps and speculative, but, I hope, not altogether useless or unentertaining" (unnumbered introductory paragraph). In fact, the latter parts of *Siris* are, for Berkeley, a perfectly natural extension into philosophy of his scientific argument, there being in it an expression of his views about the limitations of natural philosophy (science) and mathematics with respect to causes, effects, mind, and sense.

Siris was Berkeley's last and strangest philosophical writing. It was called by G. J. Warnock a "curiosity": "So Gothic a piece would seem to have strayed from some later or earlier period."* The whole impresses one as a tangled compendium of medical and scientific lore followed by a critique of scientific presumption to know the actual causes of things. Its style is not at all typical of Berkeley's earlier philosophical works.

Whether Blake read any of the first two-thirds of the book, studied those pages with care, or skimmed over them is not known. He makes no annotation until the 289th of the 368 numbered paragraphs, and all but one occur from 289 to 310.

*G. J. Warnock, *Berkeley*, Harmondsworth: Pengiun Books, 1953, 234.

In these paragraphs, Berkeley argues that God is pure mind, without sense and without body (matter). God is the real agent, the "first mover, invisible, incorporeal, unextended, intellectual source of life and being" (296). The body is an impediment. Sense and the senses are not godly because they imply body and "resistance." Corporeal forces wrongly pass for causes, yet they are merely products of hypotheses. So-called sensible things and the supposed experience of them rule, but when intellect takes over, the objects of sense prove to be but phantoms, merely natural appearances: "They are ... such as we see and perceive them" (292). It is the mind that contains everything and is the "source of unity and identity, harmony and order, existence and stability" (295).

Berkeley claims that Ancients, both Greek and Egyptian, possessed traces of this view, and both Plato and Aristotle held that because of the fleeting nature of its objects sense is not knowledge. According to both Plato and Pythagoras there were three kinds of objects. They were "a form or species that is neither generated nor destroyed, unchangeable, invisible, and altogether imperceptible to sense, being only understood by the intellect," a kind that is "ever fluent and changing, generating and perishing, appearing and vanishing," and finally "matter ... neither an object of understanding nor of sense" (306). In the mind, there is more than what is derived from sense. There are notions derived from the mind's own capacity and activity. The mind is not a *tabula rasa* on which there becomes imprinted what man experiences.

The Annotations

It is a little surprising that if Blake had read the whole of *Siris*, he had not made annotations earlier, for he was, as we know, sympathetic at least to some of Berkeley's philosophical views and might well have marked with approval, for example, the following:

> Though it be supposed the chief business of a natural philosopher to trace out causes from the effects, yet this is to be understood not of agents but of principles, that is, of component parts, in one sense, or of laws and rules, in another. In strict truth, all agents are incorporeal, and as such are not properly of physical consideration [247].

On the other hand, Blake obviously chose the part of the book that interested him most (or at all) to annotate.

In paragraph 288, Berkeley has been considering the view, which he attributed to the Ancient Greeks and Egyptians, that all things are One.

8. Berkeley's Siris

Intending to avoid a charge of atheism, he tries to distinguish his notion of the One from that of pantheism:

> Comprehending God and the creatures in one general notion, we may say that all things together make one universe or το παν. But if we should say that all things make one God, this would, indeed, be an erroneous notion of God, but would not amount to atheism, so long as mind or intellect was admitted to be the το ηγεμονικον, the governing part. It is, nevertheless, more respectful, and consequently the truer notion of God, to suppose Him neither made up of parts, nor to be Himself a part of any whole whatsoever.

This leads to the argument that God knows all, but he does not know by sense. He is bodiless, "nor is the supreme Being united to the world as the soul of an animal is to its body" (290). Blake remarks here, "Imagination or the Human Eternal Body in Every Man" and then "Imagination or the Divine Body in Every Man" (E663). But here there is a problem. Does Blake express agreement with Berkeley? Is he merely describing what he thinks Berkeley is saying? Or is he disagreeing? Or is he misunderstanding? Blake consistently identifies imagination with vision, that is, with the most intense sort of seeing. A visionary is one who imaginatively constitutes, that is, "sees" God. But Berkeley is saying that God cannot be seen but can be known in mind. In *The Marriage of Heaven and Hell*, Blake has the prophet Isaiah say, "I saw no God, nor heard any, in a finite organical perception; but my senses discover'd the infinite in every thing" (E 34). What Isaiah here calls a finite organical perception is, I believe, equivalent to the passive perception of sense data described by John Locke and rejected by Blake throughout his writings, where Blake's consistent view is that one sees the spiritual body of things *through* the eyes *with* the mind. As I read Berkeley and Blake, I have to conclude that Blake is either misunderstanding Berkeley, disagreeing with him, or expressing his own view that God and man are one in imagination. I think the fundamental difference here is that for Berkeley pure mind is free not only of sense but also of any need to experience an image, while Blake thinks of the mind (a term he rarely uses; for him it is intellect or imagination) as visionary, that is, constitutive of vision beyond the power of finite perception. At least some minds are capable of visionary perception, and possibly all minds can learn it. Thus he agrees with Berkeley that Locke is mistaken about perception, but he disagrees with Berkeley's abandonment of vision.

The matter may or may not become clearer with the next annotation. Berkeley remarks:

> Natural phaenomena are only natural appearances. They are, therefore, such as we see and perceive them. Their real and objective natures are, therefore, the same — passive without anything active, fluent and changing without anything

permanent in them. However, as these make the first impressions, and the mind takes her first flight and springs, as it were, by resting her foot on these objects, they are not only first considered by all men, but most considered by most men. They and the phantoms that result from those appearances, the children of imagination grafted upon sense, such for example as pure space, are thought by many the very first in existence and stability, and to embrace and comprehend all other beings [292].

There is a problem here that is partly semantic. Berkeley refers to "natural phenomena" in a Platonic way as products of perception that are impermanent and merely appearances. When Blake thinks of "nature" he thinks, on the one hand, of the Lockean primary qualities of experience separated from the secondary and, on the other hand, of experience as allegedly passively received by the senses. He rejects the reality of both the primary and secondary qualities and the distinction between them. Berkeley states that the imagination builds "phantoms" on such perceptions. His example is Newtonian pure abstract space. This would probably in Blake's view not be a phantom, unless there are phantoms that cannot be seen at all. It could not be a product of the imagination, being not a product of vision but only an imageless abstraction. Thus Blake's annotation must be read either as a misunderstanding or a criticism of Berkeley's statement, for Blake has written, "The All in Man The Divine Image or Imagination." He goes on to imply the identity of the senses (not Locke's senses) with imagination: "The Four Senses are the Four Faces of Man & the Four Rivers of the Water of Life" (E663). Two of the five senses, taste and touch, are here collapsed into one, bringing them into congruence with his own four Zoas and the biblical rivers out of Eden (Gen. 2:10) plus the river of Revelation 22:1, which are the waters of life. I suggest that Blake *may* have misread Berkeley, perhaps deliberately and wishfully here, for on the whole he seems to have agreed with Berkeley's criticism of Locke's form of empiricism.

Blake's next annotation draws a distinction between Plato and Aristotle, on the one hand, and Jesus, on the other. Berkeley has asserted that Plato and Aristotle considered God to be "abstracted or distinct from the world" (300). Blake distinguishes between the natural and the imaginative worlds, as he has earlier: "They also considerd God as abstracted or distinct from the Imaginative World but Jesus as also Abraham & David considerd God as a Man in the Spiritual or Imaginative Vision" (E663). This says that God can be *seen*, and Blake goes on to say that Jesus, in contrast to the Ancient Greeks considered "Imagination ... the Real Man" (E663), which suggests that the real man is all imaginative perception, constituting the world as he sees it. It is this human power to which Blake thinks Jesus alludes when he says, "I will manifest myself to you" (E 663). His appearance, after his crucifixion, to Mary Magdalene and then to his disciples and others Blake reads as an example of the imaginative power of those who saw. Innocent imagination being untrammeled by matter, Blake asserts that "little children always behold the Face of the Heavenly Father" (E 633). Blake, himself, had such an imaginative experience as a child. He regards them as truths not subject to *comparison* with visions of others, but rather expressive of metaphorical identity with the visions of others. In his *A Vision of the Last Judgment*, he writes: "The Last Judgment is one of these Stupendous Visions I have represented it as I saw it. to different People it appears differently as every thing else does" (E555).

Blake's next annotation returns to a criticism of abstractions that is more precise than Berkeley's. Berkeley has stated that human beings have a natural urge to rise above "our present sensual and low condition, into a state of light, order, and purity" (302). He then observes, "The perceptions of sense are gross; but even in the senses there is a difference. Though harmony and proportion are not objects of sense, yet the eye and the ear are organs which offer to the mind such materials by means whereof she may apprehend both the one and the other" (303). The statement is a little slippery, and Blake seizes on the notion that Berkeley may have made harmony and proportion into objects of sense after all. For Blake, they are "Qualities & Not Things" (E663). Everything — Blake offers horses and bulls, for example — have their own individual harmony and proportion, proper to their forms. The reality of each is its "Imaginative Form" (E664). This view, emphasizing the particularity of form to each thing, is expressed in Blake's attitude toward rules of art in his annotations to Reynolds's *Discourses*, where he asserts his opposition to judging one artist against another on the basis of some abstract notion of beauty by which all art is supposed to be judged.

Blake disagrees with Berkeley over how knowledge is gained and the role of reason. Berkeley writes, "By experiments of sense we become acquainted with the lower faculties of the soul, and from them, whether by a gradual evolution or ascent, we arrive at the highest. These become subjects for fancy to work upon. Reason considers and judges of the imaginations. And these acts of reason become new objects to the understanding" (303). Blake would not have liked Berkeley's introduction of "experiments" into his discussion, since for him it always leads to abstract generalization taken for truth. He is specifically concerned with Berkeley's view of the source of knowledge and the raising of reason above imagination, making it imagination's judge. That would disconnect knowledge from visionary perception. Therefore, he comments, "Knowledge is not by deduction but Immediate by Perception or Sense at once" (E664). He identifies man not with reason but imagination, as he thought Jesus did: "Christ addresses himself to Man not to his Reason" (E664).

As elsewhere, Blake is interested in distinguishing Jesus from Plato. In his annotations to Thornton's *The Lord's Prayer, Newly Translated*, he remarks, "If Morality was Christianity Socrates was The Savior" (ii, E667), a statement that occurs also in the so-called *Laocöon* (E275). Here, he writes of Jesus's emphasis on "Life and Immortality" (E664). For Blake, life *is* the activity of the imagination, and heaven is the world we are in if we see it with adequate imaginative power, just as immortality is *now*, every time and place being by synecdoche everything.

After Berkeley's favorable description of Plato as holding everything sensible to be fleeting and perishable, Blake reminds us, "Jesus supposes every Thing to be Evident to the Child & to the Poor & Unlearned. Such is the Gospel" (E664). His emphasis is on trust in the immediacy of experience; the Bible, he thinks, should be read in this way: "The Whole Bible is filld with Imaginations & Visions from End to End & not with Moral virtues. that is the baseness of Plato & the Greeks & all Warriors The Moral Virtues are continual Accusers of Sin & promote Eternal Wars & Domineering over others" (E 664). This view is fundamental with Blake. It identifies moral law with abstractions turned about to rule over imaginative perception, to reduce individuals to ciphers. Blake would have understood Jesus's irritation at the disciples when they could not understand his parable and he was forced to interpret it, abstracting from the immediacy of their experiencing it.

In these annotations, it is sometimes as if Blake is running a discourse oblique to Berkeley's, though alongside it. His comments seem not always directed toward what Berkeley has written. They are sometimes observations about views held by people Berkeley cites, thoughts brought to his mind. This is in contrast, for example, to his annotations to Reynolds's *Discourses*, which are almost always direct responses to what Reynolds has written.

The later annotations to Berkeley have to do with the views Berkeley attributes to Plato, Aristotle, and Aristotle's commentator Themistius. Aristotle, Berkeley writes, distinguishes the objects of physics, mathematics, and theology from one another: "Physics he supposeth to be conversant about such things as have a principle of motion in themselves, mathematics about things permanent but not abstracted, and theology about being abstracted and immoveable..." (307). Blake regards the remark as folly, since it seems to say that reason obliterates imagination: "God is not a Mathematical Diagram" (E664).

Berkeley describes Platonic philosophy as having "native inbred notions" (309), that is, in Lockean language, "innate ideas." Blake thought that man had at least the innate power to form ideas and said so in the Reynolds annotations. They are in the nature of his being and are what makes him what he is. However, this is not what Blake notes here. Rather, he observes, a "Natural Body is an Obstruction to the Soul or Spiritual Body" (E664), by which he means that the idea of a natural, material body gets in the way of imaginative experience and clear thought. Blake thinks that Berkeley's reference to "sensible occasions" in the following passage implies the actual objective existence of a material world:

> It is a maxim of the Platonic philosophy that the soul of Man was originally furnished with native inbred notions, and stands in need of sensible occasions, not absolutely for producing them, but only for awakening, rousing, or exciting into act what was already preexistent, dormant, and latent in the soul [309].

Blake certainly knows that Berkeley does not believe in the existence of a material world, but here Berkeley may be read to allow such a world to sneak in by implying a lower world of sense. When Berkeley writes of "sense," Blake may hear Locke.

The last annotations perform a summary. Berkeley has referred to Themistius on Aristotle's *De Anima*:

> ...according to Themistius in his commentary on that treatise, it may be inferred that all beings are in the soul. For, saith he, the forms are the beings. By the form every thing is what it is. And he adds, it is the soul that imparteth forms to matter [310].

Blake's response is at the heart of what is really his one disagreement with Berkeley: "This is my Opinion but Forms must be apprehended by Sense or the Eye of Imagination Man is All Imagination God is Man & exists in us & we in him" (E664). This is not Locke's passive sense, nor is it Berkeley's intellect. It is vision. A shapeless, imageless, mathematic Platonic form is anathema to Blake. However, he might have been receptive to Berkeley's remark, interpreting Themistius interpreting Aristotle: "... the mind is all things; taking the forms of all things, it becomes all things by intellect and sense" (310). But Blake would accept this only if Themistius meant that mind and sense are one and do not play different roles. For Blake, vision and intellect are one thing, as are God and man "in the Spiritual or Imaginative Vision" (E663).

At the end of *Siris*, Blake makes a comment that returns to his earlier contrast of Jesus to the Ancient Greek thinkers: "What Jesus came to Remove was the Heathen or Platonic Philosophy which blinds the Eye of Imagination The Real Man" (E664). A doctrine of imageless abstract forms leaves nothing for vision.

9

Annotations to William Wordsworth's *Poems* and Preface to *The Excursion*

Sometime in 1826, Henry Crabb Robinson lent to Blake his two volumes of the 1815 edition of William Wordsworth's poems.* It has been presumed that Blake is the person who marked a number of the poems with X to express his approval, though this is not known for certain. The marks could have been made by Robinson or someone else. It is, however, not uncharacteristic of Blake to make such marks, for he earlier did that in his copy of Lavater's *Aphorisms on Man* and elsewhere. Those marks were made in response to Lavater's invitation to all of his readers to do so. The practice seems not to have been uncommon at the time, even in books not one's own. It appears that books were now and then lent to acquaintances with the express desire that they annotate them. In addition to these marks, Blake made one annotation to the preface of the 1815 volumes and four to the "Essay Supplementary to the Preface," but none to the appended preface to the second edition of *Lyrical Ballads*. In 1826, Blake transcribed on four pieces of paper the last paragraph of Wordsworth's preface to *The Excursion* and 107 lines of the verse conclusion planned for the never written first book of *The Recluse*.†

All of our knowledge of Blake's opinion of Wordsworth comes from these annotations and Robinson's diary, reminiscences, and letters.§ To read only

---

*Poems by William Wordsworth: including Lyrical Ballads and the Miscellaneous Pieces of the author. With additional poems, a new preface, and a supplementary essay. 2 vols. London printed for Longman, Hurst, Rees, Orme, and Brown, Pater-Noster-Row, 1815. The copy that Blake annotated is in the Cornell University Library.

† *The Excursion, being a portion of the Recluse, a Poem by William Wordsworth*, London, Printed for Longman, Hurst, Rees, Orme, and Brown, Pater-Noster-Row, 1814. Blake's transcription is in Dr. Williams's Library, London. For mistakes or deliberate changes Blake made in copying, see E888. I give the text and page references as they are in the 1814 edition. The prose passage is on page x.

§Henry Crabb Robinson, *Diary, Reminiscences, and Correspondence*, selected and edited by

Blake's annotations is to take away but a partial sense of Blake's attitude toward Wordsworth, which in Robinson's account is far more favorable. According to Robinson, Blake "imperfectly knew" (324) Wordsworth's poetry until he had seen Robinson's volumes. Blake said to Robinson that Wordsworth was a "great man" (325) and that he was "the *only* poet of the age" (323). When Robinson offered to introduce him to Wordsworth, Blake responded with enthusiasm, but the meeting never took place. Wordsworth did, however, read some of Blake's poems, and, according to Robinson, the poems excited great interest in him.

The Marked Poems

If the X marks made to the poems are indeed Blake's, we may perhaps learn something more of Blake's taste than we get from his writings. I shall assume in the following discussion that they are, though the assumption may be wrong. The poems marked are as follows*:

"Lucy Gray," "We Are Seven," "The Blind Highland Boy," "The Brothers," "Strange Fits of Passion," "I met Louisa," "Ruth," "Michael, A Pastoral Poem," "Laodamia," "To the Daisy," "To the Small Celandine," "To the Cuckoo," "A Night Piece," "Yew Trees," She Was a Phantom," "I Wandered Lonely," "The Reverie of Poor Susan," "Yarrow Unvisited," "Yarrow Visited," "Resolution and Independence," "The Thorn," "Hart-leap Well," "Tintern Abbey," "Character of the Happy Warrior," "Rob Roy's Grave," "Expostulation and Reply," "The Tables Turned," "Ode to Duty," "The Old Cumberland Beggar," "Ode: Intimations of Immortality."

In addition, there are marks at the titles "Miscellaneous Sonnets" and "Sonnets Dedicated to Liberty."

There is enough here to make us think that Blake may well have been the person who marked the poems, for in almost all of them there is something that is likely to have pleased him. However, he would have enjoyed various poems for different reasons. It is clear from his remarks to Robinson that he could admire a poem even when he detected an attitude toward nature and a way of experiencing it with which he disagreed. Blake said to Robinson that Wordsworth was "often in his poems an *Atheist*. Now according to

---

[continued] Thomas Sadler, Ph.D. 2 vols, London: Macmillan and Co., 1869. There are some small differences between the entries in the actual diary and those in this volume, revised by Robinson. See G. E. Bentley, Jr's transcription of Robinson's remarks about Blake in the diary in *The Stranger from Paradise: A Biography of William Blake*, New Haven and London: Yale University Press, 2001, 411–19.

*The titles are as they are in the table of contents of the 1815 edition.

Blake, Atheism consists in worshipping the natural world, which same natural world, properly speaking, is nothing real, but a mere illusion produced by Satan" (323). Later Robinson reported, "Of Wordsworth Blake talked as before. Some of his writings proceed from the Holy Spirit, but others are the work of the Devil" (316). Making sense of this requires that we know what Blake meant by "nature" and "natural" as well as "Satan" and "Devil." In the annotations to Bacon, Blake remarks, "The Devil is the Mind of the Natural Frame," meaning that the Devil, as in the Swedenborg annotations, is an inner state of mind, the alien part of a mental reality (E625), and this view seems common to his later writings. I shall consider nature at some length a little later; it emerges from the annotations to Wordsworth as absolutely central to Blake's critical response.

Robinson wrote to Dorothy Wordsworth about Blake: "Dante and Wordsworth, in spite of their Atheism, were [according to Blake] inspired by the Holy Ghost. Indeed, all real poetry is the work of the Holy Ghost, and Wordsworth's poems (a large portion, at least) are the work of Divine inspiration. Unhappily he is left by God to his own illusions, and then the Atheism is apparent" (324). But Blake also said of Wordsworth, anticipating a possible meeting, "...he may convince me I am wrong about him; I have been wrong before now" (325).

It appears that Blake responded favorably to the spirit of the old English ballads and to poems written in that spirit by Wordsworth. In her careful comparative study of Blake and Wordsworth, Heather Glen rightly points out that Blake's *Songs of Innocence and of Experience* "stands at a curiously oblique angle to the official morality of its time. ... [T]hese poems seem deliberately designed to disconcert such a reader's impulses toward secure moral generalization."* In her view, Wordsworth's *Lyrical Ballads* are more straightforward than Blake's, even though they were disconcerting to readers of the time. With two exceptions, the balladic and narrative poems of Wordsworth that Blake marked allow the story to be its own message and in their way confound easy readerly conclusions: "The Brothers," "Michael," "The Thorn," and "The Blind Highland Boy." The exceptions are "Hart-leap Well" and "The Old Cumberland Beggar," in both of which a moral is explicitly offered. All hark back in spirit if not in strict form to an earlier age that produced balladic narratives. It is well-known that as an artist Blake was partial to things medieval. He championed Macpherson's Ossian poems and Chatterton's Rowley poems.

*Heather Glen, *Vision and Disenchantment: Blake's Songs and Wordsworth's* Lyrical Ballads, Cambridge: Cambridge University Press, 1983, 110. This book has fine readings of poems in both collections as well as interesting information about contemporary taste.

In his "Essay Supplementary to the Preface" (of 1815), Wordswoth expended considerable space subjecting Macpherson to criticism, beginning with ridicule:

> All hail, Macpherson! hail to thee, Sire of Ossian! The Phantom was begotten by the smug embrace of an impudent Highlander upon a cloud of tradition — it traveled southward, where it was greeted with acclamation, and the thin Consistence took its course through Europe, upon the breath of popular applause [I, 363].

Wordsworth proceeds to complain that the allegedly blind (but only with age) poet Ossian could not have written the lines of visual description in the text. Basing his argument on his own experience as a child living in mountainous country, he regards the imagery as "spurious":

> In nature everything is distinct, yet nothing defined into absolute independent singleness. In Macpherson's work it is exactly the reverse; everything (that is not stolen) is in this manner defined, insulated, dislocated deadness,—yet nothing distinct. It will always be so when words are substituted for things [I, 364].

Furthermore, the descriptions are often of physical impossibilities. Given the nature of the terrain, the poetry contains a mélange of borrowings. The supposed translation is "a motley assemblance from all quarters" (I, 364).

Quite solemnly and with no invective, Blake writes, "I Believe both Macpherson & Chatterton that what they say is Ancient, Is so" (E665). A little further on, Wordsworth writes of Ossian, "...much as those pretended treasures of antiquity have been admired, they have been wholly uninfluential upon the literature of the Country. No succeeding writer appears to have caught from them a ray of inspiration; no author in the least distinguished, has ventured formally to imitate them,— except the boy Chatterton, on their first appearance" (I, 365). Wordsworth goes on to contrast the Ossian poems, to their detriment, to Bishop Percy's *Reliques*. All of this causes Blake to assert, "I own myself an admirer of Ossian equally with any other Poet whatever Rowley & Chatterton also" (E666). Blake's straightforward remarks may be read in the light of his view of what is genuine and his statement that comparison of the value of poets is futile. The view is expressed in the annotation to "To H. C.": "This is all in the highest degree Imaginative & equal to any Poet but not superior I cannot think that Real Poets have any competition None are greatest in the Kingdom of Heaven it is so in Poetry" (43, E665). Genuine poetic power and historical authenticity are two different things. Peter F. Fisher asserts that Blake was "not the least interested in documentary authenticity" and cites Blake's jeering criticism (in his annotations to Watson's *Apology for the Bible*, above, p. 77) of the veracity of public records.* Blake's claim in his discussion of his lost painting "The Ancient Britons" that the "British Antiquities are now in the Artist's [Blake's] hands" suggests that true history is "visionary contemplations" (E542), not naked documents. The defense of Ossian and Chatterton's Rowley poems is in line with Blake's deep interest in the ancient Druids and his visionary appropriation of the popular but wildly inaccurate contemporary lore about them.

Blake may have been interested in some of Wordsworth's poems because they touch on innocence and experience: "We Are Seven," "To H. C.," and "Ruth." He also seems to have thought well of a group of Wordsworth's earlier sonnets contained in the sections called "Miscellaneous Sonnets" and "Sonnets Dedicated to Liberty." No doubt, he responded favorably because of the political views implied. What he, as a self-described "liberty boy," would have thought of the reactionary political turn of the later sonnets we can probably guess.

Most important, we can speculate on Blake's response to the moments of visionary experience that appear in Wordsworth's poetry. He responded to them positively even though they exhibit some significant differences from what Blake called vision. There is something fleeting, sometimes illusory or ghostlike, in them. Optical illusions figure prominently in "Strange Fits of Passion" and "Influence of Natural Objects" (Blake responded negatively to the title of this poem). "Phantom" and "phantasy" characterize the vision in "She Was a Phantom" and "Yew Trees," as if to suggest illusion again or at least something not retained in vision. In "A Night Piece" and "The Reverie of Poor Susan" the vision passes away. In "To H. C." the vision becomes fraught with worry. In "Resolution and Independence," the speaker's vision of the leech-gatherer is troubling, but memory of it will generate a moral lesson. For Blake, a Wordsworthian memory is not a renewed vision; it is something thought *upon*, an abstraction from a vanished past experience. In the preface to the second edition of *Lyrical Ballads*, Wordsworth, in a well-known passage, says of this, "I have said that poetry is the spontaneous overflow of powerful feelings: it takes its origin from emotion recollected in tranquillity: the emotion is contemplated till, by a species of reaction, the tranquillity gradually disappears, and an emotion, kindred to that which was before the subject of contemplation, is gradually produced, and does itself actually exist in the mind" (II, 387–8). We do not know for certain that Blake

---

*Peter F. Fisher, "Blake and the Druids," *Journal of English and Germanic Philology* 58: 4 (October 1959, 589–612). See also Fisher, *The Valley of Vision: Blake as Prophet and Revolutionary*, Toronto: University of Toronto Press, 1961, esp. pp. 32–53.

had read this. He probably had. It is fair to say, in any case, that he would have regarded "emotion" as a word that abstracts from the vision a subjective feeling now detached and thus alienated from what Wordsworth calls its origin.

Yet Blake was much moved when Robinson read aloud "Ode: Intimations of Immortality from Recollections of Early Childhood." During his reading, Robinson recalls, "I never witnessed greater delight in any listener; and in general Blake loves the poems" (324). However, that poem laments a visionary glory permanently lost, and we might speculate over whether Blake would have resisted this, even though Wordsworth finds in its stead a "primal sympathy," of which Blake would probably have approved. He may or may not have accepted the "philosophic mind" that Wordsworth finds as a recompense. Blake would, nevertheless, probably have been moved by the speaker's recovery of a relation to the world, distanced as it may be; and he probably recognized the poem's neo–Platonic imagery, which appears occasionally in his own work, in addition to the theme of innocence and experience. Robinson remarked that Blake especially liked the parts of the immortality ode that were to Robinson most obscure.

Blake seems also to have liked Wordsworth's poems of address to flowers, "To the Daisy" and "To the Small Celandine," for they, along with "To the Cuckoo," imply a sympathetic identification similar to that in some of the *Songs of Innocence*. In the last of these, the cuckoo brings a "tale of visionary hours," lost and regained, but this restoration brings also the appearance of an "unsubstantial faery place" quite in contrast to Blake's insistence that visionary experience is clear and well-defined. In "To the Daisy" the vision is vague, fleeting, and identified with

> An instinct call it, a blind sense;
> A happy, genial influence,
> Coming one knows not how, nor whence,
> Nor whither going [I, 239].

It is a vision in direct contrast to that claimed by Blake, who is always confident of the source and clarity of his own. In almost every case, Wordsworth's reader is moved by a melancholy not characteristic of Blake's work. In the immortality ode, vision ebbs into adulthood and sober thoughts "that do often lie too deep for tears." Wordsworth implies loss and sadness. Blake insists on the persistence of vision, and when he thinks it is warranted (and he often does when he looks at the society around him) he does not hold back anger.

Vision, Imagination, Nature

Blake's criticism of Wordsworth's poems is based on his notion of three words: "vision" and "imagination," which always have positive connotations, and a word he usually employs negatively, "nature." However, Blake seems tacitly to accept Wordsworth's use of "nature" when it does not explicitly refer to an otherness or what Blake thinks of as a lifeless abstraction. His apparent acceptance occurs when nature is treated as a living, benevolent spirit, as in "Strange Fits of Passion" or "Michael, A Pastoral Poem," where the "gentle agent of natural objects" is invoked, or the "natural temple" of "Yew Trees," or nature's "presence" in "Tintern Abbey."

At the beginning of the section of poems titled "Poems Referring to the Period of Childhood," Blake writes: "I see in Wordsworth the Natural Man rising up against the Spiritual Man Continually & then he is No Poet but a Heathen Philosopher at Enmity against all true Poetry or Inspiration" (I,1, E665). It is important to recognize the presence of the word "then" in this annotation. It is *when* the natural man rises up, as he is "continually" doing, to invade parts of the poems, that Wordsworth ceases to be a poet. This seems to mean that there are occasional Satanic insurrections in poems otherwise "true Poetry."

Three other annotations have to do with Blake's criticism of the "continual" rising up of the "Natural Man" in Wordsworth's writing:

> One Power alone makes a Poet.— Imagination The Divine Vision [I, viii, E665]
>
> There is no such Thing as Natural Piety Because The Natural Man is at Enmity with God [I, 3, E665]
>
> Natural Objects always did & now do Weaken deaden & obliterate Imagination in Me Wordsworth must know that what he Writes Valuable is Not to be found in Nature Read Michael Angelos Sonnet vol 2 p. 179* [I, 44, E665]

This third annotation is explained by a remark Blake made to Trusler in a letter of August 23, 1799: "The tree which moves some to tears of joy is in the Eyes of others only a Green thing that stand in the way" (E702). The latter is but a natural object, the former a vision.

It is worthwhile to expend here at some length an effort, in relation to, almost in summary of, all Blake's annotations, to discuss Blake's views as they

---

*This is the second of three poems that Wordsworth translated from Michelangelo and contains the lines: "Heaven-born, the Soul a heavenward course must hold; / Beyond the visible world She soars to seek / (For what delights the sense is false and weak) / Ideal Form, the universal mould" (II, 179). What Blake must have appreciated here is that the speaker sees into or beyond the "mortal object" to its reality. Blake would not have read "Ideal Form" as Platonic but as something available to vision, possessing an image.

are expressed in the three words "vision," "imagination," and "nature," introduced above. I begin by making two points: First, Blake was a professional engraver and visual artist, and most of his mentions of imagination have to do with visual art. His was an engraver's and painter's imagination, and for him imagination was connected literally to sight. But sight was not an adequate word for what he had in mind. He offers the word "vision," which contains much more than Locke's passive reception of sense data. Second, in his long poems, Blake was a maker of chains of metaphor that, if followed out, imply the identification of all things with each other. Thus there are no *separate* objects as such. This characteristic of his poetry has a limited parallel in his critical writings, where imagination implies vision, vision implies inspiration, inspiration implies intellect, and intellect implies imagination.

To say, however, that Blake's notion of imagination was grounded in sight requires that we understand just what he meant by vision. It may be well to remind ourselves that his generation and the poets he read had more spatially oriented imaginations than did the Romantics. The notions of imitation and *ut pictura poeisis* still had life in criticism. It is important to observe just how literally connected with seeing Blake's notion of vision was and how important for him "image" was in the word "imagination." In the letter to Trusler, Blake also writes, "This world is a world of Imagination & Vision I see Everything I paint in this World.... Some See Nature all Ridicule & Deformity & by these I shall not regulate my proportions, & Some Scarce see Nature at all But to the Eyes of the Man of Imagination *Nature is Imagination itself*" (my italics) (E702). The italicized phrase is central to Blake's thought. It states that there is no barrier between the person seeing and the so-called object of sight, that there is no such thing as objectivity or subjectivity except as a fiction of reason. This view leads to Blake's vigorous rejection of Wordsworth's lines in the preface to *The Recluse*:

> How exquisitely the individual Mind
> (And the progressive powers perhaps no less
> Of the whole species) to the external World
> Is fitted:— and how exquisitely, too —
> Theme this but little heard of among men —
> The external World is fitted to the Mind [p. xiii, ll. 63–8].

Blake is unyielding here: "You shall not bring me down to believe such fitting & fitted I know better & Please your Lordship" (E666–7). Here sarcasm directed at Wordsworth's tendency toward pomposity speaks out. One might think that the phrase "external World is fitted to the Mind" might possibly have been acceptable, but although it makes mind dominant, it is still inadequate for Blake. It gives externality a separate and alien existence.

This matter of fitting and fitted comes up again for Blake a few lines later in the preface to *The Recluse*:

> — Such grateful haunts foregoing, if I oft
> Must turn elsewhere — to travel near the tribes
> And fellowships of men, and see ill sights
> Of madding passions mutually inflamed;
> Must hear Humanity in fields and groves
> Pipe solitary anguish; or must hang
> Brooding above the fierce confederate storm
> Of sorrow, barricadoed evermore
> Within the walls of Cities; may these sounds
> Have their authentic comment, — that even these
> Hearing, I be not downcast or forlorn! [p. xiii, ll.71–81].

Blake apparently admires the lines, but he dislikes the content, which he takes to refer to a material world alien to the perceiver: "does not this Fit & is it not Fitting most Exquisitely too but to what not to Mind but to the Vile Body only & to its Laws of Good & Evil & its Enmities against Mind" (E667). The vile body is that which is abstracted into sheer matter.

Wordsworth's passage may well have reminded Blake of his own treatment of the travels of Urizen in a natural world in Night Six of *The Four Zoas*:

> For Urizen beheld the terrors of the Abyss wandring among
> The ruind spirits once his children & the children of Luvah
> Scard at the sound of their own sigh that seems to shake the immense....
> no one answerd every one wrapd up
> In his own sorrow howld regardless of his words... [E347]

Blake seems to find the Wordsworth of the preface to *The Recluse* a Urizen figure, as he seems to also in an earlier passage from that work:

> ...Urania, I shall need
> Thy guidance, or a greater Muse, if such
> Descend to earth or dwell in highest heaven!
> For I must tread on shadowy ground, must sink
> Deep — and, aloft ascending, breathe in worlds
> To which the heaven of heavens is but a veil.
> All strength — all terror, single or in bands,
> That ever was put forth in personal form —
> Jehovah — with his thunder, and the choir
> Of shouting Angels, and the empyreal thrones —
> I pass them unalarmed [at end of the manuscript page of Blake's transcription; from p. xi, ll. 25–35, E666].

Robinson reports that the preface very much bothered Blake: "... he told me, six months ago, that it caused a stomach complaint that nearly killed him. When I first saw Blake at Mrs. Aders' he very earnestly asked me, 'Is Mr.

Wordsworth a sincere, real Christian?' In reply to my answer, he said, 'If so, what does he mean by the worlds to which the heaven of heavens is but a veil? And who is he that shall pass Jehovah unalarmed?'" (324).

Blake's annotation, written at the end of his manuscript, is as follows:

> Solomen when he married Pharohs daughter & became a Convert to the Heathen Mythology talked exactly in this way of Jehovah as a very inferior object of Mans Contemplations he also passed him by unalarmd & was permitted. Jehovah dropped a tear & followd him by his Spirit into the Abstract Void it is called the Divine Mercy Satan dwells in it but Mercy does not dwell in him he knows not to Forgive [E666]

The reference is to 1 Kings 3.1 and 11.1–8, but there is no report in 1 Kings or in Chronicles of Solomon talking in this way. The Lord drops no tear. He is angry with Solomon:

> 9. And the Lord was angry with Solomon, because his heart was turning from the Lord God of Israel, which had appeared to him twice,
> 10. And had commanded him concerning this thing, that he should not go after other gods: but he kept not that which the Lord commanded.
> 11. Wherefore the Lord said unto Solomon, Forasmuch as this is done of thee, and thou hast not kept my covenant and my statutes, which I have commanded thee, I will surely rend the kingdom from thee, and will give it to thy servant.

This is the Old Testament Jehovah speaking, not the Jehovah of Jesus. Blake converts him into the latter. A merciful God follows Solomon into the "abstract void," a natural world into which he has fallen, and rescues him. Perhaps Blake's reading of 2 Chronicles, which skips over Solomon's later heathenism, led him to the notion of the Lord's forgiveness.

The fundamental way to consider Blake's statements about vision is epistemologically. In his poem *Milton*, Blake has Milton say he has come "to cast off Bacon, Locke & Newton from Albion's covering/To take off his filthy garments, & clothe him with Imagination" (E142). This is to reject the epistemology of subject and object and introduce a way of seeing that frees the mind from the abstract fiction of an independent object lacking, for Locke, the so-called secondary qualities of perception. Locke isolates those qualities from the real. Blake identifies nature with this dull objectivity. Nature is the deluding product of a faith solely in what Blake calls "general knowledge," and it is not often that Blake uses "nature" in any other way. When Blake sees in Wordsworth "the Natural man rising up against the Spiritual man Continually," "Spiritual" means the appropriate way of seeing, literally of vision. It has little, if anything, to do with mysticism as we usually think if it. Nature became for Blake the external world, unreal when regarded as apart from or even "fitted" to man. It was constructed by the dominant philosophy of the time and projected as an other. This is the nature that is the "Ridicule & Deformity" of Blake's letter to Trusler.

It is also a mistaken view of what it is to see. For Blake, the material eye as a source of vision is a delusion. We do not see passively. Our minds see *through* the eye in two senses: see through it if one is still to speak *as if* there were a material body separate from mind; see through it in the sense of recognizing it as a delusion of matter. The truth is that when the so-called outer world is seen, it is the projection of an active intellect. Imagination is intellectual, and the act is an act of imaging. In the same letter to Trusler, Blake refers to what he calls "Spiritual Sensation" (E703), a phrase he did not ever use again, probably because of "sensation's" connections to the notion of passive reception of sense data. Blake regards spirit as intellectual, rejecting such separations as reason/emotion.

But all people do not imagine the world in the same way. Some people have weak imaginations. The "greatest of all Blessings," Blake remarks, is "a strong imagination, a clear idea, and a determinate vision" (E693). Some minds see more intensely and therefore more clearly than others, but even equally strong imaginations will see things differently. In a description of his "Last Judgment," Blake writes that the Last Judgment "is seen by the Imaginative Eye of Every one according to the situation he holds" (E554).* Great artists see alike, that is, intellectually and actively rather than copying or recording a passive response of sense; yet their visions will be individual, different, though metaphorically related. Art does not improve; situations vary and change. Genius, as in the annotation to "To H. C.," can be equaled but not surpassed.

Proper seeing, or vision, as I shall call it henceforth, is grounded for Blake on clarity, which is achieved by intense concentration. There should be nothing mysterious about it. Blake rarely uses "mystery" in an honorific sense. He usually thought of it as something imposed by a priesthood or an elite in order to maintain power, and religion should be devoid of it. For him, the most important thing in art is outline and "attention to minute particulars":

> A Spirit and a Vision are not, as the modern philosophy supposes, a cloudy vapour or a nothing; they are organized and minutely articulated beyond all that a mortal and perishing nature can produce. He who does not imagine in stronger and better lineaments, and in stronger and better light than his perishing mortal eye can see does not imagine at all [E541].

---

*"Imaginative Eye" was deleted by Blake, but it does fit the statement fairly well, except that Blake thought it is the mind, not the "mortal" eye, that is the imaginative power.

9. Wordsworth's Poems and Preface to The Excursion

The passage implies a remarkable intensity of vision that seems to have been characteristic of Blake's activity when he drew what are called his "visionary heads." Allan Cunningham, one of Blake's earliest biographers, tells a story, perhaps somewhat embellished, about Blake that informs us of his practice:

> He was requested to draw the likeness of William Wallace — the eye of Blake sparkled, for he admired heroes. "William Wallace!" he exclaimed, "I see him now, there, there, how noble he looks — reach me my things!" Having drawn for some time, with the same care of hand and steadiness of eyes, as if a living sitter had been before him, Blake stopped suddenly and said, "I cannot finish him — Edward the First has stepped between him and me.*

This passage suggests a discipline of creative vision that required projection of an image (as on a blank wall) and then drawing it. When Blake said he copied imagination I think he meant something like this. If another vision gets in the way, the first vision is suspended. (Blake was having some fun here, in that Wallace was the frustrating Scottish foe of Edward I.)

All of Blake's likes and dislikes in painting, and they are vigorously expressed, arise from his emphasis on intensity and clarity of vision (we can notice that a professional engraver might very well emphasize the importance of outline): "Nature has no Outline: but Imagination has" (E270); and if there is no "determinate and bounding form" (E550), there is no "idea in the artist's mind" (E550). Copying nature ends up with only what the material eyes can see. Rubens as an influence is a "most outrageous demon" (E547) who leads followers to "blotting and blurring" (546). Chiaroscuro is an "infernal machine" (E547). The mortal eye, with which these styles work, is caught up in a flux of time and cannot seize intellectually on anything and fix it clearly in vision. Over and over, Blake's long poems emphasize proper mental vision. In *Jerusalem*, for example, Blake views time as a huge visual pattern, and elsewhere he chastises historians for reasoning on events. They should present acts for all to visualize, not theories about acts (E544). Acts alone are real, and anything that is not an action is not worth reading (E544).

Blake presents his own version of what Sir Philip Sidney treated as a poetic improvement on nature. One difference is that Sidney thinks of beautification, while Blake thinks of clarification. The latter is a different sort of improvement in that it is composed of inventions of "Intellectual Vision" (E704) that can go beyond what the mortal eye can see. Thus Blake complains that what he also calls the "corporeal" eye, separated from imagination, sees not only passively but also dully:

---

*Allan Cunningham, *Lives of the Most Eminent British Painters* (rev. ed. 1830), quoted by Mona Wilson, *The Life of William Blake*, London: Rupert Hart-Davis, 1948, 271.

> What it will be Questiond When the Sun rises do you not see a round Disk of fire somewhat like a Guinea O no no I see an Innumerable company of the Heavenly Host crying Holy Holy Holy is the Lord God Almighty I question not my Corporeal or Vegetative Eye any more than I would Question a Window concerning a Sight [E565–566].

Here Blake makes Swedenborg's spiritual sun and its reality into a product of creative imagination. In his description of an illustration he made to Milton's "L'Allegro," Blake speaks of "The youthful Poet sleeping on a bank by the Haunted Stream by Sun Set [who] sees in his Dream the more bright Sun of Imagination" (E684), but one does not have to dream to imagine; one can do it consciously looking through the eyes. Indeed, the imagination is not a state of mind that one turns on and off: Blake remarks, "It is the Human Existence itself" (E132); and he holds in his annotations to Berkeley's *Siris*, "Jesus considerd Imagination to be the Real Man" (above, p. 156, E663). The sun of the passages I have offered is not an allegorical image standing for an abstract idea. It is a visionary idea, not a substitute for a Platonic one. It is what it is and refers only to itself. As such, it communicates vision to the reader or viewer who identifies with it in a way that would be impossible with a mere external object. Writing about his "Last Judgment," Blake remarks,

> If the Spectator could Enter into these Images in his Imagination approaching them on the Fiery Chariot of his Contemplative Thought if he could Enter into Noahs Rainbow or into his bosom or could make a Friend & Companion of one of these Images of wonder which always entreats him to leave mortal things as he must know then would he arise from his Grave then would he meet the Lord in the Air & then he would be happy General Knowledge is Remote Knowledge it is in particulars that Wisdom consists & Happiness too [E560].

Blake makes an important distinction between what he calls the daughters of imagination and the daughters of memory. They are the true and false muses respectively. Inspired by the daughters of memory, a painter is "confined to the sordid drudgery of facsimile representations of merely mortal and perishing substances" (E541). "Walking in another man's style, or speaking or looking in another man's style and manner" (E547) is the same. An art based on memory cannot create, only copy and mirror the false knowledge of the passive subject.

More than an improvement on nature, indeed a denial of it, vision at its greatest intensity sees potentially into the infinite in a thing. But Blake's infinite is not a Platonic realm without image; it is the "regions of my imagination" (E705). Every moment, like every so-called piece of matter, is a window into it. The fundamental principle of imagination is the synecdoche:

> To see a World in a Grain of Sand
> And a Heaven in a Wild Flower
> Hold Infinity in the palm of your hand
> And Eternity in an hour [E493]

These are by no means casual lines. Infinity is the largest and the infinitesimal is the smallest of things, and they are identical in the sense that two sides of such tropes include both sameness and difference. Synecdoche supports Blake's notion of the individuality and yet communality (by that trope) of what imagination creates. "This World of Imagination [with its attention to the minute particular] is the World of Eternity" (E555). In the religion of imagination or the proper imagining of religion, the savior is the imagination; and the imagination is the savior. It is what saves us from a living death in the world of vegetable nature. Jesus is the spirit and power of imagination in man, no more no less. There is "no other Gospel than the liberty both of body & mind to exercise the Divine Arts of Imagination" (E231). The historical Jesus is of no importance to this view. He is an Antichrist. The Jesus of the Gospels lives only in the presentness of those books and only there and now. He never simply *was*. The past is an imaginative creation in the present of reading.

Every artistic imagination produces according to its own individuality what "Eternally Exists" (E554). A string of metaphorical identities relates all things. In *Jerusalem* there is described a receptacle of all that can be imagined and can occur:

> All things acted on Earth are seen in the bright Sculptures of
> Los's Halls & every Age renews its powers from these Works
> With every pathetic story possible to happen from Hate or
> Wayward Love & every sorrow & distress is carved here
> Every affinity of Parents Marriages & Friendships are here
> In all their various combinations wrought with wondrous Art
> All that can happen to Man in his pilgrimage of seventy years [E161]

This is the collective imagination of all art, which belongs by synecdoche to every visionary act in all of time. The apocalyptic act in *Jerusalem* is a vision: "All Human Forms identified even Tree Metal Earth & Stone" (E258). "Identified" here means both named and made identical by metaphorical relation.

Blake held Chaucer in high regard, and he describes Chaucer's pilgrims as "Visions of ... eternal principles or characters of human life" that "appear to poets, in all ages" (E536). Blake remarks that Gray's vision of eternal characters can be seen "in the person of his bard on Snowden" (E543). Every great artist enters in vision into this place, which is seen according to his or her situation. To enter it does not require servile allegiance to prior models, but to one's own individuality. Blake must have accepted Wordsworth's defense in the 1800 preface of at least some aspects of his practice. Beyond these images, each unique, but also metaphorically identical, art does not, need not, and indeed cannot not go.

But there is always danger if these humanly made images are erected into gods, or even one god, and given divine names. As such, they become destructive to humanity, for properly "All deities reside in the human breast" (E38). Objectified, they are no better and probably worse than kings, though as we see from the annotations to Bacon kings are very bad. So, too, for gods. For Blake, even Jesus is an imaginative creation. But it is a misfortune that, as Blake says, "The Nature of Visionary Fancy or Imagination is very little Known & the Eternal nature and permanence of its ever Existent Images is considerd as less permanent than the things of Vegetative & Generative Nature" (E555).

W. B. Yeats wrote of Blake that he was a "too literal realist of the imagination." For a chapter title in his *Fearful Symmetry*, Northrop Frye shortened the phrase to "literalist of the imagination."* He was right to do so. Frye was writing a book of literary criticism, and he was right also to have argued elsewhere that "literal" ought to have something to do with "literary" rather than its opposite. If that is the case, a poet cannot be too literal, and the real is what imagination literally envisions, intellectually and spiritually. It is not nature passively received or "fitted to the mind."

Who Wrote These Prefaces?

Blake was apparently not moved to comment in the margins of the preface to the second edition of *Lyrical Ballads* (1800). He could well have expressed his dislike of general knowledge, as he had in the annotations to Reynolds's *Discourses*. Wordsworth writes, "[Poetry's] object is truth, not individual and local, but general and operative" (II, 378). Blake, with faith in metaphor, denies the distinction. There was plenty of opportunity to dissent from Wordsworth's remarks on nature, for example his reference to what he called the "real language of nature," whatever, in Blake's view, that could possibly be. Or the following: "the image of man and nature" (II, 378). Or "[The poet] considers man and nature as essentially adapted to each other, and the

---

*W. B. Yeats, "William Blake and His Illustrations to *The Divine Comedy*" (1897), *Ideas of Good and Evil*, in *Essays and Introductions*, London and Stratford-on-Avon, 1903, 127. Northrop Frye, *Fearful Symmetry: A Study of William Blake*, Princeton, NJ: Princeton University Press, 1947, 85–107.

mind of man as naturally the mirror of the fairest and most interesting properties of nature" (II, 380).

What Blake does do is question ironically whether Wordsworth himself was the author of the prefaces. At the beginning of the "Essay Supplementary to the Preface," he wrote, "I do not know who wrote these Prefaces they are very mischievous & direct contrary to Wordsworth's own Practise" (341, E665). This statement is, of course, playful, even as it is serious. Blake implies that there are two Wordsworths, one visionary and one possessed of the Devil, who is "the mind of the natural frame" (annotations to Bacon, E625). At the end of the essay, he speculates that even a third author may have intervened and written the last paragraph:

> It appears to me as if the last Paragraph beginning With "Is it the result" Was writ by another hand & mind from the rest of these Prefaces. Perhaps they are the opinions of Sr G Beaumont a Landscape Painter Imagination is the Divine Vision not of The World nor of Man nor from Man as he is a Natural Man but only as he is a Spiritual Man Imagination has nothing to do with Memory [375, E666].

Wordsworth has taken up the question of whether "the judgment of the People is not to be respected" (I, 374). He has already argued that every great and original author has to "create the taste by which he is to be enjoyed" (I, 368). Now he distinguishes between the People and the Public. He argues that the People have spoken in the past and continue to speak and as a result good poetry survives through their intellect and wisdom. The Public, by contrast, is "that small though loud portion of the community, ever governed by factitious influence, which, under the name of the PUBLIC, passes itself, upon the unthinking, for the PEOPLE" (I, 374). One would not be surprised if, upon reading this, Blake thought of Robert Hunt's scathing review of his 1809 exhibition. Blake must have approved of the distinction Wordsworth made, given his own problems with those he surely thought governed by "factitious influence." But Blake, enamored of neither landscape nor portrait painting, nevertheless attributes these words to such a painter. This third author is apparently not the person Blake thinks couldn't have written the poems because the views set forth sometimes clash with the practice. This is someone who, though not the kind of painter Blake is and perhaps a "natural man," at least mentions "Vision and the Faculty Divine" and does not here glorify memory. Memory, in Blake's view, is the result of the fading of vision into abstraction. This is not Hobbes's or Hume's idea of memory, which is a different kind of imagination, and not worthy of the name, for its result is either decayed or in a lesser degree than the so-called original. Neither of these philosophers begins with Blake's idea of either vision or imagination of something greater than passive sense can produce.

In the 1815 preface, Wordsworth begins with a listing of the "powers requisite for the production of poetry" (I, viii). They are observation and description, sensibility, reflection, imagination and fancy, invention, and judgment. Imagination and fancy are the power "to modify, to create, and to associate." Later in the preface he distinguishes imagination from fancy: "Imagination ... has no reference to images that are merely a faithful copy, existing in the mind, of absent external objects; but is a word of higher import denoting operations of the mind upon those objects, and processes of creation or of composition, governed by certain fixed laws" (I, xx–xxi). Blake would probably have liked this up to the mention of objects as external to the mind's activity and of the limitations of imagination to governance by fixed laws, whatever they might be. At this point, one of the other Wordsworths has insinuated himself. Nor would Blake have liked the notion, later offered, of imagination as an "abstracting" or "endowing" or "modifying" power. What would it abstract *from*; what would it *endow*; what would it *modify*? All would imply something objective over and against a subject, something sensed and in the act changed from its real state. Blake was impatient enough with all of this to make the annotation we have already seen: "One Power alone makes a Poet.— Imagination The Divine Vision" (viii, E665).

Resolution

If the Xs are Blake's, he marks favorably certain poems that he must have liked because they give value to perseverance and steady commitment, even though they are quite different from his own poems depicting such matters. They are, at least in some passages, explicitly didactic: "Resolution and Independence," "The Old Cumberland Beggar," "Character of the Happy Warrior," and "Ode to Duty."

Blake's commitment to his art under dire circumstances and in the face of severe judgment could only have been fraught with moments of discontent, similar to the dark moment that Wordsworth describes in "Resolution and Independence":

> WORDSWORTH: "But, as it sometimes chanceth, from the might
> Of joy in minds that can no farther go,
> As high as we have mounted in delight
> In our dejection do we sink as low" [II, 28].
>
> BLAKE: "Tuesday Janry. 20. 1807 between Two and Seven in the Evening—Despair" [E694]
>
> WORDSWORTH: "'God,' said I, 'be my help and stay secure';
> I'll think of the Leech-gatherer on the lonely moor" [II, 34].
>
> BLAKE: "23 May 1810 found the Word Golden" [E695]

10

Annotations to Robert John Thornton's *The Lord's Prayer, Newly Translated*

Robert John Thornton (1768–1837) is best known for his published but unfinished botanical work, *Temple of Flora, or Garden of Nature, Picturesque Botanical Plates of the new Illustration of the Sexual System of Linnaeus* (1799–1807). Inspired by lectures on botany that he attended as a student in Trinity College, Cambridge, he set forth on a career in medicine, botany being part of the medical curriculum at the time. In 1797, at age 29, Thornton inherited the family fortune, abandoned in the main his medical practice, and began what he planned to be a three-volume work titled *A New Illustration of the Sexual System of Carolus von Linnaeus*, inventor of the binomial system of classification of plants. The third volume, the only one published, became *Temple of Flora*. It was to have been a book of some 90 images with text, but the work as it finally appeared in 1807, water-colored from engravings based on paintings by prominent botanical artists, contained only 29 to 33 images, depending on the copy. Thornton bankrupted himself trying to complete the edition, even attempting in 1812 to raise funds by sponsoring something to be called the Royal Botanical Lottery, the first prize of which was to be a quarto version of all the plates. The effort was a failure. Thornton lost his fortune and died destitute. *Temple of Flora* had a considerable influence for some time, but it became regarded as of little or no botanical value, though it was praised for its artistic value.

Blake's connection with Thornton was at least threefold. He was introduced to Thornton sometime in 1818 by the painter John Linnell.* They met

*On the Blake-Thornton relationship see G. E. Bentley, Jr., *The Stranger from Paradise: A Biography of William Blake*, New Haven and London: Yale University Press, 2001, 383, 388–392.

several times thereafter. Certainly Blake knew of *Temple of Flora*, though it is not mentioned in his extant writings. He does refer to Linnaeus in his *Descriptive Catalogue* of 1809: "... as Linnaeus numbered the plants, so Chaucer numbered the classes of men" (E 533); and he may have been led to make this comparison by his acquaintance with Thornton's book.

Thornton commissioned Blake to execute a series of woodcuts for his edition of Virgil's *Eclogues*, a series very highly regarded by the young artists who knew and revered Blake. Thornton was, however, uncertain about their quality and had to be convinced by others to use them. Today they are regarded as small masterpieces.

Finally, in 1827, the year of his death, Blake annotated a copy of Thornton's translation of the Lord's Prayer.* Whether Blake had begun to feel hostility toward Thornton over the woodcuts or for some other reason is unknown. We know that he and Thornton were of opposite political convictions. Thornton was deeply conservative in all things, an avowed royalist, and an avid hater of the French Revolution. Blake's antipathy toward Thornton's pamphlet, expressed in the annotations, was political. In any case, the prayer and Thornton's accompanying notes roused in him a response that included bitter parody.

Versions of the Lord's Prayer

Below are transcriptions of the Lord's Prayer as it appears according to St. Matthew and then St. Luke in the King James Bible. These are followed by Matthew in the Revised Standard Version and, finally, Thornton's translation. It is clear that Thornton was translating Matthew (6:9–13).

> Matthew, King James (or Authorized Version): 9. Our Father which art in heaven, Hallowed be thy name. 10. Thy Kingdom come. Thy will be done in earth as it is in heaven. 11. Give us this day our daily bread. 12. And forgive us our debts, as we forgive our debtors. 13. And lead us not into temptation, but deliver us from evil: For thine is the kingdom, and the power, and the glory, for ever. Amen.
>
> Luke, King James: 2. Our father, which art in heaven, Hallowed be thy name. Thy kingdom come. Thy will be done, as in heaven, so in earth. 3. Give us day by day our daily bread. 4. And forgive us our sins; for we also forgive

---

* The Lord's Prayer, newly translated From the Original Greek, with critical and explanatory notes by Robert John Thornton, M. D. of Trinity College Cambridge & Member of the Royal London College of Physicians, Sherwood and Co., Paternoster Row; Cox, St. Thomas Street, Borough; and Dr. Thornton, 52, Great Marlborough Street, 1827. The copy that Blake annotated is in the Huntington Library.

every one that is indebted to us. And lead us not into temptation; but deliver us from evil.

Matthew, Rev. Standard: 9. Our Father Who is in heaven, hallowed (kept holy) be Your name. 10. Your kingdom come, Your will be done, on earth as it is in heaven. 11. Give us this day our daily bread, 12. And forgive us our debts, as we also have forgiven (left, remitted and let go the debts and given up resentment against) our debtors. 13. And lead (bring) us not into temptation, but deliver us from the evil one. *For Yours is the kingdom and the power and the glory forever. Amen.*

Thornton: 9. O FATHER OF MANKIND, THOU, who dwellest in *the highest of the* HEAVENS, *Reverenc'd be* THY *Name!* 10. May THY REIGN be, *every where, proclaim'd* so that THY *Will* may be *done* upon *the Earth*, as it is in the MANSIONS OF HEAVEN: 11. Grant unto *me*, and *the whole world, day* by *day*, an abundant supply of *spiritual* and *corporeal* FOOD: 12. FORGIVE us our transgressions against THEE, AS WE extend OUR *Kindness*, and *Forgiveness*, TO ALL: 13. O ! GOD! ABANDON US *not*, when surrounded, by TRIALS; But PRESERVE US from *the Dominion of* SATAN: For THINE only, IS THE SOVEREIGNTY, THE POWER, and THE GLORY, throughout ETERNITY!!!
AMEN.

As a translation, Thornton's is certainly eccentric. It appears that he saw his job as providing commentary inside the translation, so to speak. Morton D. Paley observes, "Parts of it appear very far from the original, and it introduces words and phrases that have no counterpart in the Greek." He calls it "in part ... an explication or paraphrase."*

Prefatory Material and Blake's Responses

The Lord's Prayer, newly translated..., Thornton's last published work, is no more than a pamphlet, being but ten pages in length. Most of it is devoted to critical and explanatory notes, much of which amount more to spiritual exhortation than to explanation. The translation itself is preceded by a page on which various hands speak out, some offering the opinion that a new translation of the whole Bible is needed and some welcoming Thornton's translation of the Prayer. Thornton refers the reader to Matthew and Luke and then quotes Bishop Horne in praise of prayer. This is followed by Dr. Johnson's remark, "The Bible is the *most difficult* book in the world to *comprehend*, nor

---

*Morton D. Paley, *The Traveller in the Evening: The Last Works of William Blake*, Oxford: Oxford University Press, 2003, 284. I am indebted to Paley's discussion of Blake and Thornton's "Lord's Prayer." Readers will find there a detailed description of the text as well as a careful reading, to which I shall be referring in what follows.

can it be understood at all by the unlearned, except through the aid of CRITICAL and EXPLANATORY *notes*." He declares that to undertake a commentary performs a "very useful task" (back of title page).

Blake's response to Johnson is consistent with two of his most strongly held opinions. He was, as Northrop Frye observed, a "literalist of the imagination"* That is, he insisted that spiritual apprehension is immediate. It followed, for him, that there is nothing mysterious in the Bible, nothing arcane that requires interpretation of a mystery. He writes in response to Johnson, "Christ & his Apostles were Illiterate Men Caiphas Pilate & Herod were Learned" (ii, E 667). Of course, neither Jesus nor his apostles wrote the Gospels, but Blake is interested mainly in what Jesus says in them. More important, we see here near the outset an expression of Blake's sensitivity to class distinctions and the religious and political tyranny that he thought went with them. Blake thinks that a certain learned sophistication (in the literal sense drawn from "sophistry") is responsible for Johnson's view. He thinks that Johnson was in the "pay" of those who profit from a criminally imposed class structure: "The Beauty of the Bible is that the most Ignorant & Simple Minds Understand it Best — Was Johnson hired to Pretend to Religious Terrors while he was an Infidel or how was it" (title page). In this instance at least, Blake thinks that Johnson was not really a believer but a hypocrite. And perhaps he thought so in other instances as well. His one other extant reference to Johnson is (in the so-called *An Island in the Moon*) where a bat is seen "winking & blinking/Like Dr. Johnson" (E458). The passage seems not inconsistent with Blake's attitude here.

Bishop King is next quoted, observing that if a school-boy were to make and present a translation of the Lord's Prayer "as it appears at present in our BIBLE AND PRAYER BOOK, for a certainty he would be *very much blamed* by his master" (ii). One wonders how Thornton's translation would fare in similar circumstances.

A quotation follows from Lord Byron: "In *my mind* the highest of all *Poetry* is *Ethical*, or *Sacred Poetry*, as the highest of all earthly objects must be *moral truth*, and hence MILTON is *the first* of Poets, whose genius alone could reach it. What made SOCRATES *the greatest of men?* His *moral truths—his ethics.* What proved JESUS CHRIST to be the SON OF GOD, HARDLY LESS *than his miracles did? His moral precepts*" (ii). Blake's suspicion of those who talk of moral virtues is reflected in his annotation: "If Morality was Christianity Socrates

---

*Frye so titles chapter four of his *Fearful Symmetry: A Study of William Blake*, Princeton, NJ: Princeton University Press, 1947. Frye plays on a phrase from W. B. Yeats, who called Blake a "too literal realist of the imagination" in his "William Blake and His Illustrations to *The Divine Comedy*," *Ideas of Good and Evil*, London and Stratford-on-Avon, 1903, 127.

was The Savior" (ii, E 667).* Byron's remarks fly in the face of Blake's fundamental view that the only new but supremely important idea brought by Jesus was the concept of forgiveness. All else was present in writings of the classical philosophers. His idea is put in the forefront of *Jerusalem*, chapter one: "The Spirit of Jesus is continual forgiveness of Sin: he who waits to be righteous before he enters the Saviour's Kingdom, the Divine Body; will never enter there" (E145). This was not for Blake a ritual forgiveness, as in formal confession. Instead, "...Throughout all Eternity / I forgive you you forgive me / As our dear Redeemer said / This is the Wine & this the Bread" (from "My Spectre around me..., E 477). The Eucharist is dissolved here into a simple act between people that is identified with the divine body.

Byron's remarks are followed by those of T. W. C. Edwards, M. A., who offers several examples of the superiority of Thornton's translation and the value of his notes. The Rev. Dr. Mosely completes the puffery by claiming that Thornton's translation "ought to be *printed* IN LETTERS OF GOLD" (ii).

At the top of page one, directly above the translation itself, Blake makes an interesting observation that reflects on some of Thornton's criticism of the King James version in Matthew. For example, on page three, Thornton objects to the use of "which" in "Our Father which art in heaven," complaining that the word excludes personality and is objectionable as a reference to God. Blake's remark refers to several other similar complaints:

> Such things as these depend on the Fashion of the Age
> In a book where all may Read &
> In a book which all may Read &   are Equally Right
> In a book that all may Read
> That Man who &c is equally so The Man that & the Man which
> [1, E 668]

For his example, Blake has taken a line from his "Introduction" to *Songs of Innocence*, the third above. Then, perhaps reminding himself that "book" is inanimate, he makes the addendum, referring to animate "Man," and approves the use of "that" and "which" with it in King James. He appears to think that Thornton is merely nit-picking.

Thornton's Critical and Explanatory Notes

Thornton follows his translation with a paraphrase of it. (On the page beside the translation is a poem of unidentified authorship. It is accurately

---

*This statement also appears in the so-called "Laocoön" (E275), or as Blake seems to call it, "[Jehovah] & his two Sons Satan and Adam as they were copied from the Cherubim of Solomons Temple by three Rhodians & applied to Natural Fact. or. History of Ilium."

described by Paley as "turgid." He wonders whether Thornton himself might be the author. The poem is of thirty lines and entitled "Lines on Eternity," beginning "What *is* ETERNITY! Can aught/Paint its duration to the thought?") Much in the first of eight notes urges the seriousness of prayer. Thornton asserts that this prayer "is not a selfish one for in the *Greek* we address God, as *the Common Parent of all Mankind*" (4). The prayer must be "fervent" and from the heart. Isaiah, Malachi, Matthew, and John Milton are invoked, and those who pray are also encouraged in their "solitary musings" to behold in nature "a kind and benevolent GOD" (3). Two more poems in heroic couplets appear here, titled "Lines on the Love of God" and "Creation a Proof of the Love of God." These two have not been identified.

In the second note, Thornton comments on the first and second lines of the Prayer. God is to be contemplated, in the saying of these lines, as the "King of Kings, Lord of Lords" (3), and there must be no frivolous mention of him. He sits in "the *highest of* the *Heavens*." Here Thornton quotes a part of the prayer put by Milton into the mouths of Adam and Eve (*Paradise Lost* 5, 153–65). He emphasizes the notion of "reverence" as preferable to the King James "hallowed," as the former implies "religious awe" and the latter means only to "make holy" (3).

The Prayer is also "for the church itself and for its establishment and dissemination of the *Gospel* throughout the World" (3). In the lengthy third note, Thornton suggests that "Thy kingdom come" does not "reach the sublimity of the subject," because the emphasis should be on the fact that the kingdom is "a spiritual one only" (4). His sense of the value of Christianity in action is reflected in the following:

> Although this SPIRITUAL KINGDOM has not hither to produced its *full effect* upon *the world*, yet we can clearly trace its *influence* in *humanizing* the *manners of men*. WHEREVER CHRISTIANITY prevails, it has discouraged, and, in some degree, abolished *slavery*. It has introduced *more equality* between *the two sexes*, and rendered the *conjugal union* more *rational* and *happy*. It has abated the *ferociousness* of *war*, and in some families has already made HEAVEN upon EARTH [4].

Christianity, the spiritual kingdom, has given us the rules of conduct. Thornton mentions especially the admonition to love one's enemies. In the annotations to Watson's *Apology*, Blake earlier sided on this matter with Thomas Paine, who called "loving enemies ... another dogma of feigned morality" (see above, p. 65).

Thornton criticizes the phrase "in earth" in King James as bad grammar and insists on "mansions of heaven," indeed many heavens, there being in his view higher and lower ones: "We may perhaps part from *one* to the *other* in due succession" (4). Apparently in support of this, he produces a poem by

Isaac Watts (though not so identified), "There is *a* land of pure delight"* and Milton's lines from *Paradise Lost* as follows, though he repunctuates them, quotes them out of order, and adds a word:

> In contemplation of created things
> By *Steps* we may *ascend* to GOD!
> For one ALMIGHTY is *from* whom
> All things proceed; and *up* to HIM— return.
> If not depraved from good.
> [First two lines: V, 511–14; next three lines: V, 469–471.]

Thornton proceeds to speculate about the vastness of God's creation and seems to preach also on the vastness of the ascent that, through the voice of the angel Raphael, Milton mentions above. He observes that human beings can shape matter and "raise up" images, but only God "produces substances the *most solid!!*" (5). We should not confine our thought to one world or one sun, for there are "myriads" of suns and "more Planets than there are grains of sand upon the sea-shore" (5). Thornton knew of Newton's famous remark about sands on the sea shore, as did Blake, who refers to them and to "Newton's particles of light" in his poem "Mock on, Mock on..." (E 477–8). Blake, however, who often employs such a synecdoche, reverses infinity and in his "Auguries of Innocence" (E490) makes the grain of sand contain it. Thornton speculates that these other globes may be inhabited by "the souls of just men made perfect, and angels have here their mansions" (5). He seems to be referring to one of the lower heavens implied in his translation of the Prayer. The globes are apparently part of a great chain that connects "Earth to Heaven, from one system of worlds to another system, and centers finally in GOD HIMSELF" (5).

At this point, Thornton cites Joseph Addison, who (*Spectator* 299) admires Newton for his profound sense of the "vast machine we inhabit" (6), but Addison observes that even Newton's mind had a "narrow prospect" compared to the "ken of an angel." Paley comments (288) rightly that Addison's remarks about the "vast machine" must have reminded Blake of Urizen's "dark machines" and evoked a reaction to the idea of them as an object of worship. Addison is quoted at length. Part is below:

> It pleases me to think that I who know so small a portion of the CREATOR, and with slow and painful steps creep up and down on the surfaces of this globe, shall ere long shoot away with the swiftness of imagination, trace out the hidden springs of Nature's operations .... In ETERNITY a great deal may be done of this kind [5].

---

*Paley (287–8) notes some interesting resemblances here to Blake's "The Land of Dreams" (E486).

His hope is that he will be "advanced to a more exalted station" (5). Thornton quotes Addison again: "Dim at best are the conceptions we have of the SUPREME BEING, who, as it were, keeps the human race in suspense, neither discovering, nor hiding HIMSELF" (5). (This passage Blake comments on with three words: "a Female God," to be discussed in the next section).

Thornton is particularly concerned with the idea of God's will. He begins by asserting that man will experience the "still more *numerous, beautiful astonishing works* of the great CREATOR. It is the will of "our MAKER," "our PRESERVER," "our SOVEREIGN LORD," "our best friend." God is "MOST HOLY, *perfectly just,* infinitely wise," IMMENSELY GOOD and benign. He is "uncontrollably powerful" (6).

Among these descriptions come Thornton's warnings that it is a "Monstrous arrogance" for us to give the law to ourselves and that we can expect punishment if we offend the "sole fountain of mercy," who will "avenge the violation of his will." Because he is perfectly just, he "cannot but assert his own righteous WILL and avenge the violation thereof" (6). As a result, Thornton argues that God's will "must prevail one way or another, either with our *will* or against it." This means that he "must reign over us, if not as over *loyal subjects* to *our comfort,* yet as over stubborn *rebels* to *our confusion*" (7).

In his fourth note, Thornton criticizes the use of "give" in "give us this day our daily bread." It is "ill adapted to a supplicant," and he proceeds to object strongly to "*praying* for *this day's bread,* when the *day is past*" (7). These remarks lead him to think that careless obeying of the precepts of Christianity may be in part because of the "imperfect rendering of the LORD'S PRAYER" (7).

In his fifth note, Thornton rejects the use of "debts" and "debtors" as making the Prayer a " money account" and "trespass" as making the offense merely a simple one like "getting into a man's garden." (It is certainly an irony that Thornton should employ this example, for Blake, being accused of seditious utterances, was prosecuted as a result of forcibly removing a soldier from his garden at Felpham). Thornton recognizes an offense against the king as "treason" (the charge against Blake) and offense against God's law as "transgression," the term he chooses. He then cites the notion of forgiveness of other men and love of one's enemies, quoting Alexander Pope's "The Universal Prayer" (emphases and second semi-colon added by Thornton):

> To hide the *fault* I see;
> That MERCY I *to others show*;
> That MERCY shew to me.

(Other lines from this poem appear here and there in Thornton's notes.) And he follows the lines above with Portia's speech on mercy from *The Merchant of Venice*. It is not clear here that Thornton distinguishes love from mercy.

In the sixth note, Thornton defends his choice of "abandon us not" over "lead us not into temptation." His argument, based on the assumption that for God to tempt to sin is absurd, is also grounded on the epistle of James (1:13): "Let no man say when he is tempted, I am tempted of God: for God cannot be tempted with evil, neither tempteth he any man." (Thornton seems content with the King James version here.) Thornton's version, "O GOD! ABANDON US *not*, when surrounded, by TRIALS," he defends as follows: "... from the constitution of this world we are subject to various *trials*, and these often are BENEFITS, for what we call evil, is not truly such, for in fact by *afflictions* or *trials*, we are weaned *from the world*, and we are *ordered 'to set our affections upon things above, and not upon things on this earth.'*"

In the seventh note, Thornton argues that the translation "evil" in "deliver us from evil" is inaccurate; it should clearly refer to Satan or the evil one. (8) The eighth and last note is in its entirety as follows: "And the seventy returned again with joy, saying, 'Lord, even *the devils* (χαι παδαμοννα) are subject to us through THY NAME,' and he said unto them, 'I beheld SATAN (τονΣατοναν) as *lightning falling from heaven*'" (8). The passage, with a few small changes from King James, is from Luke 10:17–18. Thornton seems to be referring to the Prayer's "PRESERVE US from the *Dominion* of SATAN" (8).

It is clear that Thornton's translation, if we can call it that, is frequently based on his attempt to force that prayer into his conception of what it *should* say rather than what it *does* say.

Following the notes, Thornton cites comments by several persons on the need for a new translation of the whole Bible. Sir James Bland Burgess makes a summary statement: "The Translators of our *English Bible* made *their* Translations chiefly out of *JEROME'S Latin Bible*, and his was not from the original *Hebrew*, but from a prior translation into *Greek*, so that *our Bible* is in fact, only a Translation of a Translation." Furthermore, according to Burgess, the King James translators did not, by their own admission, make a new translation but rather a collation and revision of previous translations. Bishop Lowth and Thomas Blackwell speak out on the inaccuracies, Durrell and Blaney likewise, the last asking rhetorically, "Can any Scripture be profitable, except it be understood? And if not rightly understood, may not the perversions of it be proportionally dangerous?"

Thornton concludes with a call for a new translation from the original Hebrew and Greek by "*an assemblage of all the first scholars of the age*, (with marginal, and other notes, if thought necessary)." Thus we have come full circle back to the views of Dr. Johnson, quoted at the beginning.

It is interesting that Blake makes no marginal comments on the things he agrees with Thornton about, as he did years before with Lavater and even later with Reynolds. He certainly thought with Thornton that God's kingdom was a spiritual one only, though what he meant by that was surely different from what Thornton meant. He might well have commented favorably on Thornton's complaint that a passage in the King James version sounded like a "money account." As for his disagreements, although he says nothing, he might well have been critical of Thornton's claim for the generally beneficial effect of Christianity in the world, and he certainly did not agree that we should love our enemies when we forgive. This, he thought, encouraged hypocrisy. Finally, he is silent when Thornton discusses God's will, a word Blake disliked. He identified it with egoistic drive for power. He refrains until the end of his annotations from commenting on Thornton's attribution to God of universal power and capacity for vengeance. By this time Blake could well have lost patience with making specific references to Thornton's sentences. He does this only four or five times. He probably thought he had said enough and surely had more fun in writing his own version of the Prayer and his concluding parody of Thornton's.

Blake's Annotations

The first of Blake's annotations not attached to specific parts of Thornton's text is Blake's own imaginative and politically outspoken version of the Prayer:

> Jesus our Father who art in thy Heavens calld by thy name the Holy Ghost Thy Kingdom on Earth is Not nor thy Will done but Satans Will who is the God of this World   The Accuser   His Accusation shall be Forgiveness that he may be consumd in his own Shame
>
> Give us This Eternal Day our own right Bread & take away Money or Debt or Tax a Value or Price as we have all things in common among us Every Thing has as much right to Eternal Life as God who is the Servant of Man
>
> Leave us not in Parsimony Satans Kingdom liberate us from the Natural Man & want or Jobs Kingdom
>
> For thine is the Kingdom & the Power & the Glory & not Caesars or Satans Amen [3, E 668–9].

Satan, who according to Blake in the annotations to Bacon is the "Mind of the Natural Frame" (E625), that is, one's illusory material being, is not here to be consumed in flames of torment imposed from without, as in Revelation. Satan is also the accuser of sin. His act will be transformed into forgiveness by those he accuses, and as a result he will be consumed with shame and annihilated. He has been a state of mind all along.

What Blake calls "this world" is the illusionary world of matter, product of an imagination fallen under the domination of an arrogant reason and imposed on people by church and state. This world's god is actually what tradition has called Satan, tyrannical accuser, not a forgiver.

Blake's remark about Satan is unusual in its explicitness. Generally, Satan, for Blake, is a state of mind into which people fall, but for Blake "every class is individual" in the manner of Giambattista Vico, who proposed the "imaginative universal,"* in which anything abstract in present-day thought was given body by the earliest people, for they could think only in images. By this poetic logic (Vico's term), Satan is a bodily image that is a class of things. He is also his works, which are legion. As described in the conclusion to *Jerusalem*, he is not just the accuser but also the act of accusation of sin, itself. He is also human sacrifice in war and in the Druid temples (E258). In *Milton*, he is the selfhood, rational demonstration, "Bacon, Newton, Locke," and many other things Blake despised. For Blake, accusation is the negation of forgiveness, which is the one original thought Jesus brought. Elsewhere in Blake's writings, Satan is also consumed in his own flames. Here, what one might suppose is accusation against him for all his works is instead forgiveness, and his imaginative form is consumed in the fire of his own shame.

Later, Blake calls Thornton's a "Tory translation" (10). It appears that Blake has intended to meet Thornton on his own ground and write a prayer that has as its theme a revisionary economics. Blake's version follows his scathing remark, which appears just after Thornton's translation:

> Lawful Bread Bought with Lawful Money & a Lawful Heaven seen thro a Lawful Telescope by means of Lawful Window Light The Holy Ghost & whatever cannot be Taxed is Unlawful & Witchcraft.
>
> Spirits are Lawful but not Ghosts especially Royal Gin is Lawful Spirit No Smuggling real British Spirit & Truth

David Erdman remarks, "Blake was incensed at the idea of begging one's daily bread from any god."† He points out that during this period William Cobbett was attacking the use of paper money and the so-called Waterloo taxes on any number of things to pay for the war against France.§ In sarcasm Blake

---

*On Vico's imaginative universal and poetic logic and Blake's, see my *The Offense of Poetry*, Seattle, WA: University of Washington Press, 2007, 162–71.

†David V. Erdman, *Blake: Prophet Against Empire*, Princeton, NJ: Princeton University Press, 1954, 454.

§On Blake's references to taxation, all unfavorable, see Paley (291–4) for a helpful discussion of the social context.

takes the view that under the present regime anything not taxed is unlawful and of no value, including the Holy Ghost. He goes so far as to condemn private ownership of property, though such a reading turns on the meaning here of "common." Does it mean "owned by all" or does it refer to the things owned by most individuals? From what is said later, I think it is the former. At the bottom of page 2 of Thornton's notes, Blake writes, "Give us the Bread that is our due & Right by taking away Money or a Price or Tax upon what is Common to all in thy kingdom" (E668). The remark is echoed in his own version of the prayer, which immediately follows on page 3.

In addressing Jesus or speaking of him, Blake does not append "Christ"; to Blake the word suggests the kingship he so disliked. He had to have known that the Messiah ("Christ" being Greek for "Messiah") was expected by the Jews to be a king in the line of David. I take it that when Blake refers to "thy Kingdom on earth" he is both mimicking the standard prayer and declaring that such a thing — an earthly rather than a spiritual notion — is a Satanic delusion. It is surprising that he calls Jesus "father," for this has also the suggestion of external power, but I think he does this in order to have Jesus replace any notion of a father-god separate from him as he seems to have interpreted the idea of the Trinity. Furthermore, he calls Jesus the Holy Ghost, a spirit dwelling in man as interpreted in Christian tradition, immanent on earth in this way. Blake's Jesus is, in fact, the imagination in each of us. Although there was an historical figure named Jesus, Blake is not really interested in him. He is now an Antichrist. Today, he only *was*, and the only real Jesus is the one present to a reading of the gospels and internal to the human imagination. Blake is interested in the imaginative human creation that appears in a fictive (in the sense of something made) work, the New Testament, a visionary work, in his vocabulary.

Blake begins the second paragraph by inserting into his version of the prayer "Eternal" before "Day." The principle is synecdoche, for he is speaking of every day, the moment for Blake being infinitely expansive and potentially containing everything. The prayer again attacks debt, money, and taxation; here there is no ambiguity about common ownership. Spiritual (as against monetary) values are identified with eternal life. God is declared a servant, being identified with the imaginative power, common to all.

Blake seems first to have written "Leave us not in Poverty," but that had already been implied in the foregoing. Here he turns to parsimony, in the sense of miserliness. The natural man, next mentioned, is the man without an effectively working imagination, self-trapped in a world like that of Urizen in *The Four Zoas*, and thus certainly in spiritual want. The prayer asks for liberation from that state and from poverty as it befell poor Job, who, in Blake's view, came under the dominion of a false god. S. Foster Damon remarks, "Job's prime error was admitting this Accuser [Satan] into his heaven [his mind, what Blake calls here his "kingdom"]; and from this Satan all the disasters proceed."* Satan has introduced doubt and guilt into Job's mind. Blake's use of "kingdom" here is surely ironic, as Job's kingdom is really Satan's, a projection of his own error and pride; the word, for Blake, suggests tyranny.

The concluding line of Blake's prayer mentions kingdom, power, and glory, as in King James; but Blake's prayer, addressed to Jesus, specifically separates that kingdom from Caesar's and Satan's. The fact that "kingdom" is employed by Blake here may simply be a nod to the conventions of the prayer, but it runs against Blake's own dislike. This is the reason, perhaps, that Blake comes in one of his last notes to distinguish "kingdom" from "kingship": "I swear that Basileia (βασιλεια) is not Kingdom but Kingship," that is, the institution of monarchy (10, E669). He doesn't erase the problem of having used it, but he chooses here a term that emphasizes the position of the tyrant. In short, Blake implies that Thornton's prayer requires drastic revision because it is addressed to the false god, an illusion of the natural world, in which men have no better power of imagination than to worship god as if he were merely a temporal tyrant.

Blake next comments on a part of Thornton's long quotation from Joseph Addison, where Addison describes our conceptions of god as "dim at best" (5) and declares that the supreme being "keeps the human race in suspense, neither discovering, nor hiding HIMSELF." Blake comments: "A Female God" (E669). In his poetry, that is Vala, the nature goddess of *The Four Zoas*—a seductress, tempting man but withholding consummation. This is the "female will" of Blake's poems who invokes the moral law of chastity. Thornton's discussion of will follows, and it is enough to draw from Blake a summary concluding address to the reader: "So you See That God is just such a Tyrant Augustus Caesar & is not this Good & Learned & Wise & Classical" (5, E669). Now we learn that not only are "Caiphas, Pilate & Herod" (Blake's villains are always triple-formed) learned men, but also Blake sarcastically identifies the classics with them. The reason is the tyranny of Augustus Caesar, and also the tradition of war and conquest in Greek and Latin literature, especially as represented by Virgil's *Aeneid*. (See *On Homers Poetry* and *On Virgil* [E269–70].) Blake's theme here extends to his comment at the bottom of page 9, where various writers are cited by Thornton in support of a new translation of the whole Bible. The annotation is cryptic: "The only thing for

---

**Blake's Job: William Blake's Illustrations of the Book of Job*, with an Introduction and Commentary by S. Foster Damon, New York, E. P. Dutton, 1969, 8.

Newtonian & Baconian Philosophers to Consider is this Whether Jesus did not suffer himself to be Mocked by Caesars Soldiers Willingly & to Consider this to all Eternity will be Comment Enough" (E 669).* Blake identifies Caesar's soldiers with the culture of war, conquest, and materialism — just as he identifies the philosophies of Bacon and Newton with the era of British empire. Jesus would suffer the soldiers' mockery to reveal their own natures as tools of the violence of empire and, I think, to imply forgiveness — but not love. As we have seen, Blake did not think one needed to or should love one's enemies. To profess such, crosses the line into hypocrisy. The Jesus of Blake's prayer is a political radical and preacher of forgiveness.

Blake's Parody

The blank, last page of the text contains a summary statement describing Thornton's translation: "This is Saying the Lord's Prayer Backward which they say Raises the Devil" (10, E669). Blake alludes to Thornton's Tory politics and remembers Burgess's statement that King James is a translation of a translation. He playfully conflates the King James version with James's Scottishness, and he implies in his preface to his parody that the James version is the Bible corrupted by classical and Scottish influences that keep it hidden from readers; he will now reveal what is hidden in it: "Doctor Thorntons Tory Translation Translated out of its disguise in the Classical & Scotch language into the vulgar English" (10, E 669).

Here is the text of the parody:

> Our Father Augustus Caesar who art in these thy Substantial Astronomical Telescopic Heavens Holiness to thy Name or Title & reverence to thy Shadow Thy Kingship come upon Earth first & thence in Heaven Give us day by day our Real Taxed Substantial Money bought Bread deliver from the Holy Ghost so we call Nature whatever cannot be Taxed for all is debts & Taxes between Caesar & us & one another lead us not to read the Bible but let our Bible be Virgil & Shakespeare & deliver us from Poverty in Jesus that evil one For thine is the Kingship or Allegoric Godship & the Power or War & the Glory or Law Ages after Ages in thy Descendents for God is only an Allegory of Kings & nothing Else Amen

The reference to astronomy harks back to Thornton's discussion of the telescopic study of the heavens and the possibility of other worlds. It is there, in

---

*What we have here is a revision. After the ampersand, Blake originally wrote "and I hope they will." When he erased this, he added the "to." Or, as Paley puts it with respect to Blake's apparent loss of interest in translation, "[Blake] at this very late point in his life regarded the real meaning of the Bible as something to be intuited rather than translated" (290).

the abstract space of the false material universe, that Blake locates Caesar. In his work, "holy" appears in both pejorative and honorific senses, more often pejorative, as here. It is usually identified with secrecy and mystery and connected with a god only whose shadow we are permitted to see. Caesar's kingship will first be temporal. Then he will be turned into a false god. Blake again criticizes taxation and ironically brings the Holy Ghost down to earth, but not in spirit, rather as nature, a word Blake came almost always to use negatively, it being associated with the illusion of matter.

It is not surprising that Virgil is invoked here. Blake has already identified him with conquest and empire in his *On Virgil* (E270). Shakespeare may be more difficult to explain, unless one decides that Blake is thinking of the history plays and the countenance of kingship they imply. Blake constantly opposes a language that treats God in terms of kingship. In the end here, Blake makes the prayer atheistic by turning God into an allegory of kings. There is kingship only on earth, kingdom in heaven. ("Kingdom" somehow escapes, for Blake, the pejorative connotation of "kingship.") In a any case, Blake is convinced that Thornton can think of God only on the allegorical model of a temporal tyrant.

The note that follows (somewhat garbled) continues the attack on Thornton's prayer. It begins with the claim, as we have seen, that the translation should say "kingship" rather than "kingdom," and then it proceeds by irony, indicating that natural philosophy and religion create a false man, in whose fallen imagination priests and kings hold the power to declare what sort of god exists. The model for that god is once again kingship; such a god is the unpleasant odor emanating from priest and king:

> I [referring to what immediately follows] Nature Hermaphroditic Priest & King Live in Real Substantial Natural Born Man & that Spirit is the Ghost of Matter or Nature & God is The Ghost of the Priest & King who Exist whereas God exists not except from their Effluvia [10, E669]

The priest who speaks here and in whom are conflated nature and king is hermaphroditic in Blake's language because he is composed of ideas that cannot be resolved with each other, especially strife about sexuality, but also the negation matter/spirit. This priest thinks of the natural world, of which he is a synecdoche, as the real world and the spiritual world as but a ghost.

Blake carries on his implied criticism of mystery and holiness, "Here is Signed Two Names which are too Holy to be Written," alluding to Jewish belief that the name of God should not be spoken. That he says two names are signed suggests the hermaphrodite already mentioned (10, E670). He then proceeds to summarize sarcastically:

> Thus we see that the Real God is the Goddess Nature & that God Creates nothing but what can be Touchd & Weighed & Taxed & Measured all else is Heresy & Rebellion against Caesar Virgils Only God See Eclogue i for all this we thank Dr Thornton [10, E670].

In Virgil's first "Eclogue," poor Meliboeus has been evicted from his farm, and Tityrus has traveled to Rome to plead his own case not to be evicted from his. The authorities there have allowed him to stay on. In the aftermath of Julius Caesar's assassination, there was civil war in Italy, and Octavian (later the Emperor Augustus) appointed commissioners to seize land for veterans who had served him. This history illustrated for Blake everything that was wrong with empire, kingship, authority, and war, all of which he identified with Thornton's Tory politics.

11

Addendum

Erdman's edition (E670) notes two other annotations, one alleged by Edwin J. Ellis to be in Cennino Cennini's book on fresco *Trattato della Pittura*, published in Rome in 1821.* Erdman reports (in his textual note, E888) from Alexander Gilchrist's *Life of Blake*, that John Linnell gave Blake a copy of this book. However, Erdman can find nothing in that book to which Blake would have made the annotation printed by Ellis. Recognizing Ellis's notorious inaccuracy, Erdman proposes that the annotation may have been to Benvenuto Cellini's *Trattato dell' Oreficeria*, first published in 1568, but appearing again in 1795 or 1811. Blake's remark, according to Ellis, is as follows: "The Pope supposes Nature and the Virgin Mary to be the same allegorical personages, but the Protestant considers Nature as incapable of bearing a child" (E670). The statement, though dubious for most Protestants, is consistent, as Erdman points out, with Blake's view as it is expressed in one of his annotations to Reynolds, "This [natural] World is too poor to produce one Seed" (E656).

Erdman treats as an annotation the titles that Blake places on the spines of books in his water-color illustration of Edward Young's *Night Thoughts*, Night the Fifth, lines 735–6, which read,

> But you are learn'd; in Volumes, deep you sit;
> In Wisdom shallow: pompous ignorance!

The books represented are Plato, *Phaedo; or, A Dialogue on the Immortality of the Soul*; Cicero, *De Natura Deorum; or, On the Nature of the Gods*; Plutarch, *Moralia*; and John Locke, *An Essay on Human Understanding*. Blake abbreviates the titles. There is no comment by Blake, but for him these books do express "pompous ignorance." Plato's soul, abstracted into bodilessness, is hardly Blake's. Cicero's title alone would have irritated him, nature for Blake

---

*Edwin J. Ellis, *The Real Blake*, London: Chatto & Windus, 1907, 420.

being a human fantasy of the reason. Plutarch's title also would not sit well, as Blake was suspicious of anything associated with the so-called moral law. Locke's book, with its division of perception into primary and secondary qualities, Blake thought the source of much modern error.

12

A Note on Blake's Reading

In the writings about Blake in his time and sometimes since, a number of false ideas about him or ideas with little or no foundation in fact have appeared and have been repeated: that he was as innocent as the children of his poems, that he was insane, that he had Muggletonian forebears, that he wanted to introduce a concubine into his household, that he was socially isolated. It is true that Blake was untutored (except for his having attended drawing school). He had no formal education. In later life, he declared himself opposed to it. Henry Crabb Robinson reports that he said, "There *is* no use in education. It is the great sin. It is eating of the tree of the knowledge of good and evil. This was the fault of Plato. He knew of nothing but the virtues and vices, and good and evil."* Robinson also tells us, "Nor would he admit that any education should be attempted, except that of the cultivation of the imagination and fine arts" (308). He rejected what he thought of as formal education's coercive discipline:

> Thank God I never was sent to school
> To be flogd into following the Style of Fool [E510].

He must have held these view at least from early in his career, as his poem "The School Boy," placed in *Songs of Experience*, spoken by a child, seems to show. He was, however, an avid and eclectic reader and in his later years a student, probably self-taught, of Greek, Hebrew, and Italian. Our sources for knowledge of Blake's reading are, of course, his own writings and the reports and scholarship of others. In addition, there are the many books to which he contributed designs and/or engravings.† Of these he may have read little or

---

*Henry Crabb Robinson, *Diary, Reminiscences, and Correspondence*, selected and edited by Thomas Sadler, London: Macmillan and Co., II, 303.
†For interesting lists that include these, see G. E. Bentley, Jr., *Blake Books*, Oxford: Clarendon Press, 1977 ("Part III: Commercial Book Engravings"), 507–647, and *Blake Books Supplement* Oxford: Clarendon Press, 1995 ("Table of Contemporary Commercial Engravings by and

much. What follows here is a brief effort to give a general idea of the scope of Blake's reading. It is not meant to mention all of Blake's books.

Almost fifty years ago, Sir Geoffrey Keynes reported on the seventeen and perhaps nineteen volumes that still exist and were then known to have been owned by Blake.* They are, in addition to the books he annotated, Johann Joachim Winckelmann's *Reflections on the Painting and Sculpture of the Greeks*, 1765, translated by Henry Fuseli; *The Tragedies of Aeschylus*, 1779, translated by R. Palmer; Thomas Chatterton's *Poems by Thomas Rowley*, 1778; John and Charles Wesley's *Hymns for the Nation in 1782*; James Barry's *An Account of a Series of Pictures in the Great Room of the Society of Arts, Manufacture, and Commerce at the Adelphi*, 1783; Horace Walpole's *Catalogue of the Royal and Noble Authors of England*, 1792; Percy's *Reliques of Ancient Poetry*, 1765; and Chapman's *Homer*, 1616. Keynes also mentions *Works of Peter Pindar* and Young's *Night Thoughts*, though he had not himself examined these volumes. In any case, we know that Blake had read the latter, for which he had made illustrations. In his biography of Blake,† G. E. Bentley, Jr., mentions books Blake is known to have bought: Joseph Hallett, Jr.'s, *Free and Impartial Study of the Holy Scripture recommended*, 1729; Jacob Duché's *Discourses on Various Subjects*, in addition to the Wesleys' book mentioned above. He lists as probable *The Works of Jacob Behmen* (Boehme), 1764, translated by William Law; perhaps works by Paracelsus and Cornelius Agrippa. Behmen, Paracelsus, and Agrippa were certainly known to Blake.

Bentley also notes that in *An Island in the Moon* Blake quotes from Joseph Addison's *Cato*, James Hervey's *Theron and Aspasio* and *Meditations*, Henry Wotton's *Reliquae Wottonianae*, William Sherlock's *Practical Discourse on Death*, Edward Young's *Night Thoughts*, Pliny, and Robert South (26n).

Among poets to whom Blake alludes are Pindar, Corinna, Ovid, Virgil, Chaucer, Tasso, Ariosto, Spenser, Camoens, Orcilla, Hervey, Pope, Prior, Dryden, Macpherson (Ossian), Klopstock, Goethe, Cowper, Churchill, Gray, Barbould, and Byron. In addition to these he owned the books of the following: Chapman's Homer, Cowper's Homer. Cary's translation of Dante, Vellutello's Dante, Milton, Young, Blair, Chatterton (Rowley), Hayley, Shenstone, Falconer, Gay, Hurdis, and Wordsworth. For some of these he did designs, engravings, or woodcuts.

He mentions several of Shakespeare's plays: *Richard III*, *Henry IV*, *Henry*

[continued] After Blake"), 186–89. For the contents of this chapter I have drawn heavily on Bentley's heroic scholarship in these books.

*Sir Geoffrey Keynes, "Blake's Library" *Times Literary Supplement*, November 6, 1959, 648.

†G. E. Bentley, Jr., *The Stranger from Paradise: A Biography of William Blake*, New Haven and London: Yale University Press, 2001, 126.

12. A Note on Blake's Reading

VIII, Julius Caesar, Hamlet, Romeo and Juliet, Othello, King Lear, Macbeth, and *The Tempest*. For many of these he did illustrations. Other dramatists he mentions are Addison, Aeschylus, whose *Tragedies* he owned, and Otway.

Among writers of narrative prose whom he mentions by name (or books by them) are Bunyan, Rousseau, Voltaire, Goethe, Wollstonecraft, Defoe, Richardson, and Bage. His knowledge of Arthurian legend no doubt came from Malory.

We know he read books of art, literary criticism, and aesthetics: Edward Bysshe's *Art of English Poetry*, Cennino Cennini's *Trattato della Pittura*, Benvenuto Cellini's *Trattato dell' Oreficeria*, Fuseli's *Lectures on Painting*, Rees's *Cyclopaedia*, Edmund Burke on the sublime and the beautiful, George Cumberland's *Thoughts on Outline, Sculpture, and the System*, Charles N. Tatham's *Three Designs for the National Monument...*, Raphael's designs. These he had at some time owned. He mentions Dr. Johnson, though no specific work, and William Gilpin on picturesque scenery.

He was familiar with or knew of the work of philosophers: Pythagoras, Democritus, Epicurus, Plato, Aristotle, Cicero, Descartes, and Hume. He owned books by Bacon, Berkeley, and Locke.

Among historical works, he owned William Gordon's *History of the Rise, Progress, and Establishment of the Independence of the United States of America*, Hay's *The History of Chichester*, and Stedman's *Narrative* of the slave revolt in Surinam, for which he did engravings.

He owned two books of hymns by the Wesley brothers and Joseph Thomas's *Religious Emblems* in addition to having much knowledge of the Bible, and he did commercial engravings for *The Protestant Family Bible* and *The Royal Universal Family Bible*. Among his commercial engravings are works on mathematics, medicine, including surgery, botany, geography, physiognomy, and archeology as well as poems, prose fiction, and drama. He seems to have read Newton.

As we know from the annotations, Blake was an avid critic and commentator, and I have little doubt that if he did not annotate he spoke his mind to others about what he read. It is a shame that the annotations he claims to have made to Burke's *Philosophical Inquiry*, Locke's *An Essay on Human Understanding*, and Bacon's *Advancement of Learning* are presumably lost, for they might have told us much more about his philosophical and aesthetic views.

Index

Abraham 156
accident 15–18, 118, 125
Achilles 76, 101–2
Ackrill, J.L. 16
Adam 63, 75, 181n, 182
Adams, Hazard: *Antithetical Essays* 123n; *Offense of Poetry* 16n, 30n 187n; *William Blake: A Reading* 34n
Addison, Joseph 83, 183–4, 189, 197; *Cato* 196
Aeneas 102
Aeschylus: *Tragedies* 196, 197
Agamemnon 99, 101
Agrippa, Cornelius 196
Albion 169
allegory 79, 122, 172, 191, 193
Allentuck, Marcia 7n
angels 17, 32–3, 36, 40–2, 45, 47–9, 51, 57, 168
Anjou 104
Antichrist 30, 173, 188
Aphorism 9, 19
Apollo 51, 55, 124
Ariosto, Ludovico 196
Aristotle 10, 15–6, 19, 87, 92, 103, 118, 154, 156, 158, 197; *De Anima* 159
Augustine, Saint 56

Bacon, Francis 5, 95, 121, 125, 129, 133, 146, 147n, 148–9, 162, 169, 174–5, 186–7, 190, 197; *Advancement of Learning* 3, 81–2, 197; *An Advertisement ...* 91; *Colours of Good and Evil* 81; *Confession of Faith* 91; *Essays* 81–96; *Novum Organum* 82; *Religious Meditations* 81, 92; "Of a King" 81, 84–5; "Of Atheism" 92; "Of Cunning 87"; "Of Expense" 91; "Of Faction" 87; "Of Nobility" 85–6; "Of Sedition and Troubles" 85, 88; "Of Superstition" 93; "Of the True Greatness" 88; "Of Travel" 95; "Of Truth" 94; "Of Usury" 90
Bage, Robert 197
Bajezet 102
Baker, H. Kendra 83n
Baldwin, James Mark: *Dictionary of Philosophy and Psychology* 141
Barbould, Anna Laetitia 196

Barry, James 110, 116; *Account of a Series of Pictures* 196
Basire, James 4
Beaumont, George 175
Behmen, Jacob (Boehme): *Works* 196
Bellin, Harvey F.: *Blake and Swedenborg* 29n
Bentley, G.E., Jr. 62, 147n; *Blake Books* 195n, 196; *Blake Books Supplement* 195n; *Stranger from Paradise* 148n, 161n, 177n, 196n
Berkeley, George 14, 42, 197; *Principles of Human Knowledge* 150–1; *Siris* 150–9, 172
Bible 17, 61–80, 158, 177–92, 197; Chronicles 64, 169; 2 Chronicles 169; Daniel 68; Decalogue 102; Deuteronomy 67; Genesis 156; Gospel 79, 173, 182; Isaiah 68, 155, 182; Jeremiah 68; Jerome's Latin Bible 185; Job 65, 188–9; Jonah 77; Joshua 64, 68; King James (Authorized) Version 87, 178, 181–2, 185–7, 190; James 185; 1 Kings 21; 1 and 2 Kings 64, 68, 169; Luke 178–9, 185; Malachi 182; Matthew 16, 178–9, 181–2; New Testament 64–5, 188; Old Testament 64–5, 68, 75, 79, 169; Pentateuch 67–8, 76; Philippians 56n; Proverbs 65, 79; Revelation 156; Revised Standard Version 178–9; Samuel 20, 64, 68; Scripture 102
Blackwell, Thomas 185
Blair, Robert 196
Blake, William, works by: *All Religions Are One* 9, 42, 84; *America* 62; "Ancient Britons" 164; "Auguries of Innocence" 183; "Chaucer's Canterbury Pilgrims" 16, 24, 173; *Descriptive Catalogue* 77, 123, 178; *Europe* 62; "Everlasting Gospel" 78; *Four Zoas* 14, 23, 33n, 168, 188–9; "Introduction to *Songs of Innocence*" 181; *Island in the Moon* 180; *Jerusalem* 52, 148, 173, 181, 187; "Land of Dreams" 183; *Laocoön* 158, 181n; "Last Judgment" 170; *Marriage of Heaven and Hell* 15, 23, 28–9, 33–4, 40, 44, 71–2, 93–4, 100, 102, 144, 155; *Milton* 31, 33n, 34, 105, 169, 187; *On Homers Poetry* 189; *On Virgil* 189, 191; *Public Address* 114–5, 149; "School Boy" 195; *Songs* 30; *Songs of Experience* 195; *Songs of Innocence* 165, 181; *Songs of Innocence and of Experience* 162;

199

200   Index

"Thank God, I never was sent to school" 195; *There Is No Natural Religion* 75; *Urizen, Book of* 14, 34; "Virgil's Eclogues" 178; *Vision of the Last Judgment* 45, 157, 172; "William Cowper Esqre" 148
Blaney, Rev. Dr. 185
Bolingbroke, Henry St. John 73
Boswell, James 111
Boyd, Henry: *A Translation of the* Inferno 97–108
Brand, C.P.: *Italy and the Romantics* 97–8
Browning, W.R.F.: *Dictionary of the Bible* 56
Bruni, Leonardo 97
Bunyan, John 197
Burgess, James Bland 185, 190
Burke, Edmund 81, 111, 115–6, 124, 133–4; *Revolution in France* 115–6, 119; *Sublime and Beautiful* 3, 134, 197
Butts, Thomas 110n
Byrd, Max: *Visits to Bedlam* 148
Byron, George Gordon Lord 180, 196
Bysshe, Edward: *Art of English Poetry* 197

Caesar, Augustus 83, 93, 96, 104–6, 189–92
Caesar, Julius 192
Caiaphas 180, 189
Calvin, John 13, 56, 58
Camoens, Luiz vaz de 196
Capanius 103
Caroline College 7
Carte, Thomas: *General History of England* 83
Cary, Henry Francis: translation of Dante 97–8, 196
Catholic Church 140, 144
Cellini, Benvenito: *Trattato dell'Oreficeria* 193, 197
Cennino Cennini: *Trattato della Pittura* 193, 197
center and circumference 14, 44
Chalcographic Society 149
Chapman, George: translation of Homer 196
Charmont 102
Chatterton, Thomas 114, 162; *Poems by Thomas Rowley* 196
Chaucer, Geoffrey 16, 173, 178, 196
cherubim 181n
chiaroscuro 171
Church of England 72
Church of Ireland 98
Churchill, Charles 196
Cicero 197; *De Natura Deorum* 193
Cobbett, William 187
Collegium Humanitatis 7
conception 125
copying 117, 120–2, 129; *see also* imitation
Corinna 196
Correggio, Antonio da 126
correspondences 33–4, 48–9
Cowley, Abraham 83
Cowper, William 67, 146, 196; "Cast-Away" 147; *Memoir* 148; translation of Homer 196

cranioscopy 140
Croce, Benedetto: *Aesthetic* 114
Cromwell, Oliver 13
Cumberland, George 102; *Thoughts on Outline* 197
Cunningham, Allan: *Lives* 171

Dale, David 66
Damon, S. Foster: *Blake's Job* 189
Damrosch, Leopold: *Symbol and Truth in Blake's Myth* 12
Dante 97–101, 104–5, 107–8, 162; *Inferno* 97, 99; *Paradiso* 97; *Purgatorio* 97
David 156, 188
Defoe, Daniel 197
Deism 61–2 65, 68–9, 70, 80, 93, 100
Democritus 121, 197
Descartes, René 82, 129, 197
De Sua, William: *Dante into English* 97–8
D'Ewes, Semonds: autobiography 82
Dictionary of Philosophy and Psychology 141
Dido 102
Druid 187
Dryden, John 102, 114, 196
Duché, Jacob: *Discourses* 196
Dürer, Albrecht 124–5
Durrell, Rev. Dr. 185

Eaves, Morris: *Blake's Theory of Art* 136n
Echard, Laurence 78
Edda 75
Edgar 102
Edgcumbe, Richard Lord 111
Edinburgh Review 82
Edward I 171
Edwards, T.W.C. 181
Elizabeth I 84
Ellis, Edwin J.: *Real Blake* 193; *Works of William Blake* 3, 143, 146
enthusiasm 20, 50, 107, 121, 131
Epicurus (and Epicurean) 11, 25, 92, 95, 106, 112, 121, 131, 133, 197
Episcopal Church 66
equilibrium 54
Erasmus, Desiderius 13
Erdman, David V.: *Blake and His Bibles* 61; *Complete Poetry and Prose of William Blake* 4, 6, 37–8, 193; *Prophet Against Empire* 187
essence 15–17, 43–4
Eve 17, 63, 75, 182
execution 114–5, 118, 124–5
expression 114, 122, 127, 137
externalization 114
Ezekiel 94

Falconer, William 196
Fenelon, François 13
Fingal 75
Fisher, Peter F. 163–4; *Valley of Vision* 164n
Flemish painters 118
Florence 104–5

Florentine painters 134
France, Anatole: *Penguin Island* 55n
Franklin, Benjamin 62
Frye, Northrop: *Fearful Symmetry* 174, 180
Fuseli, Henry 7–9, 111, 196; *Lectures on Painting* 197

Gainsborough, Thomas 127
Gall, Franz Joseph 139–40, 144
Garrick, David 111
Gates, Gen. Horatio 62
Gay, John 196
generalization (and general knowledge) 94–5, 115, 118–20, 124–6, 128, 133–4, 150–1, 157, 169, 174
George III 110, 112–3, 119
Ghibellines 104
Gibbon, Edward 78, 111
Gilchrist, Alexander: *Life of William Blake* 30, 82, 193
Gilpin, William 197
Gladiator 124
Glen, Heather: *Vision and Disenchantment* 162
Goethe, Johann Wolfgang 196–7
Goldsmith, Oliver 111
Gordon, William: *History of ... United States of America* 197
Gray, Thomas 173, 196
Guelphs 104
Guiccardi, Francisco: *History of Florence* 104n

Hallett, Joseph, Jr.: *Free and Impartial Study of the Holy Scripture* 196
Hancock, John 62
Hartley, David 117, 137
Haslam, John: *Observations on Madness* 142, 146
Hay, Alexander: *History of Chichester* 197
Henry IV 13
Hercules 124
Hermes Trismegistus 34
Hermione 102
Herod 180, 189
Herodotus 78
Hervey, James: *Meditations* 196; *Theron and Aspasio* 196
Hesketh, Harriet Lady 147–8
Hilles, Frederick W.: *Literary Career of Reynolds* 111n
Hindmarsh, Robert 29
Hipple, Walter J. 136n
Hobbes, Thomas 175
Hogarth, William 124
Holcroft, Thomas 8
Homer 98, 101, 123; *Iliad* 75, 99, 100–1; *Odyssey* 99
Horne, Bishop George 179
Hudson, Thomas 111
Hume, David 13, 78, 92, 95, 131, 175, 197
Hume, Joseph 97
Hunt, Robert 139, 175

Hurdis, James 196
Hutcheson, Francis 102

Iago 102
identity 43–4, 120, 123–4, 151, 157, 174
imagination 14, 16, 19, 21, 30–1, 35–6, 42, 44, 46, 51, 62, 65–6, 75, 81, 115, 117, 119, 122–4, 127–8, 130, 133–4, 134–8, 144, 151, 155–8, 166–7, 169–76, 186–8, 195
imitation 117–8, 121–2, 128–9, 163; *see also* copying
insanity 139–49, 195
intuition 114
invention 114–5, 119, 125, 128, 176
Isaiah 155

Jackson, H.J. 4–5; *Romantic Readers* 12n, 109n
James I 190
James, G. Ingli 4
Jeffrey, David Lyle: *A Dictionary of Biblical Tradition* 55–6
Jehovah 103, 169, 181
Jesus Christ 1, 9, 29, 63, 65, 68–70, 73, 76–80, 83, 91, 94, 96, 103 156, 159, 169, 172–3, 180, 187–8, 190
Johnson. Joseph 61n, 70
Johnson, Mary Lynn 8n
Johnson, Samuel 111–2, 115, 179–80, 185, 197
Jupiter 103, 123

Keppel, Augustus 111
Keynes, Geoffrey 84, 196
King, Bishop 180
King, James: *William Cowper* 147
kings and kingship 59–62, 67, 84–7, 89, 174, 188–9, 191
Klopstock, Friedrich Gottlieb 196

Lang, Bernhard 31
Last Judgment 29, 46
Lavater, Johann Caspar: *Aphorisms* 7–27, 93, 140, 150, 186; *Essays on Physiognomy* 140n; *Physiognomische Fragmente* 8
Law, William 196
Lee, Gen. Henry 62
Leibniz, Gottfried Wilhelm 82
Lessing, Gotthold Ephraim: *Laocoön* 127n
Lichtenberg, G.C. 8, 9n
Linnaeus, Carolus 178
Linnell, John 143n, 177
Linnell, John, Jr. 143n
Linnell, William 143n
Lipking, Lawrence: *Ordering of the Arts* 109–10
Livy 7
Locke, John 14, 42, 71 81, 83, 94–5, 113, 117–20, 129, 132–4, 137, 145–6, 147n, 149, 151, 156, 158–9, 167, 169, 187, 197; *Human Understanding* 3, 150, 193–4, 197
Los 35
Lowth, Bishop Robert 185
Luce, A.A. 153

Lucian 92
Luther, Martin 7, 13, 28, 105

Machiavelli, Niccolo 84
Macpherson, James 162-3, 196
madness 139-49
Malone, Edmond 109, 111, 114-6
Malory, Thomas 197
Martin, Peter: *Edmond Malone* 114n
Mary Magdalene 157
Mathews, Nieves: *Francis Bacon* 82-3
maxim 9
McFarland, Thomas 4
Melibaeus 192
Mellor, Anne K. 139n, 145n
memory 53, 117, 121, 137, 164, 172, 175
metaphor 31, 120, 123-4, 157, 167, 170, 173-4
Methodism 24, 146, 148
Michelangelo 126-7, 129, 135-6, 138, 166
microcosm 55
Milton, John 30, 32, 34, 71 108, 169, 180, 196; "L'Allegro" 172; *Paradise Lost* 77, 182-3; *Reason of Church-Government* 121
minute discrimination 117-9, 125
minute particular 34, 122, 124, 151, 170, 173
Modiano, Raimonda 127n
Morgan, Thomas 23
Mortimer, John Hamilton 111
Mosely, Rev. Dr. 181
Moses 64, 68, 72, 77, 78
Moskal, Jeanne 24; *Blake, Ethics, and Forgiveness* 24n
Mudge, Zachariah 115
Muggletonian 195

nature 20, 22, 40, 47, 59, 65, 69, 75, 95, 100, 117-8, 120, 122-6, 128, 133, 151,153-6, 159, 161, 166-9, 175, 189, 191, 193
Nero 79
New Jerusalem Church 29-30, 47-53
Newton, Isaac 83, 94-5, 113, 133, 146, 147n, 149, 156, 169, 183, 187, 190
Noah 172
Nurmi, Martin, K.: *Blake's Marriage of Heaven and Hell* 29

Orcilla 196
Ossian 162-3, 196
Otway, Thomas 197
outline 118-9, 122-3, 125, 128, 170-1
Ovid 196
Oxford English Dictionary 9, 54

Packer, James I. 55-6
Paine, Thomas 62, 70, 75-6 78-80, 92; *Age of Reason* 61-73, 77, 182; *Common Sense* 61-2, 67
Paley, Morton D. 4, 61n, 70, 147, 182-3, 190n; *Energy and the Imagination* 72, 147, 182-3, 190n; *Traveller in the Evening* 179
Palmer, R. 196
Paracelsus 196

Parr, Henry 4
Paul, Saint 65, 69
Peltonen, Markku 89n; *Cambridge Companion to Bacon* 89n
Penelope 99, 101
Percival, Melissa: *Physiognomy in Profile* 8n
Percy, Thomas 111; *Reliques* 163, 196
Phaedo 193
Phidias 123
phrenology 8-9, 139-42, 146
physiognomy 8-9, 14, 21
Pilate, Pontius 94, 180, 189
Pindar 196
Pindar, Peter (Wolcot, John): *Works* 196
Plato (and Platonism) 72, 79, 118, 123, 154, 156, 158, 165, 166n, 172, 193, 195, 197;
Pliny 196
Plutarch 78; *Moralia* 193-4
Poetic Genius 42, 94, 106
Polybius 106
Pope, Alexander: *Dunciad* 83, 196; *Essay on Man* 82; "Universal Prayer" 184
Porphyry 68
Portia 185
Poussin, Nicolas 128
predestination 55-9
Priam 69
Prior, Matthew 196
Proclus 123
Prometheus 103, 131
prophecy 12, 29, 68, 77
Protestant Family Bible 197
providence 54-5, 57, 59
Pythagoras 154, 197

Quid the Cynic 112-3

Racine, Jean: *Berenice* 102
Rafael (angel) 183
Raphael 13-4, 16, 110, 112, 117, 126-7, 129, 132, 197
Rapin, Paul de 78
Rees, Abraham: *Cyclopaedia* 197
Reynolds, Joshua 5, 82, 93, 186, 193; *Discourses* 80, 109-38, 151, 157-8; *Works* 109, 111, 114
Richard III 102
Richardson, Samuel 197; *Clarissa* 101
Robinson, Henry Crabb: *Reminiscences* 28, 29n, 32n, 43, 51n, 90, 95, 160-2, 195
Rogers, Charles 97
Rogers, Pat: *Reynolds's Discourses* 111
Roman painters 125
Romney, George 148
Rosa, Salvator 128
Rousseau, Jean-Jacques 13, 197
Rowley, Thomas 114, 162
Royal Academy of Art 4, 110, 113, 131
Royal Universal Family Bible 197
Rubens, Peter Paul 13, 122, 128, 171
Ruhl, Darrell: *Blake and Swedenborg* 29n
Ryscamp, Charles: *William Cowper* 147

Index

St. Clair, William: *Reading Nation* 5n
Sandler, Florence 61n
Satan 20, 51, 63, 75, 83, 103, 110, 113, 117, 162, 166, 169, 181n, 185–9
Schevill, Ferdinand: *History of Florence* 104n
Scipio Africanus 112
Seneca 79
Shaftesbury, First Earl of 102
Shakespeare, William 101, 114, 191; *Hamlet* 102, 197; *Henry IV* 196; *Henry VIII* 196–7; *Julius Caesar* 197; *King Lear* 102, 197; *Macbeth* 197; *Merchant of Venice* 185; *Midsummer Night's Dream* 30–1; *Othello* 102–3, 197; *Richard III* 196; *Romeo and Juliet* 197; *Tempest* 197
Shenstone, William 196
Sheridan, Richard Brinsley 111
Sherlock, William: *Practical Discourse on Death* 196
Shroyer, R.J. 4, 7n, 9
Shylock 102
Sidney, Philip 171
Smith, William: *Smith's Bible Dictionary* 21
Snart, Jason Allen: *Torn Book* 5–6
Socrates 72, 158, 180
Solomon 169, 181n
South, Robert 19
Spenser, Edmund 196
Spurzheim, J.C.: *Observations* 3, 8n, 139–49; *Recherche sur la système* 140
states 33, 39, 42
Stedman, John: *Narrative of ... the Revolted Negroes of Surinam* 197
Stern, J.P.: *Lichtenberg* 8, 9n
Stoeffer, F. Ernst: *German Pietism* 11n
Stoics 95
sublime 10, 118, 123–4, 126, 134
substance 15, 17, 19, 49–50
Suction 112–3
Swabia 104
Swedenborg, Emanuel 4, 28–60, 162; *Divine Love* 12, 34, 36–54; *Divine Providence* 28, 38, 54–60; *Earths in the Universe* 35; *Earths in Our Solar System* 28, 35–36; *Heaven and Hell* 28, 30–38, 50; *Worlds in Universe* 35
synecdoche 19, 40, 43–4, 55, 123, 151, 172–3, 183

Tacitus 77
tar-water 152–3
Tasso, Torquato 101, 196
Tatham, Charles N.: *Three Designs* 197
Telemachus 99
Themistius 158–9
Theseus 30–1
Thomas, Joseph: *Religious Emblems* 197
Thornton, Robert John: *Lord's Prayer Translated* 4, 158, 177–92; *New Illustration* 177; *Temple of Flora* 177–8
Tindal, Matthew 73
Tintoretto 126
Titian 126
Titus 103
Trusler, Rev. Dr. John 81, 166, 170
Tucker, Nathaniel 56–7, 59
Tytler, Graeme: *Physiognomy in Profile* 8n

Ulysses 99, 101
Urizen 14, 35, 73, 168, 183, 188
Uzzah 20–1

Vala 189
Velutello, Alessandro: *Dante* 196
Venetian painters 119, 125–6, 134
Veronese, Paolo 126
Vickers, Brian: *Francis Bacon: The Major Works* 81n, 86
Vico, Giambattista 16, 187
Virgil 98, 196; *Aeneid* 99, 101–2, 189; *Eclogues* 178, 192
vision 41, 45–6, 48, 51, 75, 115, 117, 120, 122–3, 133–4, 138–9, 148–9, 155–9, 164–7, 170–5
Voltaire 13, 78, 112–3, 197

Wallace, William 171
Walpole, Horace: *Catalogue of the Royal and Noble Authors of England* 196
Ward, Aileen 110n
Wark, Robert R.: *Discourses on Art* 136
Warnock, G.J.: *Berkeley* 153
Warren, Gen. Joseph 62
Warton, Thomas 97, 111
Washington, George 62
Watson, Bishop Richard: *Anecdotes* 66; *Apology for the Bible* 4, 5, 61–80, 93, 164, 182
Watts, Isaac 183
Weldon, Anthony: *Court and Character of King James* 82
Wesley, Charles: *Hymns for the Nation* 196–7
Wesley, John: *Hymns for the Nation* 196–7
White, Harry 94, 95n
will 34, 37–8, 41, 50, 52–5, 145, 184, 186, 189
Wilson, Arthur: *Annals of King James I* 82
Wilson, Mona: *Life of William Blake* 171n
Winckelmann, Johann Joachim: *Gedanken über die Nachahmung* 127n; *Reflections* 196
Wollaston, William Hyde 102
Wollstonecraft, Mary 197
Wordsworth, Dorothy 162
Wordsworth, William 22, 160–75, 196; "Blind Highland Boy" 161, 162; "Brothers" 161, 162; "Character of the Happy Warrior" 161, 176; "Essay Supplementary" 160, 163, 175; *Excursion* 3, 160; "Expostulation and Reply" 161; "Hart-leap Well" 160, 162; "I Met Louisa" 161; "I Wandered Lonely" 161; "Influence of Natural Objects" 164; "Laodamia" 161; "Lucy Gray" 161; *Lyrical Ballads* 160, 162, 164; "Michael" 161, 162, 166; "Miscellaneous Sonnets" 161, 164; "Night Piece" 161, 164; "Ode: Intimations of Immortality" 161, 165; "Ode to Duty" 161, 176; "Old Cumberland Beggar" 161–2; *Poems* 3, 161; "Poems to Childhood"

166; Preface to *Lyrical Ballads* 174; *Recluse* 160, 167–8; "Resolution and Independence" 161, 176; "Reverie of Poor Susan" 161, 164; "Rob Roy's Grave" 161; "Ruth" 161; "Sonnets to Liberty" 161, 164; "Strange Fits of Passion" 161, 164, 166; "She Was a Phantom" 161, 164; "Thorn" 161, 162; "Tintern Abbey" 161, 166; "To H.C." 163–4, 170; "To the Cuckoo" 161, 165; "To the Daisy" 161, 165; "To the Small Celandine" 161, 165; translation of Michelangelo's sonnet 166n; "We Are Seven" 161, 164; "Yarrow Unvisited" 161; "Yarrow Visited" 161;"Yew Trees" 161, 164, 166

Wotton, Henry: *Reliquae Wottonianae* 196

Yeats, W.B. 3, 143, 146, 174, 180n; *Works of William Blake* 3, 143, 146

Young, Edward: *Night Thoughts* 193, 196

Zoas 156

Zwingli, Huldrich (Ulrich) 7n

www.ingramcontent.com/pod-product-compliance
Lightning Source LLC
Chambersburg PA
CBHW032057300426
44116CB00007B/787